P9-CTP-916

THE EARLY STORIES

OF

LOUISA MAY ALCOTT

1852–1860

THE EARLY STORIES

OF

LOUISA MAY ALCOTT

1852–1860

With an Introduction by Monika Elbert

IRONWEED PRESS
NEW YORK

Introduction © 2000 Ironweed Press, Inc.
All rights reserved.

Ironweed Press, Inc.
P. O. Box 754208
Parkside Station
Forest Hills, NY 11375

Manufactured in the United States of America.
Ironweed American Classics books are printed on acid-free paper.

Cover painting: Robert Vonnoh, detail,
"In Flanders Field—Where Soldiers Sleep and Poppies Grow,"
1890, © 1914. Oil on canvas, 58 in. x 104 in.
Courtesy of The Butler Institute of American Art.

Library of Congress Cataloging-in-Publication Data

Alcott, Louisa May, 1832–1888.
    [Short stories. Selections]
    The early stories of Louisa May Alcott, 1852–1860 / with an intro-
duction by Monika Elbert.
        p.   cm. — (Ironweed American classics)
    Includes bibliographical references (p.).
    Contents: The rival painters — The masked marriage — The rival
prima donnas — The little seed — A New Year's blessing — The sisters' trial — Little Genevieve — Bertha — Mabel's May day — The
lady and the woman — Ruth's secret — The cross on the church
tower — Agatha's confession — Little sunbeam — Marion Earle; or,
Only an actress — Mark Field's mistake — Mark Field's success —
The monk's island — Love and self-love.
    ISBN 0-9655309-6-5 (alk. paper)
    1. Young women—Social life and customs—Fiction. 2. Man-
woman relationships—Fiction. 3. Sex role—Fiction. 4. Feminism—
Fiction. 5. Love stories, American.   I. Title.   II. Series.
PS1016   2000a
813'.4—dc21   99-053595

CONTENTS

ACKNOWLEDGMENTS

Special gratitude is owed to the following individuals and institutions for the courtesies extended: Philip Lampi, Dennis Laurie, and Russell Martin, Newspapers and Periodicals Department, American Antiquarian Society; Jane Victor, Leonard H. Axe Library, Pittsburg State University; Microtext Department, Boston Public Library; and Massachusetts Historical Society.

INTRODUCTION

Louisa May Alcott's early stories, published between 1852 and 1860, bear the hallmark of her later works and indicate the divergent directions her mature writing would take. These stories, most of which appeared in the *Saturday Evening Gazette* while Alcott was in her twenties, are strikingly different from her first published book, *Flower Fables* (1855), a collection of fairy tales for children. With their moral lessons and sunny endings, these fairy tales are a far cry from the stories of pain and sorrow in this volume. Alcott's first two stories, "The Rival Painters: A Tale of Rome" (1852) and "The Masked Marriage" (1852), do betray a certain lack of depth, as does her first novel, *The Inheritance,* a sentimental juvenilia which, though written in 1849, was not published until 1997. The two exceptions aside, the stories in this collection are less pat and more realistic than *The Inheritance* and at times offer a remarkably mature and pessimistic perspective on life. Alcott moved away from the popular gothic and sentimental framework of then-contemporary fiction and began to experiment with the earliest forms of realism. It is not surprising that Alcott admired Nathaniel Hawthorne's *The Scarlet Letter* (1850); even though her mother found the book not altogether wholesome, Alcott insisted that she was drawn to the "lurid" quality of Hawthorne's writing and found it "true and strong also."

Alcott had an intensely close relationship with her parents, and their influence upon her early fiction is unmistakable and profound. The mother figures in the stories reflect Louisa's idealized picture of her nurturing, charitable, and resourceful mother, Abigail May Alcott, who, by her untiring effort, managed to keep the family out of the poorhouse. The strong, practical father figures often function as surrogates for her real father, Amos Bronson Alcott, an impractical, pedantic man who was never able to provide for his family. Though a less visible figure in her stories, he played a major role in shaping his daughter's moral vision, one that served as a constant point of reference in her fiction. A progressive educator and founding member of the transcendentalist movement, Bronson imprinted her with his philosophical idealism and, to no lesser degree, his moral obsessiveness. He impressed upon his daughter at an early age the importance of discipline and duty, assigning her a rigorous schedule of exercise, lessons, and household chores. Of the four Alcott sisters, Louisa suffered the most from the parental union of seemingly disparate traits, and she struggled to reconcile and integrate these contradictory influences through her writing.

The commingling of parental character traits in the writer child is best described by Hawthorne's sister-in-law, Elizabeth Palmer Peabody, who was a prominent New England intellectual and close family friend of the Alcotts. Shortly after Abigail's death, Peabody sent Louisa a letter of condolence, in which she celebrates the memory of her mother: "I have never known a greater, more devoted, more tender, more self-sacrificing human being; and it was all pure moral force and *character,* for she owed nothing to the *imagination.* . . . There was no froth on the cup of life for her—it was all the reality down to its very dregs . . . uprightness and downrightness and plain speech—but *an infinitely tenderer* heart." Peabody goes on to commend Louisa for having been a faithful daughter and "the first person who ever did sufficiently to do justice to her." In a telling passage Peabody describes Louisa as an amalgam of both parents: "Gifted by God with your mother's heart and your father's ideality, you united them in yourself, and saw them both in God's idea of them."

Alcott's early fiction deftly captures these competing influences and portrays her parents in an almost reverential manner. If her mother represented the Christian reform impulse at the communal level, her father represented a broader, more abstract vision of improvement for humanity through the application of transcendentalist philosophy. Despite the difference in their impulses, both firmly believed in self-abnegation and in personal growth through the fulfillment of duty, which for Abigail and Bronson hinged upon some divinely ordained or inspired employment that would further some higher moral objective. A sense of duty and a desire to find and fulfill one's personal mission for the betterment of humanity lie at the heart of Alcott's early stories. This view was not an idiosyncratic one imparted by her parents, but rather a vision based on the Protestant work ethic and the legacy of the Puritan forebears and shared by most New Englanders at the time. For Bronson and other transcendentalists, the Protestant cultural heritage was translated into the redefinition of work as a spiritual pursuit.

In Alcott's work the image of her mother looms much larger than that of her father. Alcott transformed her into a cultural icon of her texts and immortalized her as "Marmee" in *Little Women* (1868, 1869). Alcott's fictional universe is a distinctly mother-centered one, in which children seek a nurturing home, husbands maternal warmth in their wives, and orphans a mother-surrogate. In "The Rival Painters: A Tale of Rome" the maternal image is endowed with almost magical powers; this cautionary tale seems to suggest that greatness comes to those who obey and revere their mothers.

For Alcott, motherhood is not limited to its biological definition. In "Marion Earle; or, Only an Actress!" (1858), Alcott, perhaps inspired by her younger sister's death from scarlet fever in the spring of that year, tells the story of Marion Earle, an actress who devotes her life to bringing up her orphaned sister, May. The girl's sudden death stirs even stronger maternal feelings in Marion, and she becomes the great nurturing mother to all, proclaiming that since her sister's death "for every child I feel a yearning tenderness and love them for her sake." The benevolent, self-sacrificing mother-surrogate is a staple of Alcott's fiction and reappears in "Little Sunbeam"

(1857), "Mark Field's Mistake" (1859), and its sequel, "Mark Field's Success" (1859).

But Alcott did not rigidly uphold the image of blessed maternity; in "Ruth's Secret" (1856), for example, the image of the mother is far from sacred. Unlike many sentimental women writers of her era, she did not sacrifice verisimilitude for the sake of evoking emotion. Granted, Alcott was not exempt from the sentimentality and melodrama of the "scribbling women" of her time; but with her social consciousness she was much more like Fanny Fern, whose novel *Ruth Hall* (1855), noted for its realistic appraisal and exposure of social ills, appeared during this period. It could be maintained that Alcott was influenced by the sentimentality of Charles Dickens or the romanticism of Sir Walter Scott, both of whom were among her favorite authors when she was a young girl. Nonetheless, Alcott's plots are not neatly tied together in the traditional sentimental fashion—by a happy ending revolving around the marriage of long-lost lovers, or a joyous reunion between mother and child that would endure forever.

In Alcott's fictional universe the paternal figure plays an equally important role as its maternal counterpart. To understand her idealized father figure, as portrayed in the stories, and often in contradistinction to her real father, one must turn to Alcott's adolescence. Though Bronson's visionary qualities profoundly influenced his daughter, it seems unlikely that she modeled the father figures in her early fiction directly on him. From 1843 to 1844, Louisa witnessed the failure of her father's utopian experiment, Fruitlands, which she later parodied in "Transcendental Wild Oats" (1873); with the experiment's failure, Bronson suffered a nervous breakdown from which he never fully recovered. The successful, capable father figures were most probably based on Ralph Waldo Emerson, whom she called "Master" and "the god of my idolatry," and on Johann Wolfgang von Goethe, whose work, significantly enough, was introduced to Louisa by Emerson. The two older writers served as catalysts to her sexual awakening, which occurred during what she later referred to as her "romantic" or "sentimental" period "when I fell to writing poetry, keeping a heart-journal, and wandering by moonlight instead of sleeping quietly." As a teenager, she found in Emerson's library a copy of Goethe's *Correspondence with a Child* (1835), a collection of letters exchanged by Goethe and fifteen-year-old Bettine von Arnim, and "fired with a desire to be a Bettine," made her "father's friend my Goethe." Thus Louisa became the inquiring girl, Bettine, and Emerson her Goethe. As her biographer Ednah Cheney points out, girls of Alcott's generation, lacking access to education or a full intellectual life, often engaged in such hero worship; Cheney suggests that Goethe's *Correspondence with a Child* "led more than one young girl to form an ideal attachment to a man far older than herself, but full of nobility and intellectual greatness." Emerson also gave Alcott a copy of Goethe's *Wilhelm Meister* (1796) during this time— another gesture that merged for her the love of her mentors Emerson and Goethe. Alcott wrote in her journal that "from that day Goethe has been my chief idol." Some three decades later she would pay homage to Goethe with her novel *A Modern Mephistopheles* (1877), which was inspired by his *Faust* (1808, 1832).

In a journal entry from 1852, Alcott listed Charlotte Brontë's *Jane Eyre* (1847) as one of her favorite novels, and the power dynamics manifested in Alcott's father-daughter stories replicate those of the master and governess in *Jane Eyre*. In "Bertha" (1856), the setting of which, perhaps not coincidentally, is Germany, Ernest Lennartson, a prominent musician, discovers the singing talent of the poor orphaned child Bertha and subsequently takes her into his home and trains her. Years later, Bertha goes out into the world and becomes an acclaimed singer, and Ernest thinks she has abandoned him; but she ultimately returns to her "dear master" to become his wife and to care for him in his impoverished old age, as he had provided for her earlier. The father-daughter theme is further developed in "Love and Self-Love" (1860), which appeared in the *Atlantic Monthly* and proved to be a turning point in Alcott's literary development. Its male protagonist, Basil Ventnor, an older bachelor, marries the sixteen-year-old Effie, moved by a promise he has made to the girl's guardian on her deathbed. But Basil reveals himself as cold and egocentric: "I was a master, content to give little, while receiving all she could bestow." After toying with her affections and returning to an earlier love, Basil sends Effie back to her grandfather. Soon after, Basil loses his fortune, and Effie gains her inheritance from her grandfather. She then returns to Basil to declare her love and claim him as her husband, but now as his equal in terms of emotional depth, worldly experience, and material wealth.

Perhaps the single most influential idea that permeates almost all of Alcott's early stories is the Emersonian principle of self-reliance, translated into a feminine and feminist ideal by Margaret Fuller in her *Woman in the Nineteenth Century* (1845). This work, along with Emerson's essay "Self-Reliance" (1841), profoundly influenced Alcott's own manifesto on self-reliance, "The Lady and the Woman" (1856), in which its female protagonist, Miss Kate, serves as Alcott's representative. Miss Kate is able to convince the rather sexist and initially misguided Mr. Windsor that she is the ideal woman by evincing "masculine" courage in the face of a flood that threatens to kill the members of their travel expedition, while showing "feminine" compassion to her invalid brother and their hosts' children. At the opening of the story, Miss Kate asserts that a woman should possess a balance of masculine and feminine traits: "I would have her strong enough to stand alone and give, not ask, support. Brave enough to think and act, as well as feel. Keen-eyed enough to see her own and others' faults and wise enough to find a cure for them. I would have her humble, though self-reliant; gentle, though strong; man's companion, not his plaything; able and willing to face storm as well as sunshine and share life's burdens as they come." In a voice resonating with Fuller's prophecy for equality between the sexes, Miss Kate looks forward to a more equitable time: "Give the brothers and sisters of our great family an equal share of the pleasures, duties, benefits, and rewards of life, and in time you will see the beautiful result."

The feminism evidenced in Alcott's early fiction is strikingly modern. Frequently underscored in her stories is the need for a sisterhood to sustain women who find themselves at the mercy of untrustworthy men. The type of sisterhood that Alcott would later celebrate in *Little Women* is already evident in such stories as "The Sisters' Trial" (1856) and "Marion Earle; or, Only an Actress!" which stand in sharp contrast to their negative counterparts of betrayed sisterhood, exemplified by "The Rival Prima Donnas" (1854), "Mabel's May Day" (1856), and "Agatha's Confession" (1857).

Alcott's own experiences may have contributed to the darkness of some of her early fiction. Though she may have inherited her melancholy from her father, it was exacerbated by what she described in her journals as the two most significant losses in her life to that point, losses that she felt were connected—the death of her younger sister Lizzie in March 1858 and the betrothal of her older sister, Anna, a month later. Louisa's overwhelming sense of loss forced her into an almost suicidal despair. She perceived these events in a highly peculiar manner, linking death with marriage and resenting both powers for robbing her of her sisters: "Death and love have taken two of us away."

Yet this kind of perversity is characteristic of many of her early stories, some of which represent her first forays into the "thriller" genre. Though there are aspects of gothic horror, the tone is more grotesque than gothic. For example, in "Agatha's Confession," Agatha, in Poesque fashion, allows her rival to be buried alive; Alcott's use of the first person lends a particular intensity and poignancy to Agatha's insanity. There are many other inexplicably grotesque endings. Beatrice, the fallen prima donna of "The Rival Prima Donnas," driven to despair by her unfaithful lover, kills the reigning prima donna by dropping on her head an iron crown hidden in a garland of roses, and the story concludes with Beatrice's incarceration in an asylum, where she "constantly wove garlands and, like a swan, died singing mournfully." "Monk's Island: A Legend of the Rhine" (1859) is perhaps the most subversive piece in this collection; implicit in its grotesque ending is the suggestion that the fulfillment of duty is detrimental to one's ultimate happiness.

For all her enduring popularity, Alcott is still an underappreciated writer. Only since the republication of her thrillers has she begun to shed her erstwhile reputation as a children's writer. Ironically, Alcott herself was in large measure responsible for undermining her own posthumous reputation. When juvenile fiction proved to be a lucrative niche, she rarely strayed from the genre and, ever the businesswoman, went to great lengths to cultivate her public image as the "Children's Friend" in order to enhance the marketability of her fiction. Not surprisingly, she sought to distance herself both from her thrillers of the 1860s and from her early stories, some of which, because of their sensationalist or macabre elements, would have been embarrassing for the "Children's Friend" to acknowledge as her own. Records indicate that during the period covered in this volume, Alcott published at least eight other stories, which are presumed lost; and five of these appear to have been thrillers. Of the nineteen stories presented in this collection, only "The Cross on the Church Tower" (1857) was reprinted during her lifetime. Had the Alcott scholars Madeleine Stern and Leona Rostenberg not uncovered her thrillers, her canonized image as the patron saint of children's literature would undoubtedly have remained intact.

Though not all of Alcott's early stories are successful, they represent a vital part of her oeuvre. In them Alcott laid the foundation for her later canon. Admittedly, she was not yet wholly free from the influences of her literary predecessors—Dickens, Poe, Hawthorne, Brontë—but the results were Alcott's alone. Drawing on her antecedents, she created something original and fresh, imprinting her fiction with her own unique genius. In June 1857 she wrote in her journal, "Wonder if I shall ever be famous enough for people to care to read my story and struggles. I can't be a Charlotte Brontë, but I may do a little something yet." She never did become a Charlotte Brontë, but she became something just as good. She became Louisa May Alcott, a literary icon in her own right.

Monika Elbert
Montclair State University

THE EARLY STORIES

OF

LOUISA MAY ALCOTT

1852–1860

THE RIVAL PAINTERS

A TALE OF ROME

"Farewell, my son, go trustingly forth. Carve thine own fortunes by untiring efforts, and it will be doubly enriched by the memory of those years of patient toil that gained so much happiness for thee. The world is bright and beautiful to a young heart, but its light and loveliness pass away. Set not, therefore, too great value upon its riches. Walk calmly in the quiet path that leads to thy duty, envying none, loving all, and a purer and more lasting joy will be thine than the praise and homage a flattering world can give thee. Fear nothing but sin and temptation; follow only the dictates of thine own innocent heart. Be faithful to thy friends, forgiving to thine enemies, true to thyself, and earnest in thy love to God; and with a mother's blessing on thy head, fare thee well."

And with nothing but a deep love for his beautiful art and a heart filled with pure and lovely feelings, Guido, a young Florentine painter, left his quiet home for the great city of Rome, where all his hopes and desires were centered. There, in the studio of some great master, he would seek honor and wealth for himself and a luxurious home for his mother, who with all a woman's patient constancy had toiled to gain enough to place her son where his exalted genius might be guided and taught till he could gain all that she so fondly hoped. When the time came, she freely gave up all that made life pleasant to her—cheerfully bade farewell to her noble son, and in her lonely room toiled on, that he might lack nothing to cheer and help him on his way. Nor was all the mother's self-sacrificing love unappreciated or unfelt; it kept her son from temptation and cheered him on to greater efforts, that he might repay with unfailing care and tenderness the sacrifice so nobly made. Nothing could stay or turn him aside while his mother's words lingered in his ear. No harm could fall on a head made sacred by her blessing, and no evil enter a heart filled with such holy love.

And so amid all the allurements of a luxurious city he passed unharmed and labored steadily on till he won his way among the first of the highborn young artists who crowded the studios of the great masters; and as time went on, honor and wealth seemed waiting for him, but not happiness.

The kind old painter with whom he had spent so many happy years had a fair young daughter whom he had loved long and silently, happy that he could be near one so good and beautiful. He never thought of asking more till a fellow student, possessed of wealth and rank, comely in person and courtly in manner, sought her hand; and then, only when he feared it was too late, did he gain courage to plead his love so well and earnestly that the old painter could not refuse to leave the choice to his daughter.

"Tell me truly, Madeline," he said, "and he you love shall be thine with my blessing. But pause and consider. Young Ferdinand hath wealth, rank, a splendid home, and a heart full of love for thee. Guido has nothing—nay, blush not so proudly, my child! I meant no *earthly* riches; he hath a noble soul and a rare talent for painting, but in this cold world these are uncared for, where gold and honors are prized more highly. Judge for yourself, Madeline, which will bring thee most happiness: the pomp and show of a countess, or a humble painter's home, subject to all the care and sorrow poverty brings. Wealth or love—few maidens would pause; and yet 'tis a hard choice—both so noble and comely, I wonder not at your indecision."

The image of the pale young painter came oftenest to the girl's heart—all his silent acts of kindness, his humble, self-denying life, and most of all his deep and earnest love for her—and the gay, gallant Count was forgotten. A flower from

Guido was more highly prized than all the costly gifts her titled suitor laid at her feet. But she knew her father longed to
see her the wife of some highborn lord. His own life had been
darkened by hours of poverty and sorrow, and he fondly
hoped to spare her that pain which he had borne unmurmur-
ingly. So with a daughter's self-denying love, she answered:

"Father, as a painter's daughter, my life has been one of
perfect happiness—why not as a wife? The Count loves the
beautiful art only as a means of gaining honor, and even that
love will soon pass away and some trifling thing succeed it.
Guido is poor and his art is his all. I know the deep, earnest
love he bears for all that is great and good. Beauty and purity
he worships with a true painter's steadfastness; and while he
humbly toils for bread, the noble genius which lies hidden
now will awake and, hallowed by such a purpose, will bring
him honor and wealth. But I am young, Father, and the world
is new to me. Judge as your own wise love counsels, and by
that judgment will I abide."

"So let it be, Madeline! And if I do not greatly err, our
choice will be the same," he replied, and passed out and left a
loving heart behind, struggling with the gentle memories that
thronged so tenderly about it. But with a woman's strength all
thoughts of love were banished, and she waited to fulfill her
duty, hard though it might be.

"Signori," said the old painter when he joined the rivals,
who together sought to learn their fate, "my daughter leaves
the choice to me, and as a father, I would ask what you would
give up to win her love? Maidens are fond and foolish things
and would be hardly won. My lord, how highly do *you* prize
the love of a simple girl?"

"More than life, liberty, wealth, or honor," replied the
Count with a glance at his humble rival, who possessed so little to sacrifice.

"And you, Guido?" said the old man.

The bright blood mounted to the pale face, and the clear
light glowed deeper in his dark eye as he answered with a low,
sad voice, "I would give up that which is more precious than
life or liberty; that for which I would toil and suffer long

years—that for which I would most gladly give the little honor, wealth, or happiness that I possess. All these were trifles, useless and vain, if that one thing were not gained."

"And this is what?" asked the wondering painter.

"Your daughter! Her happiness is more to me than all the earth can offer. Let her bestow her love where she will, and God protect him who is so blessed as to possess it. My deepest, truest joy will be the knowledge of her own. Cold and selfish were the hearts that did not find pure happiness in the joy of those they truly love. My rival hath all that can make life fair and beautiful; I would not bring a cloud to darken her bright sky. But when all the blessings that the world can give are hers, I would only ask a passing thought of one whose earnest life and abiding love will ever link all bright and happy memories with her."

"It is enough! Hear my decision. Three weeks hence is the Carnival; he who before that time hath painted a picture the most perfect in grace and beauty of form, design, and coloring, to him will I give my daughter. Strange as it may seem, I feel a painter's pride in bestowing my only earthly wealth on one worthy the glorious art that wins her. Three weeks hence, at the gallery of ——, we meet again. Till then, farewell."

And as the two rivals turned away, his eye rested proudly on Guido as he whispered with a smile, "He is worthy of her and will succeed."

The hours went by, and rumors of the strange trial between the rival painters were rife through the city. Many were the wondering thoughts of the people; gay jests went around, and happy visions of fame from the hand of the painters filled many a fair lady's heart.

The beautiful Madeline sat alone and strove to banish the thoughts that would come, bringing a picture she would not look upon; and so the time went on, the days were spent, and the Carnival was in progress.

Gallery after gallery filled, and still the crowd poured in till the dim old halls were brilliant with the fair and noble of the gay city. The sunlight stole softly in through the richly stained windows, throwing strange, bright hues on the old pictures within, and the air was heavy with the fragrance of the flowers twined around statue and pillar.

Two dark, mysterious curtains hung side by side, and before them stood the rival painters—a strange contrast. The young Count—his proud face glowing with joy, his costly garments glittering with embroidery, and his plumed cap heavy with jewels—stood proudly forth, and many a light heart beat and fair cheek flushed as his dark eye glanced over the galleries, bright as an Eastern garden with the loveliest flowers of Rome.

But they soon turned from him to his rival and lingered there. His humble dress and threadbare mantle were unheeded for the noble face that looked so pale in the dark shadows where he stood. But a ray of sunlight lay softly on the long dark locks that fell heavily around his face, and unconscious of the eyes upon him, he stood looking calmly on the sweet face of a Madonna above.

A crowd of the first painters stood around a canopied seat, conversing with the father, who listened, silently watching the dial as it first approached the appointed hour. Beside him sat Madeline; the long veil folded so closely could not hide the lovely face that blushed beneath; and the hand that clasped the victor's wreath trembled with the emotions of hope and fear that made the dark eyes fill with tears and the gentle heart beat wildly.

As the twelve silvery chimes died away, the Count sprang forward and exultingly flung back the curtain. A long breathless pause, and then loud and long sounded the applause till the vaulted roof rung again.

It was Madeline—beautiful as love could make her. Beneath the picture, traced in golden letters, were courtly words of love and flattery, and before it the Count knelt gracefully and with uncovered head.

Then the pale young painter lifted his dark curtain, and not a sound broke the deep stillness as with fascinated eyes they gazed. Tears were on many a cheek, for the simple word "Mother" traced below brought back to many a careless heart the long-forgotten hours of innocence and youth; it was strangely beautiful. The silvered hair lay softly around the gentle face, and the mild, dark eyes seemed looking down on her son with all a mother's fondness while the golden light that fell from the high window seemed to shut the world of sin and shadows from them.

The silence was broken by a burst of applause that shook the old walls, and often as it died away, it was again renewed. Plumed caps waved and flowers fell at his feet. Still with folded hands he stood, heedless of all, for his thoughts were far away. He saw only the gentle face before him, heard only her low, sweet voice, felt only her hand laid in blessing on his head; and all else was forgotten.

Then clear and deep above the murmuring crowd sounded the voice of the old painter, saying—"Guido of Florence hath won the prize; and, more than this, he hath gained our love and honor, for one whose holy affections prized above the young and lovely the face that first smiled upon him, the heart that first loved. I ask no greater wealth for my child than the love of so noble a son. She is thine, Guido, with my fondest blessing."

And amid a burst of triumphant music the wreath fell upon his head and Madeline upon his breast. The noblest painters crowded around him, fair ladies scattered flowers in his path. Even his rival, shrouding his own fair picture, flung a bright wreath over the other and, with tears on his proud face, stood humbly before it while gentle memories came stealing back, bringing a quiet joy, long unknown, to his ambitious heart; and he rose up a better man for the holy lesson he had learned.

And while noble painters and beautiful women paid their homage to the humble artist, and the deep-toned music rolled through the bright halls, high above all the calm, soft face looked proudly down on the son, whose unfailing love for her had gained for him the honor and love he so richly deserved.

THE MASKED MARRIAGE

The summer moon looked softly down on the silvery waters of the Arno, whose cool waves washed the marble steps of the noble palaces upon its banks. Rich music pealed from those lighted halls; lovely forms floating in the dance were seen through the open casements, whose heavy curtains were flung back by the cool night wind which swept in, laden with the perfume of the orange groves below. Stately knights and fair ladies stood on the balconies, soft words were spoken, and tender vows were made while the quiet stars looked down on many a blushing cheek and downcast eye.

From one of these gay mansions a cavalier emerged and, hastily descending to the waterside, sprang into a light gondola, which darted away through the starlit waves.

On it went, amid drooping boughs and fragrant flowers slumbering in the soft moonlight that fell so brightly on the countenance of him who looked so sadly at the quiet evening sky. It was a pale and noble face with nothing of the "Italian" in it, save the dark, lustrous eyes and the raven hair the night wind flung so freely back, while the unadorned and simple dress told that, though brave and true, a humble fortune must be his.

Meantime, the light boat sped along by lighted palaces and moonlit gardens till the high, dark walls of the Convent of St. C—— rose before him. The faint, low chant of the evening prayer rose softly on the quiet air, and as the solemn sound of the holy music ceased, the gondola glided into the dark shadow of the walls. A moment more and it was moored beneath a solitary casement, while in a low, sweet voice these words were sung:

> "The summer wind is sighing
>   Across the moonlit sea,
> And bears my bark, dear lady,
>   Through whispering waves to thee.
> O wake! for the evening star
>   Casts her soft light o'er me:
> Thou art my star, and I the wave,
>   Reflecting naught but thee."

As the song ceased, the casement opened and a light female form appeared in the balcony, where the moonlight revealed a young and lovely lady. It was no nun, for the silken robe was clasped with jewels and no close veil hid the bright locks that fell so softly around the fair young face. Bending from the balcony, she said:

"Ah, Ferdinand, why hast thou ventured forth tonight? They will miss thee at the palace, and all may be discovered."

"Pardon, dearest Alice, but I could not rest till I had told thee what I this day learned. Tomorrow thou wilt leave the convent where till now thy life has flowed along beneath a cloudless sky. The gay world thou wilt enter is too full of sin and sorrow for one so pure and gentle as thou art. O Alice! My heart is filled with sad forebodings for thee."

"Nay, why fear for me, dear Ferdinand? Amid the sins and follies of the world, my heart shall be a holy shrine where all the pure, undying love I bear thee shall be gathered up and, with all a woman's constancy and faith, be treasured but for thee."

"That bright dream is over, dearest," replied her lover, and his voice was sad and low. "This is why I could not rest. I would be the first to tell you all our sorrow and share the grief I bring thy gentle heart. Thy father has betrothed thee to Count Antonio and by solemn vows hath bound himself to wed thee only unto him, the heir of those rich English lands he so long hath coveted. I knew not of this till it was too late to claim the hand where I had won the heart. I cannot doubt the tidings; our happy visions for the future are no more. Thou must be led a victim to the altar, and I, amid the ruins of my life's fair hopes, will seek for patience to bear this sorrow as I ought."

He ceased and bowed his head, and the few heavy tears that fell showed how hard a struggle love and honor made within that noble heart.

"How can I free myself from this unholy marriage?" said the gentle girl, while the bright tears fell like summer rain. "I cannot give my hand where my heart can never follow. Ah, save me, Ferdinand, from such a fate!"

"Alice, what a heart's best love can do shall not be wanting now. I'll plead as never lover pled before, and if I cannot win my suit, hard as the task may be, we must teach our hearts to share the sorrow nobly and forget the joy that hath been ours."

"Thou shalt not bear this grief alone; these idle tears shall never dim the light that leads me to my duty. Thy noble words have stilled the deep despair of this poor heart. The happy dream that made my life so bright and beautiful is gone; those hopes and joys have passed away—all but my love and constancy to thee. They may wed me where they list, my heart is ever thine."

"God bless thee, dearest, and reward thee as thy true heart's tenderness deserves. But hark! The convent bell is sounding. I must leave thee, but not yet forever; we shall meet again. Till then, bear bravely up. And now farewell, dearest. May good angels guard and comfort thee."

"Farewell," said the weeping lady. "If we must part, may you find a heart as true and tender as the one now sorrowing for thee, is the prayer of thy poor Alice."

The boat was gone, the balcony deserted, and the moon's soft light fell only on the bright waves rippling below.

II

The Count de Adelon was a proud and highborn Italian, wedded in his youth to a lovely English lady, who had borne him one fair child and then, like the sweet but short-lived southern flowers that bloomed around her, faded gently away and was borne to the tomb of the proud de Adelons.

Years went by, and the mother's child found a calm and happy home among the gentle nuns of St. C—— and grew up amid the holy sisterhood lovely as a poet's dream, pure and gentle as the saints she worshiped with such pious love.

A father's tenderness and care she had never known; for he had brought another bride to his stately home and, amid the many joys that rank and wealth can bring, forgot the gentle child who was growing into womanhood and beauty in the dim old convent.

At length poverty stole into his luxurious home, for years of careless splendor had brought the proud Count's fortune low. Then, while wandering through the stately halls where no trace of the coming ruin was yet seen, he remembered that a lovely daughter yet unknown to the gay world dwelt within the gloomy convent. She might wed some lord whose wealth would well repay the honor done him by the noble house of Adelon.

He sought the daughter he had so long neglected, and with wondering delight, beheld a form and face that well might grace the proudest home in Italy. Tender memories rose in his cold heart, and with kind and loving words he won his daughter's love and from time to time had taken her to his splendid home, that others might see the loveliness of his fair child.

It was there she had seen and learned to love Ferdinand de Vere. Young, brave, and rich in manly virtues, he soon won the heart he longed for. Amid the proud and highborn guests who thronged her father's halls, the English stranger was the only one whose image did not fade like a bright dream when in the silent convent she forgot the gay scenes that had passed before her. And thus ere long the loving hearts were joined, and the bright waves rippling by St. C—— bore on their bosom the happy lover to the little cell where all his earthly happiness was found.

Little dreaming of the tender scenes the moon looked down on through those long summer nights, the Count de Adelon was winning for his child the hand of Count Antonio, an Italian noble, whose unbounded wealth would build up the broken fortunes of the bride's father.

And at length the young lord, won by the daughter's beauty and the father's rank, besought the Count's leave to bring her from the convent to his own noble palace as his wife. That leave was given, and the lovers' happy dream was broken by the summons of the gentle Alice home.

III

The setting sun stole with a softened light through the curtains of a humbly furnished chamber where sat Ferdinand de Vere, pale and sad, struggling to calm the bitter sorrow of a hopeless love.

A low tap broke the deep silence, and a servant entered, saying, "Signore, a stranger waits below, entreating you to see her. Shall I admit her?"

"Nay, Bertoni, I can see no stranger now; yet, if she is poor or in sorrow, it were cruel to refuse. I will see her, whoever it be."

A light step sounded on the stair, and a young girl stood before him, wrapped in a dark mantle, but the veil so closely folded ill concealed the bright, dark eyes and clustering hair.

"Signore, I come on a strange errand," she said, "but to me a sad one. My mother lies upon her deathbed and cannot die in peace till she has revealed to thee a secret which will bring thee wealth and honor. Wilt thou trust me as thy guide and follow quickly?"

"'Tis a strange summons," said the young man. "How can I, a stranger here, be known to thy mother? Nay, do not weep, poor child. I will follow thee if my presence can bring comfort to a suffering spirit."

And with his unknown guide he passed into the silent streets.

Twilight shadows were deepening and the soft light had faded away as the young girl stopped before a ruined gate. Then, passing in, she led the way through a deserted garden to a low door, which was opened by an old servant, who said:

"The Virgin be praised, you are not too late! Come quickly—she is with the priest."

Up a flight of narrow stairs they went, into a darkened room, where on a low couch lay a woman in whose pale and haggard face traces of great beauty still were seen. Beside her stood a gray-haired priest holding a golden crucifix before her fading eyes.

"Mother, he is here," said the young girl, kneeling beside the couch while her tears fell thick and fast.

"Ah!" said the dying woman. "Lift me higher, Rosalie, and do thou, holy Father, bear witness to the last words of this sinful heart. Young man, draw nearer. Is thy name Ferdinand de Vere?"

"It is," replied he, wondering at the strange scene before him.

"Then listen while I unfold to thee the tale of sin I could not carry to the grave with me.

"Thy father, years ago when he was gay and young, wooed and won a simple village maiden's heart. It was her only wealth, and she gave it freely, asking for no return but constancy and truth. She knew not that her humble lover was a rich and noble knight. He vowed to love and wed her, and she believed him. Happy days passed, and then she was left to sigh in lonely sorrow. He was wedded to a noble lady and forgot the warm heart he had won. I was that poor maiden, and in the bitter hour of agony and grief I vowed a fierce revenge.

"That vow I kept. Years rolled away, and I was wedded to a wild mountain robber and sought in the stirring scenes of a wandering life to still the voice that whispered of forgiveness. But an evil demon drove me on, and my vow was at length fulfilled. Thy father's life had been a long bright dream of happiness and love. Wealth such as few possess was his, and 'twas all gathered up for thee. Thou wert a fair, unconscious child.

Often did I wander to thy home to look upon thy mother bending over thee and with all her heart's love blessing thee as mothers only can. Her life seemed all bound up in thine, and I hated her for possessing the joy I could not win.

"At length thy father died. Thou canst not remember thy mother's grief, nor her wonder and alarm when no will was found, and thus all the wealth so hoarded up for thee passed to thy kinsman Count Antonio. Thou wert left fatherless and poor.

"My revenge was gained. I had stolen the will that left all to thee, and thou and thy mother were penniless. Death took her hence, and thou hast made thyself loved and honored for thy nobleness and truth. My cruel work was done, and for years I wandered over the earth a sinful, sorrowing outcast.

"Think not, young man, I called thee hither to learn this sad and simple story for no purpose. I can give thee *now* thy father's wealth. My life is well-nigh spent, and I would perform one good deed ere I depart. My child, bring hither the ivory casket; thou knowest the secret hiding place."

The weeping girl stole out and a deep silence followed.

No words can tell the wonder, joy, and tender grief the dying woman's tale had stirred within the breast of the young listener. Thoughts of Alice, golden dreams of wealth and happiness, and sad memories of the mother who had so deeply suffered for the sins of the wild, revengeful woman who now, long years after, lay dying here before him—these came crowding to his mind like a troubled dream till the silence was broken by the return of Rosalie, bearing the casket in her hand.

"Unclasp it, love," said the dying woman faintly. "My strength fails, and my work is yet undone. These papers," she continued in broken accents, "will prove thy right to all thy father's wealth. Would it could buy this poor soul its pardon and forgiveness!

"Now, farewell. I cannot die in peace with a face so like thy father's bending over me. I have told all. This good priest will counsel thee. Now go, and may this last deed repay thee for the great wrong this sinful heart hath done thee."

"May God forgive thee as freely as I do, and grant thee

peace," whispered the young man, and with a few words to the old priest, he stole softly out into the silent night.

IV

Days had passed; the dead was buried and Rosalie in a safe home. Long and anxious were the counsels of the priest and young de Vere. The strange discovery had brought many difficulties; those who had witnessed the will were to be found. After a long and careful search they were at length traced to Rome. Messengers were dispatched to bring them secretly to F——.

Amid all these wearisome duties one thought still cheered the happy lover on—thought of the hour when he might claim Alice as his own—and this he could not hope to do until his right to all the English wealth was clear.

So he eagerly hurried on the work, and thus the weeks rolled on, when tidings reached him that in three days the nuptials of the Count Antonio would take place. Then in the wildest haste he sought the priest for comfort and advice.

"My son," said the old man, "there is but one way left thee. Go to thy lady's father and ask her hand. Thou hast virtue and an honorable name. She loves thee, and if he bear a father's heart within his breast, he will never sell her for Count Antonio's gold when her heart is given to thee. Say nothing of the strange tale thou hast lately heard, for if he makes his daughter's happiness by giving up his worldly hopes, then it will be a fit reward when he shall learn that the fortune he so coveted is thine."

He went and pled his love with all his heart's deep devotion, but in vain. The ambitious Count had set his worldly heart on the wealth of Count Antonio and with haughty coldness answered the young lover's prayers, saying as he turned to go:

"My daughter is the last of her noble name, and whoso wins her hand must possess the wealth and rank befitting such an honor."

"My lord," replied the young man, while the light shone in his dark eyes, "the name of de Vere is noble as your own. I am not poor and can give your daughter a happy home and a heart whose only care shall be to spare her every sorrow. Count Antonio's wealth may pass away. Where then will be the happiness you now seek for your child in paltry gold and a titled name?"

"Enough, young man," exclaimed the Count. "When you can boast a name and fortune noble as the Count's, I will yield my daughter when and where you please to claim her."

And with a scornful smile he turned away.

"Stay, my lord!" cried Ferdinand. "Did I hear aright? Will you give your daughter's hand when I shall bring you wealth like that Antonio now possesses? I take you at your word. Remember it is pledged. Three days hence I will claim my bride."

And with a proud, triumphant smile he passed out.

"Three days, sayest thou?" muttered the Count. "Thy bride shall then be another's, and thou wilt claim her then in vain. 'Tis a strange vow I have made; I fear I have said too much. But no, it cannot be; no mortal could in three days gather up such boundless wealth as Count Antonio brings my child. 'Tis a foolish fear; I'll think of it no more."

And in dreams of grandeur yet to come, the haughty noble thought not of the sorrowing heart that beat so sadly in the bosom of his gentle child.

The three days were nearly spent, and well had the old priest done his work. The witnesses were come, all was proved, and Ferdinand de Vere was lord of the English wealth.

Count Antonio had yielded all his generous rival would accept and secretly left Italy.

The morning of the third day came, and proudly went the Count de Adelon through his lordly home, for that night would the barter of his fair young daughter bring all the wealth he coveted.

As thus he mused, a paper was placed in his hand. It was in the writing of Count Antonio, and thus it ran:

"My Lord:—This night, according to my promise, your

daughter shall wed the heir of Lord Devereux's unbounded wealth. Pardon whatever mystery may appear when next we meet. Ask nothing, and all shall be explained when the ceremony is over."

"Some romantic folly," thought the Count. "I care not what. He shall have no cause to chide me, for not a word will I speak till all is over. And now to Alice; she must know of this new whim."

And he passed on to where his daughter sat pale and still, striving to banish the tender thoughts as they rose in her sorrowing heart.

V

Gondola after gondola swept up to the marble steps and deposited its lighthearted occupants to swell the brilliant throng that filled the stately halls of the Count de Adelon.

Plumes and gay hearts fluttered, jewels and bright eyes flashed, soft words were spoken, tender glances given, and jests went around. Knights and ladies, elves and pages, kings and flower girls, all mingled gaily in the dance; sweet voices and rich melody filled the air; and so with mirth and music the masquerade went on.

"Has your highness seen the Lady Alice?" asked a stately knight of the fairy queen who stood beside him. "Lovely she has ever been, but tonight her beauty is beyond aught I have ever seen."

"Her dress is well chosen," replied his gay companion. "That bridal robe is but a token of the one she will shortly wear, for Count Antonio claims her hand; and if I do not err, the next time we tread these halls it will be to dance at the sweet lady's bridal. But look! Yonder comes the Count Antonio. I know him in spite of his mask, by the star of the Devereux upon his breast."

"He too is attired as for a bridal," said the knight, "but never did I see him bear himself so nobly as tonight. Did you mark that whisper as he offered Lady Alice yon white rose she seems so proud of?"

"That I did," answered the lady with a gay laugh. "I wish all knights grew as strangely graceful and gallant when a fair lady smiles on their suit. I must ask Alice for the charm she has used to change the awkward, rude Antonio into yon graceful cavalier in the white velvet doublet. The music sounds; do you dance?"

And knight and lady passed away through the flower-decked halls.

Many were the wondering remarks at the bridal dress of Alice and her lover, and ere long it was whispered through the crowd that the proud Count de Adelon had drawn them hither to celebrate the nuptials of his fair daughter with the young lord so many hearts had tried to win, not for his bravery or love, but for the name and fortune he possessed. And when at length the priest appeared, a low murmur passed through the crowd.

Then the Count de Adelon stepped proudly forth, saying, "My friends, pardon this little plot, but I desired to show all honor to the noble Count who this night weds my child; and where can they more fitly pledge their faith than here, amid festivity and joy, surrounded by happy hearts and loving friends? Father, we wait your services."

A deep stillness fell upon the throng as the bridal party stood before the priest, but a murmur of astonishment was heard when the bridegroom took his place, for the mask he had so carefully worn was not removed. All had wondered at the unbroken silence of the young Count. To none but Alice had he spoken; all others he had carefully avoided, and many had noticed the graceful ease of the once uncouth Count.

Curiosity and wonder were at their height, but respect restrained all questions till the solemn words were spoken. Then the eager crowd gathered around the Count de Adelon and poured forth their unbounded astonishment at the strange scene they had witnessed.

"Gladly will I tell you when I am told myself, my lord," he said, turning to the bridegroom. "Patiently have I borne my part in this strange masquerade of yours. The bridal is now over, and I claim your promise of revealing your reason for so mysterious an act."

"It shall be given," replied the bridegroom. The next moment the mask was off, and the noble face of Ferdinand de Vere appeared, glowing with joy and manly beauty, his stately form drawn proudly up, the brilliant star of an English earl flashing upon his breast, and Alice, radiant with happiness, leaning on his arm.

Not a sound broke the stillness that followed after the first low murmur of astonishment till the tones of his musical voice sounded through the long hall, saying, "My lord, you bid me claim your daughter when I could show as high a name, as boundless wealth as Count Antonio. I can do more, and even your ambitious heart can find naught to wish for when the son of the Earl of Devereux, with all the English wealth you covet, and his own fair fortune, is the happy husband of the child you would have sold for the worthless gold that cannot buy a noble woman's love.

"My right is proved, and Count Antonio has left Italy. And now, my lord, no longer as a simple knight, but Ferdinand Earl of Devereux and de Vere, I claim this hand, dearer than aught the earth can give, for with it comes a heart wealth could not buy, nor titles tempt. Kind friends," continued he, turning gaily to those knights who gathered warmly around him, "my best wish is that you may gain as fair a fortune and as true a bride as I have won by this masked marriage."

THE RIVAL PRIMA DONNAS

The opera house was filling fast with a gay and brilliant audience, empty boxes grew bright with lovely women, jewels sparkled, plumes waved, and fans began to move. The lively murmur of conversation filled the air, and all was in that state of pleasant confusion which precedes the first notes of the orchestra.

But on this night something of greater interest than usual seemed to possess the audience. All seemed to talk with eagerness of some important event about to take place, and opera glasses were leveled with untiring curiosity at one particular box, just above the stage, the curtains of which were closely drawn.

"My dear Giulio," said Lord N. to his friend Count P., "what is the meaning of the great interest everyone seems to feel in yonder box? What fair divinity is there enshrined? I am a stranger here, so pray explain, for I am curious as a woman."

"Listen, then," replied the Count, "and perhaps you too can share in the excitement of those about you. That box belongs to Beatrice, our fair prima donna, whose place Theresa the young debutante takes tonight. Beatrice has long been the pride and favorite of the public, as much for the blameless life she leads as for her beauty and unequaled voice, and until tonight no one has ventured to usurp her place. But suddenly an unknown singer has appeared, who by her loveliness and talent has won friends, and they desire she should make her first appearance here, well knowing that if she succeed in

37

pleasing our fastidious judges, her fortune will be made else-where. And Beatrice, instead of striving to outrival her, has generously yielded up the stage entirely that nothing might be wanting to secure a favorable reception for the young artist. Tonight, therefore, is to decide the success of one prima donna and perhaps the banishment of another, for if Theresa be suc-cessful, she will doubtless be engaged and Beatrice must go elsewhere; and thus all are anxious to see how each will bear her part in the coming trial."

"Now I shall indeed share your interest," replied Lord N., "but tell me more of this Beatrice who generously yields her place to a rival. Few women would so calmly step aside and let another win the laurels she might have gained. Is it not somewhat strange?"

"Nay, not so strange as one might fancy, Arthur," said his friend, "for it is whispered, and with truth I fear, that she will bestow the hand so many have sought in vain upon the hand-some painter yonder. He is a worthy person, but not a fitting husband for a truehearted woman like Beatrice; he is gay, careless, and fickle too. I fear she is tender and confiding, lov-ing with an Italian's passionate devotion if he be true, and tak-ing an Italian's quick revenge if he prove false; therefore, I pity her and hope she will place her happiness in better hands. But hush, the overture begins, and I must join my sister."

The two friends parted, the curtain rose, and amid a breathless silence the young cantatrice appeared, beautiful in-deed but pale and trembling with suppressed emotion.

Slight was the applause that greeted her; that she was yet to win. But a few kind faces smiled upon her, and with an ef-fort she began, faintly and low at first, but as the music swelled, her voice grew stronger till it rang clear and sweet as a silver clarion through the vast house. As if carried away by the resolution to win confidence and approbation from those who seemed to look so coldly on her, she sang on till the en-thusiasm she felt sent a bright glow to her pale cheek, a deeper light to her eye, and a richer music to her wonderful voice. Stiller and stiller grew the multitude before her, and when the last clear notes died lingeringly away, they still sat spellbound till a garland fell at her feet and a woman's glad voice cried "Encore! Encore!"

At that sound every eye was turned to the mysterious box. The curtains were flung back, and radiant in beauty stood the generous Beatrice. Forgetful of all but the trembling singer before her, she clapped her white hands and cast the flowers from her own bosom at her wondering rival's feet.

Then from pit to gallery thundered the applause and showered the bouquets till, overcome by her own victory, the cantatrice was borne from the stage and the curtain fell.

When it again rose and the opera went on, the box of Beatrice was deserted, and the young painter had vanished from the crowd. They now stood together on the vine-covered balcony of her splendid home, and the summer moonlight falling on their faces revealed the happy tears that shone in Beatrice's dark eyes and the forced smile upon her lover's lips as he looked down upon her, saying in a troubled voice:

"I fear you will repent your choice, Beatrice. What can I give you in return for all you lose in thus becoming mine? You will miss the pleasant flattery of the world and pine for the homage that has so long been yours. You will soon sigh to be again the queen of many hearts, the loved, admired, and happy woman whose power so many felt and owned. It is not yet too late; remember, I can give you nothing but a painter's home, which you will soon grow weary of and long again for the brilliant life you leave so gladly now."

"How little do you know me, Claude," said Beatrice. "Have I not tried the world and found its flattering homage false? Have I not sought for happiness in wealth and fame and sought in vain until I found it in your love? What then do I leave but all I am most weary of? And what do I gain but all I prize and cherish most on earth? The painter's home I will make beautiful with the useless wealth I have won, and the painter's heart I will make happy by all the blessings a woman's love can give! Then do not fear for me. What can I lose in leaving a careless world for a husband and a home?"

And as she spoke, she laid her proud head trustingly upon his breast, little dreaming of the bitter disappointment her fond words brought to the false heart where all her hope and faith were placed. As thus they stood, a sound broke on the silent air, and soon along the moonlit street, her carriage drawn by a shouting crowd, with torches gleaming around her and flowers falling thick and fast, came Theresa, the successful prima donna; and Beatrice looked smiling down, hidden by the vines, and watched the bright train as with joyful cries and waving garlands it swept by.

"See, Claude, how soon I am forgotten by these admiring followers of mine. They bore me home in triumph once as they are bearing young Theresa now. One day she will be forgotten for another as I am even here, and then may she find a faithful friend who never will forsake her and a heart that never can forget. Success and fame be hers, and happiness like mine when she is weary of the world," she said as the last sound died away.

"But must you leave me now, Claude?" she added fondly as the young man threw his mantle around him and prepared to go.

"I must, for it grows late and I must be early at my studio tomorrow. Therefore, good night, love, and pleasant dreams," replied the painter, bending down to kiss the fair face lifted to his own, and as he did so, from his breast a little paper fell unheeded to the ground. They parted, and with fond hopes stirring in her heart, she watched his tall figure till it vanished in the distance; and then she was alone with her own happy thoughts.

Long she sat musing in the silvery moonlight while the cool night wind fanned her cheek and rustled softly through the blooming vines that clustered around her. At length the echo of the distant clocks as they rang twelve dispelled her pleasant dreams, and as she rose to leave the balcony, before her lay the paper that had fallen from her lover's breast.

"It is some tender song from Claude. He dared not give it me, but left it at my feet to read when he was gone. Dear Claude, how fond and faithful he has ever been," thought Beatrice as with an eager hand she raised the note and hastened to the lighted room beyond, where with a joyous smile she opened it and read these words:

"My Claude, if I succeed and all goes well, then come to me at midnight when I am alone, and let me hear from your dear lips the praise I value far beyond the flattery of the world. For your sake only do I thus seek wealth and fame, that I may become more worthy of the generous love you have given to, *Theresa.*"

Pale and paler grew the reader's face as each word met her startled gaze. White and still as a marble statue she stood till all was read, and then sank down like one smitten by a heavy blow. Not a sigh or a tear escaped her as she lay there amid the ruins of her young heart's hope and joy. Her sorrow was too deep for tears, and she would only seek to realize the bitter truth that came thus suddenly upon her. She had loved fervently and trusted with a woman's perfect faith—and now, in one short moment, all was changed, love forgotten, faith betrayed, and bright hopes vanished like a dream, while all the light and loveliness of life seemed gone forever. When at length she rose, a sudden blight seemed to have fallen on her; for the face so lately radiant with love and joy was now pale and haggard, her dark eyes shone with a troubled light, and her white lips moved but made no sound. Still, in her grief and deep despair she struggled to be calm, and a faint smile shone upon her pallid face as she read the note once more and whispered, "It may *not* be true. Some enemy to Claude's peace and my own may have placed it there, and yet he was so cold tonight and seemed to leave me so gladly. Ah, it all comes back upon me now, and he whom I have loved so fondly has deserted me at last. But no, I *will* not doubt him yet. I will believe him true till I can prove his falsehood plainly. But alas, how can I know and whom can I trust now!"

With a bitter sigh she bent her face upon her hands, while doubts and hopes and fears came thronging thick and fast. Suddenly she started up, saying hurriedly, "There is one way left and that is my last hope. I cannot live in doubt and will know all tonight," and with a hasty step she vanished into an inner room.

The silver clock in the deserted chamber was just striking half past twelve as from a private door beneath the balcony there emerged a slender figure muffled in a cloak, whose face was hidden by the dark plumes of his hat. For a moment he lingered in the shadow of the door and then with a light, quick step passed down the quiet street.

In a luxurious apartment, silver lamps shed a soft light on a velvet couch and gleaming mirror, and the cool night wind floated in heavy with the breath of flowers. All was beautiful and bright and still. Theresa the young cantatrice was sitting with the painter Claude at her feet. Jewels still glittered in her hair and on the graceful robe she wore; the garlands and bouquets she had won lay scattered around her. Never had she looked so beautiful as then, when joy and triumph sparkled in her eyes and glowed upon her cheek. With a fond, proud smile she looked upon the painter, saying:

"Am I not worthy of you now, Claude? Have I not shown my love to be as strong as yours? I am no longer poor, unknown, and friendless, but a glorious future lies before me. Fame and wealth I will soon win. What greater happiness do I ask than to share all with you? But you are sad, dear Claude, and this night should be one of joy alone. Then, why so gloomy? Tell me all and let Theresa charm your grief away."

"What sorrow would not vanish in the light of such a smile?" replied the painter, gazing passionately into the lovely face that bent above him. "Can you doubt my joy that you have won from others love and admiration like my own? It is not that which makes me sad—it is the memory of Beatrice. Forgive me if I speak a name you cannot wish to hear, and do not doubt my constancy to you. My love for her died long ago, and now I only pity. But tonight the image of her in her bitter grief, when she learns all, *will* rise before me even here. She has loved me as few women love, and my heart rebukes me for the sorrow I must give her in return. Each generous deed she does for you, each gentle word she speaks, but makes me seem more false and cruel still and almost turns my pity into love again."

A dark frown gathered on Theresa's face, and her eyes flashed scornfully upon her lover as he spoke. When he turned away, forgetful for a moment even of her, she rose proudly up and stood before him, saying with a haughty smile upon her lips:

"If Beatrice be still so dear to you, I fear there is no place in your heart for me. Therefore, choose now between us, for I will have no rival in your love. If Beatrice be dearest, then go and share with her the quiet home she longs for, and in her calm affection may you find the happiness you seek. But if your many vows be true and Theresa most beloved, then come and tread with me the path that lies before us. Share with me the wealth and fame I go to win; and in the gay, brilliant world, find all that makes love pleasant, and happiness in my fond, faithful love. Both are before you; therefore, choose and let all doubts be ended here forever."

With wonder, love, and admiration stirring in his heart, the painter gazed upon her as she spoke. When she stood silently before him with her white arms folded proudly on her breast and her clear eyes shining on him with a deeper light than the jewels flashing in her hair, while on her lips there played a smile half scornful and half fond, he would have paused no longer in his choice; but a tender face rose up before him with dark, reproachful eyes that seemed to warn and win him back. He thought of Beatrice—her generous, trusting love, her faith in him, her wild sorrow and despair when she should find that faith betrayed—and his heart whispered that no joy, no peace, would brighten life for him while haunted by the memory of wrong and falsehood such as this. As these thoughts passed through his mind, his better angel for the moment triumphed. He seized his cloak and turned to go, saying half aloud, "I cannot break her heart. *She* is my truest love. I will not wrong her thus." But the words died on his lips, for there before him stood Theresa with the proud light banished from her eyes, which now shone on him through bright tears as with a tender, pleading smile she stretched those fair arms toward him, whispering softly:

"Have you chosen, dearest Claude?"

The cloak dropped from his hand. Beatrice was forgotten, and his only answer was to lay her bright head on his breast and whisper as he folded her closer still: "Yes, I *have* chosen, and nothing now can part us more." As thus they stood, Theresa, with a sudden cry and a face white with terror, pointed trembling to the window, through which the moonlight dimly shone as the drooping curtains floated to and fro.

"Did you see it, Claude?" she whispered fearfully. "A wild, pale face with gleaming eyes looked in upon us through the leaves, and as you turned, it vanished. Oh, do not leave me, for it may return."

"Fear nothing, dearest. I am here to guard you. Nay, do not tremble so; 'twas but your fancy or a passing shadow. Sit here and let me sing to you, for now my only joy is to cheer and watch above *you.*"

And all night long the quiet moon looked down upon the happy lovers as they sat, forgetful of the world, wrapped in a blissful dream of love and joy.

And all night long the same quiet moon shone on a brokenhearted woman as she paced her splendid chamber with clasped hands and tearless eyes, struggling with her bitter sorrow and despair in a stern silence far more terrible to see than the wildest, saddest tears a woman ever shed.

II

The noonday sunlight shining through crimson curtains cast a rosy glow on the pale cheek of the painter Claude as with a look of troubled joy he stood before his easel, from which Theresa's face looked back upon him.

"I cannot give these lips the proud, bright smile she wears, and yet, if I had never looked on her, this would seem most beautiful to me," he murmured half aloud as he bent nearer still to gaze upon his lovely work.

"It *is* most beautiful, dear Claude," echoed a low voice at his side, and turning with a guilty start, he met the dark eyes of Beatrice bent on him with a strange, searching look, before which his own gaze fell.

"Why have you never let me see this lovely face before? Did you fear I should grow jealous, Claude? If so, you wronged me, for I well know the love you bear me and I shall never doubt it more," said Beatrice. A dark smile passed across her face as she watched her lover standing pale and silent by her side, fearing to look upon her whom he had so wronged.

But as she looked, with a sudden effort he shook off the spell that held him silent and, in a voice he strove in vain to render gay, replied, "Then you can trust me to look daily on a face like this, and never fear that it may teach me to love you less. Ah, Beatrice, you do not truly love me, or some jealous fear would stir your woman's heart and waken tender doubts of me. If I should love another, you would soon forget me."

"Never! I should not forget you nor forgive you if you were false. But tell me, Claude, you do not love Theresa? She is younger, lovelier than I, but she will never be to you all I will be—can never cling to you with half the faith and constancy as I have done. Look in my face, dear Claude, and answer truly. *Do* you love Theresa?" A sudden light flashed in her eyes; a sudden passion trembled in her voice as Beatrice thus spoke. With a fond, imploring glance she looked up into the face half averted as he answered hastily:

"Foolish Beatrice, you can doubt me then, but do not fear. Theresa is no more to me than yonder picture, a lovely thing to look upon and then forget."

"Nay, Claude, look in my face, and as you love me, answer. If she be dearest, tell me truly, but oh, deceive me not. Choose now between us—Theresa with her beauty or Beatrice with all her love. Speak, Claude, I will pardon all for the truth's sake," urged Beatrice, still looking with strange earnestness into her lover's changing face.

He turned away and for a moment struggled with the wish to tell her all and trust her generous love to pardon him. But his eye fell on Theresa's lovely face; as it smiled upon him from his easel, he remembered that he had already chosen. Now as then passion conquered; he thought only of Theresa, but with a false smile on his lips, he turned to Beatrice, softly saying as he drew her to his side:

"Banish these doubts and let no fear of another cloud your joy, dearest. Look up and smile again, for I have made my choice."

"You have, you have! And I am not the chosen one. Oh,

Claude, false to the last," murmured Beatrice in a low, broken voice as she bent her face upon her hands, for she read his heart and her last hope was gone. The painter only caught his whispered name, and after casting one fond glance at the fatal picture, he looked down upon the bent head that rested for a moment on his breast, with mingled pity, shame, and triumph stirring in his heart.

A sudden tap at the studio door broke the silence. As her lover left the room, Beatrice raised her face and pressed her hands upon her breast, as if to still her bitter grief, and her white lips whispered:

"May God forgive him for this cruel wrong. I sought to win him to a generous confession of his fault, and that should have atoned for all. But 'tis in vain; he would deceive me to the last and turn the pure, devoted love I bore him into scorn and pity for his weakness and the double falsehood he has shown. Oh, Claude! I could have borne to lose your love, but not to see my tender trust so cruelly betrayed. But hush, he comes. I cannot steal away, and so will look my last and then depart forever."

And as his step drew near, she stilled her sorrow, dashed away the tears that lay upon her cheek, and sinking on a couch, half unconscious of what she did, began with trembling fingers to make a garland of some rare flowers heaped in a vase that stood beside her.

The painter frowned as he saw her thus employed, for the flowers were destined for another. But concealing his anger, he gaily said as he resumed his palette and brush: "These were gathered for you, dear Beatrice. You see, they are roses, Love's own flowers; then will you not wear them tonight for my sake?"

"Shall I not rather weave them into a garland for the lovely Theresa, for whom they are fitter ornaments than for me? I will crown her with roses, that the world may see I neither fear nor envy her. Think not that I slight your gift, Claude, but I know it will give you pleasure to see it resting on her beautiful head," said Beatrice with a bitter smile, bending still lower to her task to hide her sorrow-stricken face. Claude cast a quick, fearful glance upon her as she spoke, but there was no sign of anger or suspicion on her half-averted face, over which the crimson drapery cast a warm, bright glow. With a sigh of relief he gently replied:

"I shall indeed delight in seeing a wreath of your weaving on your rival's head, for it will only prove to the world more plainly still how generous and noble a heart beats in your breast. Beatrice, this will indeed be a garland fit for a queen," he added, looking with admiration at the graceful band of flowers she had woven with her utmost skill. "But put in no more roses, or you will *crush* instead of crown her, Beatrice, for this wreath, light as it is, will fall heavily from the height whence you will drop it on her head. It might be a pleasant death for one to die crushed with flowers in our hour of joy; but we cannot lose Theresa yet, so weave the garland lightly, and you can add no other charm to your lovely work."

And with these words upon his lips, he turned away and soon seemed unconscious of all but the beautiful face before him.

Beatrice did not speak. But as her lover's words fell on her ear, she started and some dreadful thought seemed to flash into her mind. For her cheek grew paler still, a fierce, dark smile shot across her face, her eyes gleamed with a sudden light, and her lips moved silently, as if she muttered spells above the flowers she wove. Her lover seemed to have forgotten even her, and as he bent eagerly to his work, she watched the color deepen in his cheek, the smile rise to his lips, the sparkle to his eye, as with a rapid, skillful hand he gave fresh beauty to the fair face of her rival. And as she watched, sterner and darker grew her face, sadder and heavier the load of her grief upon her heart, stronger and deeper the wild thoughts that stirred in her troubled brain. At length she rose, folded her mantle around her, and with the flower crown in her hand, glided to the painter's side, saying:

"I must leave you now, Claude, but we shall *meet tonight.*"

He started like one in a dream and, with a hasty word and a careless glance, bade her farewell. Then, seeming to remember that he had a part to play, he took her hand, saying in a tender voice, "Farewell, dear Beatrice. I fear I have been but a dull companion, but Theresa leaves us soon and would think little of my skill if her picture were not done.

"I shall not fail to join you tonight, for I long to see the flower crown given. So adieu till then."

And bending down to shun the gaze of her clear, dark eyes, he softly kissed her cheek as she passed out. He turned to his work, saying half aloud as he bent to touch with his own the smiling lips of Theresa:

"My part has been well played. Beatrice trusts me blindly still, and now one kiss from those beautiful lips shall be my best reward." As he lifted his head, a dark shadow flitted away from the half-open door and vanished in the gloomy gallery beyond.

It was Beatrice!

Never had the Opera House been so full as now. Gallery after gallery filled, and still the crowd poured in. For the fame of the lovely singer had flown far and wide, and hundreds gathered there to wonder and admire.

The purple curtains were undrawn in the box of Beatrice, but the painter Claude stood with folded arms in the shadow of the gallery opposite and watched with a strange interest all that passed before him. He turned often from the gay, brilliant throng to look with sorrow and regret toward that still, dark curtain, behind which sat the woman he had so wronged and deceived. All her fond, tender words and loving acts of kindness came freshly to his memory that night. Her trusting love had never seemed so beautiful as now, when he had lost all right to seek or claim it, for that night he had vowed to fly with her fair rival and it was now too late to sigh and sorrow for the true heart he had cast away.

The curtain rose and the rustling crowd was still as music filled the air. Norma, the white-robed priestess, glided in among her vestals with the sacred oak leaves in her hand. Never had Theresa looked so beautiful as now, for love, ambition, joy, and triumph lent a radiant beauty to her face, a statelier grace to her fair form, and a deeper, richer music to her magical voice, which echoed with a strange, sweet melody through the vast house and seemed to grow more fresh and beautiful as she poured forth in music all the sorrow, jealousy, and love of the unhappy Norma, whom she personated with such tenderness and passion.

The painter still lingered in the shadow, but his eyes no longer rested on the lonely box. They never moved now from the fair enchantress, who in all her sorrow and despair seemed but to sing for him alone. Her eye turned often to meet his with a glance of love and pride that seemed to say, "All this I do for your dear sake, and all my triumph will I share with you." The memory of Beatrice had vanished like a dream beneath the spell of such an hour, and all was now forgotten but love and the beautiful Theresa.

Meanwhile, behind the drooping curtains of the prima donna's box sat one who could have acted Norma, the deceived, deserted woman, with a truth and power that would have thrilled the hearts that beat so quickly now. Beatrice sat in the purple shadow like a marble statue, pale, still, and cold, her hands clasped tightly on her breast and her dark, gleaming eyes fixed on her lover's face, which through a narrow opening could be seen, while before her lay the rose crown she had woven for her rival. So amid the music, light, and bursts of joyful applause she sat unmoved and never turned her steadfast gaze from the face that looked with such fond passion and delight upon the happy singer, who was acting, just below her, all the bitter grief and desolation she so keenly felt.

At length the opera ended. The priestess's doom was spoken, the fatal veil was folded around her, and with her wild, sad farewell lingering on the air, she was borne away; and all was over. But soon, amid the welcoming shouts of those who had sat spellbound by her power, she reappeared, no longer pale and sorrow-stricken, but radiant with smiles and bright in youthful joy and loveliness as with folded hands she bowed before the admiring throng, who carpeted her path with flowers and vented their delight in joyful cries and echoing applause.

Suddenly there was a pause, and a deep stillness fell on

the excited multitude as every eye turned from the lovelier singer to a fairer, stranger sight. The curtains were thrown wide apart, and the stately form of Beatrice stood proudly forth, glittering with a strange magnificence. Jewels sparkled on her velvet robe and shone like stars in her dark hair, a deep changing color glowed upon her cheek, and a wild brilliance flashed in her dark eyes as they glanced rapidly about the up-turned faces looking into hers.

"Look up, look up, Theresa, and receive the crown," cried a distant voice that she well knew. Lifting her wondering eyes, the lovely singer shuddered as she met the dark glance that flashed upon her from the haggard face of the rival she had wronged, and in that glance each read the other's meaning. While Theresa bowed her head in shame and fear, Beatrice, with a sudden smile, raised her white arms high above her head and stood a moment gracefully holding a flower crown while her eye sought out some distant object. Then the garland *fell,* and high above the tumultuous applause that shook the walls roared the death shriek of Theresa. And Beatrice, pointing to her as she lay amid the flowers with the *iron* crown concealed among the roses on her blood-stained hair, cried in a voice that never ceased to echo in one guilty hearer's ears: "You bade me crown her, Claude. See, I have done it! Better to 'die *crushed with flowers*' than live to be what you have rendered me!" And with a wild, fearful laugh she vanished from the sight of the horror-stricken crowd.

Years passed away. In a lonely convent lived and died a sad, gray-haired man, worn and wasted with remorse, and in a quiet home for the insane dwelt a beautiful, pale woman who constantly wove garlands and, like a swan, died singing mournfully—and these were Claude and Beatrice.

THE LITTLE SEED

Deep in the ground, folded in withered leaves, lay a little seed, and longed for the time when it might spring up to the light and air above. But the snow lay deep and cold over the earth, and no sunlight came to call it forth; so patiently it waited and watched meanwhile what went on below. All around slept the flower roots, and the little ants lay safe in their warm cells. But when the snow melted and the cool drops stole down to wake and freshen them after their long sleep, then each one sent forth its tender shoot and watched daily over it, that it might gain strength to reach the light above; and as they were thus employed, many were the gay thoughts of the long and happy hours they soon might spend on the pleasant earth. Each longed to see the friends from whom it parted when it sank to sleep beneath the autumn leaves. All had friends and kindred but the little seed, who did not even know what flower name it bore nor how the green earth looked. Listening to the merry tales the flowers told, it grew ever more and more eager for the time when it might join the happy flowers and find friends to love. Till now it had slept and knew nothing, and when it woke, found itself a stranger among the roots and seeds of many unknown plants.

At length, one by one the flowers sprang up to bloom in the soft spring sun. Still all alone and friendless lay the little seed, and heard the flower voices singing gaily above and watched the busy ants as they came to store up food for the wintertime; and from them it learned how bright and beauti-

ful the earth had grown, how the ugly seeds that had lain beside it had changed to lovely flowers and now were dancing in
the spring wind.

"Ah," sighed the little seed, "why may not I too enjoy these
pleasant things? Why must I live sad and solitary in the dark
earth while my sister flowers are leading happy lives above? I
will not stay alone; I will bloom as fair as the rose which the
flowers call their queen, and live here no longer."

Then a wise little ant said to the impatient seed: "If thou
goest too soon, thy life will be short and sad. The winds are
too cold yet for thee; and thou must be content to stay yet
longer in the warm earth and gather strength, for thou art as
yet too young to take fit care of thyself. I will bring thee tidings of what goes on above, and do thou wait here the time
when thou mayest spring up."

So, long lay the little seed, and when at length it gathered
strength and put forth its shoots, they soon found their way to
the light and grew daily green and strong. Then at last the
brown seed was a plant and saw the earth it had so longed for.
The sunlight came to strengthen and the dew to feed it. The
soft wind blew to brush the dust from its tender leaves, and
the gentle rain came down to moisten its young roots. Yet still
it was not happy, for no flower came; and though it stood
straight and tall, no little fragrant bud peeped from the green
leaves. So among the garden flowers it found no friends, and
they looked with wonder at the tall plant which bore only
broad green leaves. Thus through the summer lived the nameless one, but found no more joy than when it lay a poor brown
seed below the earth.

But when the flowers sank to sleep again after their short
summer life, the plant did not become a seed again. But one
by one the leaves fell off, and naked and alone it stood while
the cold winds blew and the winter snow came down. Then
was it left friendless and solitary through the dreary months
when no soft rain fell nor dew came, and yet it still lived on
and did not suffer. Gentle thoughts and grateful feelings came,
and it began to think it could not be alone, for someone still
thought of the lonely little tree. Then it said within itself, "I
sought to make no friends, but lived a discontented life amid

all sweet things, unmindful of the loving care taken of one who so ill deserved it. I might have won by gentle words the love of the fair flowers I envied; and they perhaps would have taught me how to bear sweet blossoms like their own, or if that could not be, with such loving friends I should have no longer felt alone. I may yet do this, and if they blossom near me when the summer comes again, they shall find that while they slept in the warm earth, I, amid snow and bitter winds, have learned to find joy in my own heart and happiness in loving others."

Then through the long, cold winter stood the little tree, and grew ever stronger, both in heart and form. When the winds swept rudely by, gently it bowed its head, and thus no harm came to it. Though the snow and ice lay around it, below in the warm earth the roots sent fresh sap to the stem above and fitted it for summertime.

Soon the earth grew green again, and the flowers showed their smiling faces. The wind went singing by, and the soft sunlight brought strength and beauty to their tender forms.

Then they wondered at the little tree, for it grew faster than any of them and soon spread its slender boughs above their heads. They no longer smiled because it bore no flowers, but looked up to it for shelter. At first they dared not speak to it, for they remembered how proud and selfish it had been. But soon this fear passed away, for the tree drooped lovingly over them, spread its broad leaves to shield them from the sun and rain, and whispered gentle words to them and prayed to be their friend. Then little vines folded their soft arms about its strong stem and, leaning on the kindly tree, spread their bright flowers and blossoms on its breast, striving in sweet odors to tell their love. Birds made their homes among its boughs, and tenderly the tree spread its leaves above their nests, that no cruel hands should harm them as it softly rocked the little ones to sleep.

Thus the once friendless tree was loved by all. Flowers trustingly looked to it for shelter and blossomed on its breast. Birds' sweet voices sang among its branches, and bright-winged insects found homes amid its leaves. Then was life truly pleasant; and thus lived the tree many summers. Though in the wintertime it stood alone, yet pleasant thoughts of the gentle little friends who lay sleeping all around filled its heart; and thus it never felt as solitary as before it learned to seek for happiness in gentle deeds.

When spring came and the flowers opened their bright eyes, they looked always first at their friend the tree and seemed to gather around the flowerless one, as if to cheer and thank it for its kindly care of them. Thus amid a garden of loving friends grew the tree ever more strong and lovely. At length, as if to repay it for the patient love it bore within, came the first blossoms on its boughs, and as the white petals unfolded, a soft blush spread among them, making more lovely the contrast with the deep-green leaves, while their breath was sweeter than the lily or the rose.

Then the flowers rejoiced that blossoms fairer than their own had been given to their gentle friend. Golden butterflies spread their bright wings above them, and bees, with their low voices, drank the honey from their cups.

Thus for many days they bloomed, but at length withered and died. Then the other flowers wept and mourned for their friend; but the little tree had learned to trust one wiser than itself, and patiently it waited what should come.

As the summer days passed on, tender green fruit appeared upon its boughs, and as the warm sunlight kissed them, brightly glowed their rosy cheeks. When the summer flowers passed away, their last look fell upon the tree, now grown tall and graceful, while among the deep-green leaves hung crimson fruit, glowing in the autumn sun.

Thus, as years went by, larger grew the tree till its broad branches cast their shadows far and wide while beneath, sweet flowers bloomed, the tall grass waved, and gentle birds brooded about their nests. Happy children played around, and their voices sounded gaily as they sang among the flowers and gathered in the rosy fruit.

And thus the friendless little seed, after long waiting, became a noble tree, stronger and fairer for all that it had learned.

A NEW YEAR'S BLESSING

It was New Year's Eve. While other homes were lit up with a cheerful glow that glimmered pleasantly into the snowy street, deeper seemed to grow the gloom in old John Owen's spacious room. A fire burned dimly on the marble hearth, and through the half-drawn curtains twilight shadows seemed to steal in, bringing with them cold and darkness from the outer world.

With a frown on his stern, wrinkled face the old man sat in his lonely home, uncheered by a single friend. No children gathered about his knee, filling the silence with the music of their little voices.

No wife sat at his side recalling tenderly the many happy festivals they had enjoyed together. No New Year's greetings fell kindly from his lips, and no New Year's memories rose up warmly in his heart.

The past was a bitter one and he would not look back upon it. The present was joyless and dark and the future a dull blank with no cherished hopes to be fulfilled, no generous aspirations to be realized.

Life, instead of strengthening with its joys and sorrows, had soured and hardened his once kind heart. Time had silvered and bowed his head, but passion and pride had left still deeper marks on the dark, furrowed face that brooded gloomily above the waning fire in the twilight of that New Year's Eve.

A plain, mild-eyed woman entered bearing lights and a tray, which she placed on a table at his side. As she was about to leave the room, she said with a friendly interest in her pleasant voice: "There is a little girl below, sir, who desires to see you. Shall I show her up? She is no beggar, sir, but a pretty, sweet-spoken child," she added quickly as the old man turned to her.

"Send her away—I will not be disturbed," he said harshly, with an angry frown on his brow. "She would not come here if she were not a beggar. I have nothing for her, so bid her go."

"She wants nothing of you, sir, and only asks to hand you a letter; surely that is no great favor. Let me bring her up—it will cheer you this dull evening to see a young thing at your fireside, though it be but for a minute," said the woman, looking at him with pleading eyes while her voice trembled with strange eagerness.

"Let her come, then, for I see I shall have no peace till it's over. But mind, Martha, I will have no more of this; it troubles me and wastes my time."

Speaking thus with an impatient sigh, the old man sank back in his cushioned chair while the woman with a glad smile hastened out, leaving him lost in a reverie so deep that he neither saw nor heard what passed around him till a low voice said close beside him:

"Grandfather, Mother sends you this with a New Year's greeting."

Startled at the unknown voice breaking the deep silence, the old man looked hastily up and saw before him a dark-eyed, slender child holding a letter toward him and looking into his face with a glance of such imploring earnestness that he unconsciously obeyed it and took the letter, gazing silently at the beautiful pale little figure, as if it were an apparition come to him from the sorrowful past.

On the paper he held were traced these words in a feeble hand, blurred here and there by the writer's sudden tears:

"My father, on this New Year's Eve, when I trust some tender memories of me are warm about your heart, I venture to appeal to you once more, not for myself, but for my child who brings you this. Ten years ago, when your curse fell on me for obeying what I felt to be my duty, and you sent me from the shelter of my home because I could not break the solemn vow I had made him who is now dead, you bade me never cross your threshold more, nor seek to see you. I obey, and standing in the winter night without my father's door, I send my child to you with this last prayer.

"By the great love you bore me long ago, I now beseech you to protect and cherish her who soon will be both father-less and motherless in this great troubled world, for I am spent with sorrow, pain, and labor and shall soon be in the only home now left me. Oh, my father, grant me this. Take my lit-tle child, and she will prove a household angel to your deso-late home, gladdening it with her young life and filling a daughter's place in your empty heart.

"She knows nothing of my request, and I have parted from her in this world. So if she stays, be tender with her grief and tell her death itself was far less bitter than this long separa-tion, but I could not leave her friendless and shall pass away in peace knowing she is safe in the dear old home I have lost.

"Talk with Alice. Let her simple eloquence plead for her, and may her youth and innocence soften your heart until it take her in.

"I will return in a single hour, and if you grant my prayer, place a light in the window of the room where I so often sat beside your knee long years ago. Its soft light shining forth into the gloom about me shall be your silent answer, and I will go away blessing you forever. God keep my child and warm your stern heart, Father, toward your Margaret."

Paler and paler grew John Owen's dark face as he read. When the last word, long unseen, unspoken, met his sight, the paper fluttered to the ground, and shading his eyes with his hand, he sat buried in thought so deep that all else was for-gotten till a patient sigh recalled him. Glancing up, he saw the little figure standing in the firelight, which seemed to flicker lovingly upon it.

With an eager, troubled eye he looked and saw how poorly clad his grandchild was, how blue and cold the small feet looked in their worn coverings, how thin the scanty cloak that poorly screened her from the wind. And with a strange pity (strange because so new) he saw the traces of snowflakes lying on the long fair hair that fell about her colorless face and a little trembling hand lifted to wipe away the quiet tears that glittered there.

A sudden mist passed before his eyes, and in a voice whose natural harshness he strove unconsciously to soften, he bade her come to him.

She silently obeyed and, standing at his knee, looked freely and confidingly into the anxious countenance bent over her and met its eager gaze with a wondering smile.

Long the old man scanned the young face lifted to his own, and saw with a secret joy all his lost daughter's gentle beauty shining there—her strength and courage in the small firm mouth, her tenderness in the clear light of the large mild eyes, her noble intellect in the broad tranquil brow—and over all the warm glow of her generous heart seemed playing like the red light of the flames that showed all this to the keen eyes of old John Owen.

As he looked thus, a sudden pallor blanched the child's thin face, and with a low cry as of pain, she caught his hand as if to save herself from falling. Instinctively the old man encircled her with his strong arm and drew her upon his knee. Then, looking anxiously down upon the white face pillowed on his breast, where no head had lain for ten long years, he whispered with strange tenderness in his stern voice as he uttered his dead wife's name:

"What is it, Alice? Are you in pain? Tell me, and you shall not suffer if I have the power to help you."

The child lay silent for a moment, bravely struggling to repress the tears that trembled beneath her closed lids. Then, stealing one arm around his neck, she nestled closer to his bosom, saying softly:

"How kind you are to me, dear Grandfather. I am not sick; only the warm fire and the sight of those nice things made me weak and dizzy for a minute. Indeed, I could not help it, sir."

"Good God! My child, are you faint with *hunger?* Have you had no food today?" cried the old man with a start.

"We don't get much to eat, now that Mother is so ill; she

cannot work, sir. And she *would* make me take the last we had, because she said it might be a hard night for me and I needed it the most. But I knew the hungry look in her eyes, and when I saw those tempting things, I could not help wishing she had some to make her well and strong again. I didn't mean to cry, Grandfather, but the tears *will* come when I think of her so cold and sick," and speaking thus in a broken voice, little Alice dropped her head on his shoulder and sobbed bitterly.

Closer the old man's arm was folded around her while the light touch of the small hand on his neck and the warm drops falling there seemed to melt the ice that years of loneliness and sinful pride had formed about his heart, and won back gentle feelings that had long been strangers there.

Silently he lifted the slight form of the child, and drawing from a distant corner a small chair long unused, he placed her in it at the table. Then, heaping a plate with delicate food, he bade her eat. Looking gratefully up through her half-dried tears, she timidly said, taking a little biscuit or two:

"Could I save these for Mother, sir? I should enjoy mine more if she had some too. I do not mean to beg, but could you *spare* her these, Grandfather?"

Her wistful look and the silent tale of want and suffering so plainly read in the hollow cheek and eye smote old John Owen with such a pang of keen remorse that he turned hastily away, bidding her take all—take anything she liked.

Then, bowing his head upon his hands, he sat in silence while there rose before him faithful pictures of the past called up by that true wizard Memory, which sought out a secret chamber in that worldly heart, above which the one word "Father" shone, and unlocked it. Forth floated a band of tender memories, hopes, and feelings, which gathered around the lonely phantom of a young girl sitting at his knee. He seemed to hear her cheerful voice, to feel her fond kiss on his cheek and the loving pressure of her hand as he had felt them long ago.

But this vision passed, and again the fair phantom was at his feet, not smiling now, but bathed in tears, and kneeling there in earnest supplication, praying to be heard before his

curse fell on her head. A figure fainter than her own passed
between them and, looking upon Margaret with deep love and
sorrow in its brave, true face, led her silently away into the
gloom which seemed to fall upon the old man's heart as the
third vision of his daughter rose before him.

He saw her paler and more shadowy, still standing in the
bleak winter night at his closed door, waiting meekly at the
threshold of her once happy home to make the last sacrifice
and part forever from the dearest thing she loved on earth.

With death floating dimly over her, with poverty and sorrow at her side, bowed with care and spent with labor, but
brave and generous to the last—so stood the phantom Margaret at the portal of her father's heart, where her little child
had knocked till it opened wide and took her in.

With a low groan the old man lifted his white head and
glanced fearfully about the wide, luxurious room, as if it were
still peopled with the mournful images his troubled mind had
conjured up. But all was still, the lights gleaming clearly on
the costly objects around him. The warm air was fragrant with
the odor of the rich wines on his table, and the red glow of the
fire filled each nook with generous warmth.

But these things brought no comfort to him, for over all fell
the pale shadow of the patient figure at his door.

The child had noiselessly gathered up and fed the dying
embers till they cheered the gloomy room and now flickered
brightly on her as she sat in her low seat with a heavy gilded
book lying open on her knee, at whose rare pictures she was
intently gazing.

"Read to me, Alice," said the old man suddenly, longing to
break the silence that oppressed him and to still the low reproaches conscience whispered sternly in his ear.

With a glance of silent wonder the child in a sweet, reverent voice read from the costly book, kept but for show and
never opened, the simple story of the holy child whose birthday had been celebrated but a week before far and wide over
the earth by human hearts purified and gladdened by His sacred life and love.

Silently the old man listened to the music of that clear

young voice and looked upon the meek face, brightened by the golden shadows of falling hair that bent above the book, whose worth and beauty he had never truly felt till now, when each word fell like dew upon his heart, melting its icy pride, cooling its long-cherished passion, and calling up like flowers all pure affections and generous impulses till in his breast nothing remained but deep remorse for years of sinful cruelty and a wild yearning to behold again his exiled daughter.

The hour was nearly gone, and she would soon return never to depart; but ere she came, he would try the child's love for her and feel the full depth of the sacrifice and sorrow he now had the will and power to spare them both. "Alice, come to me," he said as she looked up and closed the book.

With the quiet instinct of her true child's nature, she read aright the change which had taken place, and leaning on his knee, waited with a glad smile what should come.

"My child," he said, laying his hand tenderly upon her head and speaking in a voice whose humble, sorrowing tones wounded his young hearer's sympathies, "will you come and live with me? I am very lonely here and should love to have a little friend like you. Your mother in this letter gives you to me, and I will gladly make you mine."

The paper rustled in his trembling hand and his eye brightened, as he marked the brief terror written on the child's frank face as she drew back and gazed at him as he went on.

"Choose, Alice, now between two things—a pleasant home with me, where every pleasure wealth can buy is yours and your life will be a beautiful, untroubled one—or to go back and suffer hunger, cold, and sorrow with your mother, who longs to spare you that and here implored me to keep you in my home to cheer and comfort me. Think well and then decide."

Alice looked earnestly into the eager countenance before her, but its meaning did not change. Then she glanced at her own poor dress, the grateful fire, and the cold winter night without. For a moment her childish heart was stirred by a natural wish for rest and ease; but true to the generous love that could not falter, the temptation passed, and with a sudden flush of color on her cheek and quick, reproachful tears shining in her eyes, she said:

"My mother has no friend in the whole wide world but me. Then do not ask me so cruelly to leave her all alone when I can be a little help and comfort to her. Oh, do not make me stay, sir. It would break my heart to live so pleasantly while she was hungry, cold, and sick, with no little Alice to kiss her poor white face and love her dearly, dearly. You are very good to me, dear Grandfather, but I cannot live without my mother even for your sake, so thank you and good-bye." Taking his hand, she pressed it warmly in both her own small palms, kissed it gratefully, and turned steadily away to the hard lot she had freely chosen.

His heart struck by the child's innocent rebuke, John Owen rose up from his seat trembling with deep emotion, and bending till his silver locks mingled with her golden ones, he whispered a few glad words in her ear. Then with a cry of joy the child darted away, and leaning on his chair with hushed breath and eager eyes piercing the outer gloom, the old man waited for his daughter's coming.

Quick footsteps sounded on the stair; and then in the room, for ten years darkened by her absence, stood the pale shadow that had haunted it. No longer a young, blooming girl, but a worn, sorrow-stricken woman, whose bent form and wasted face wrung her father's heart with a remorse too bitter to find utterance in words.

Blinded by the heavy drops that fell upon his withered cheek, he could only stretch his arms to her and in a broken voice sob her name.

Little Alice, the sweet link that bound them thus together, guided his wandering hands to her mother's head, which was bowed low before him as she whispered tenderly, "The curse is taken from me, and we are at peace with one another now, thanks to the silent magic of my little child. God bless you, Father; you have blotted out with these sweet tears the mournful past and won *two* daughters to your lonely heart and home by welcoming in the holy spirit of love, which should find place at every fireside on this blessed New Year's Eve."

THE SISTERS' TRIAL

Four sisters sat together around a cheerful fire on New Year's Eve. The shadow of a recent sorrow lay on the young faces, over which the red flames flickered brightly as they lit up every nook of the quiet room, whose simple furniture and scanty decorations plainly showed that Poverty had entered there hand in hand with her sister, Grief.

The deep silence that had lasted long, as each sat lost in sad memories of the past or anxious thought for the future, was at length broken by Leonore, the eldest, a dark-haired, dark-eyed woman, whose proud, energetic face was softened by a tender smile as she looked upon the young girls, saying cheerily:

"Come, sisters, we must not sit brooding gloomily over our troubles when we should be up and doing. Tonight, you know, we must decide what work we will each choose by which to earn our bread. For this home will soon be ours no longer, and we must find some other place to shelter us, and some honest labor to maintain ourselves by, that we may not be dependent on the charity of relatives till our own exertions fail. Tell me what, after your separate search, you have each decided to do. Agnes, you come first. What among the few pursuits left open to us have *you* chosen?"

The color deepened in Agnes's cheek and the restless light burned brighter in her large eyes as she hastily replied, "*I* will be an actress. Nay, do not start and look so troubled, Nora. I am fixed, and when you hear all you will not oppose me, I feel

63

sure. You know this has been the one wish of my life, growing with my growth, strengthening with my strength, haunting my thoughts by day, my dreams by night. I have longed for it, planned for it, studied for it secretly for years, always hoping a time might come when I could prove to you that it was no idle fancy, but a real desire, and satisfy myself whether I have in truth the power to succeed, or whether I have cherished a false hope and been deluded by my vanity. I have thought of it seriously and earnestly during my search for employment and see but one thing else that I can do. I *will* not chain myself to a needle and sew my own shroud for a scanty livelihood. Teaching, therefore, is all that remains. I dislike it, am unfitted for it in every way, and cannot try it till everything else has failed.

"*You*, Nora, have your pen, Ella her music, Amy her painting. You all *love* them and can support yourselves well by them. *I* have only this one eager longing that haunts me like a shadow and seems to beckon me away to the beautiful, brilliant life I feel that I was born to enjoy."

"Set yourself resolutely about some humbler work, and this longing will fade away if you do not cherish it," said Leonore earnestly.

"It will not. I have tried in vain, and now I will follow it over every obstacle till I have made the trial I desire. You are calm and cold, Nora, and cannot understand my feelings; therefore, do not try to dissuade me, for an actress I must and *will* be," answered Agnes resolutely.

A look of sudden pain crossed Leonore's face at her sister's words, but it quickly passed. Looking into her excited countenance, she said gently, "How will you manage this? It is no easy thing for a young and unknown girl to take such a step alone. Have you thought of this? And what are your plans?"

"Listen and I will tell you, for all is ready, though you seem inclined to doubt it," replied Agnes, meeting her sisters' wondering glances with a look of triumph as she went on.

"Mrs. Vernon, whom our mother loved and respected (actress though she is), has known us long and been a friend to us in our misfortunes. I remembered that; after seeking vainly for some employment that I did not hate, I went to her and, telling all my hopes and wishes, asked for her advice.

"She listened kindly, and after questioning me closely and trying what little skill I have acquired, she said that if you consented, she would take me with her to the West, train and teach me, and then try what I can do. There is an opening for me there, and under her protection and motherly care, what need I fear? I should have told you this before, but you bade us each to look and judge for ourselves before we asked for your advice, making this our first lesson in self-reliance, which now is all we can depend on for support and guidance. Now, what is your answer? Shall I go as I *wish,* safely and properly with Mrs. Vernon, or as I *will,* alone and unprotected if you deny me your consent? Ah, do say yes, and you will make my life so beautiful and pleasant that I shall love and bless you forever."

As Agnes spoke, Leonore had thought rapidly of her sister's restless and unsatisfied life; her unfitness for the drudgery she would be forced to if denied her wish; of their mother's confidence in the kind friend who would be a faithful guardian to her. Looking in the eager, imploring face lifted to her own and reading there the real unconquerable passion that filled her sister's heart, she felt that hard experience alone could teach her wisdom and that time only could dispel her dream or fix and strengthen it forever. So she replied simply and seriously, "Yes, Agnes, you may go."

Agnes, prepared for argument and denial, seemed bewildered by this ready acquiescence till, meeting Leonore's troubled glance fixed anxiously upon her, she saw there all the silent sorrow and reproach she would not speak. Coming to her side, Agnes said gratefully and with a fond caress: "You never shall have cause to repent your goodness to me, Nora, for I will be true to you and to myself whatever else may happen. So do not fear for me. The memory of *home* and *you,* dear girls, will keep me safe amid the trials and temptations of my future life."

Leonore did not answer, but drew her nearer as if to cherish and protect her for the little time they yet could be together, and with dim eyes but a cheerful voice, bade Ella tell *her* plans.

"*I,*" said the third sister, turning her placid face from the fire, whose pleasant glow seemed shining from it as if attracted there by kindred light and warmth, "I shall go to the South as governess to three motherless little girls. Aunt Elliott, who told me of it, assured me it would prove a happy home, and with my salary, which is large, I shall so gladly help you and mite by mite lay by a little store that may in time grow large enough to buy our dear old home again. This is my future lot, and I am truly grateful it is such a pleasant one."

"How can you be content with such a dreary life?" cried Agnes.

"Because it is my duty, and in doing that, I know I shall find happiness," replied Ella. "For twenty years I have been shielded from the rough winds that visit so many. I have had my share of rest and pleasure, and I trust they have done well their work of sweetening and softening my nature. Now life's harder lessons are to be learned, and I am trying to receive them as I ought. Like you, I will not be dependent on relations rich in all but love to us, and so must endeavor to go bravely out into the world to meet whatever fate God sends me."

The light of a pure, unselfish heart beamed in the speaker's gentle face, and her simple, childlike faith seemed to rebuke her sister's restless doubts and longings.

"I come next," said Amy, a slender, graceful girl of eighteen, "and my search has been most successful. While looking for pupils, I met again my dear friend Annie L——, who, when she learned my troubles, bade me look no farther but come and make my home with her. That I would not do till she agreed that I should take the place of her attendant and companion (for she is lame, you know) and go with her to Europe for a year. Think how beautiful it will be to live in those lands I have so longed to see, and pass my days sketching, painting, and taking care of Annie, who is alone in the world and needs an affectionate friend to cheer the many weary hours that must come to one rich, talented, and young, but a cripple for life. I shall thus support myself by my own labor, though it is one of love, and gain skill and knowledge in my art in the only school that can give it me. This is my choice. Have I not done well, sisters?"

"You have indeed, but how can we let you go so far from us, dear Amy?" said Leonore as they all looked fondly at her; for she had been the pet and sunbeam of the household all her life, and their hearts clung to her, fearing to send her out so young to strive and struggle with the selfish world.

But she met their anxious gaze with a brave smile, saying, "Fear nothing for me. It is what I need, for I shall never know my own strength if it is never tried; and with you it will not be, for you cherish me like a delicate flower. Now I shall be blown about and made to think and judge for myself, as it's time I should. I shall not seem so far away as you now think; for my letters will come to you like my voice from over the sea, and it shall always be loving and merry that nothing may be changed as the year rolls on, and I may ever seem your own fond, foolish little Amy. Now, Nora, last not least, let us know in what part of the globe you will bestow yourself."

"I shall stay here, Amy," answered Leonore.

"Here!" echoed the sisters. "How can you when the house is sold and the gentleman coming to take possession so soon?"

"Just before our mother died," replied Leonore in a reverent voice, "she said to me in the silence of the night, 'Nora, you are the guardian of your sisters now. Be a watchful mother to them, and if you separate, as I fear you must, try to secure some little spot, no matter how poor, where you may sometimes meet and feel that you have a *home*. Promise me that, for I cannot rest in peace feeling that all the sweet ties that now bind you tenderly together are broken and that you are growing up as strangers to each other, scattered far apart.'

"I promised her, and this is why I longed so much to have you all remain in B——, that we might often meet and cheer each other on.

"But as it cannot be, I have decided to remain here, for Mr. Morton is a kind old man with no family but a maiden sister. They need few apartments, and when I told him how things were and that I desired to hire one room, he willingly consented and, naming those they wished, left the rest to me. I chose this one, and here, surrounded by the few familiar things now left us, I shall live and by my pen support myself, or if that fails, seek for needlework or teaching.

"It will be a quiet, solitary life, but tidings of *you* all will come to cheer me. When another New Year shall come around, let us, if we can, meet here again to tell our wanderings and to spend it on the spot where we have passed so many happy ones.

"This is my decision. Here I shall live, and remember, dear girls, wherever you may be, that there is one nook in the dear old home where in sickness or sorrow you can freely come, ever sure of a joyful welcome, and in this troubled world one heart that is always open to take you in, one friend who never can desert you."

The sisters gathered silently about her as Leonore rose. Taking from a case three delicately painted miniatures of their mother, she said in a faltering voice as she threw the simply woven chains of her own dark hair about their necks:

"This is my parting gift to you, and may the dear face Amy's hand has given us so freshly prove a talisman to keep you ever worthy of our mother's love. God bless and bring us all together once again, better and wiser for our first lesson in the school of life."

The fire leaped up with a sudden glow and, from the hearthstone where a tenderly united family once had gathered, fell now like a warm, bright blessing on the orphan sisters folded in each other's arms for the last time in the shelter of their home.

The year was gone, and Leonore sat waiting for the wanderers to come, with a shadow on her face and a secret sorrow at her heart.

The once poor room now wore an air of perfect comfort. Flowers bloomed in the deep windows, sheltered from the outer cold by the warm folds of graceful curtains; green wreaths framed the picture faces on the walls, and a generous blaze burned red upon the hearth, flashing brightly over old, familiar objects beautified and freshened by a tasteful hand.

A pleasant change seemed to have fallen on all there but the thoughtful woman, in whose troubled face passion and pride seemed struggling with softer, nobler feelings as she sat there pale and silent in the cheerful room. As the twilight deepened, the inward storm passed silently away, leaving only a slight cloud behind as she paced anxiously to and fro, till well-known footsteps sounded without and Ella and Amy came hastening in.

They had returned a week before, but though much with Leonore in her pleasant home, they had playfully refused to answer any questions till the appointed night arrived.

Time seemed to have passed lightly over Ella, for her face was bright and tranquil as of old, while some secret joy seemed treasured in her heart, which, though it found no vent in words, shone in the clear light of her quiet eyes, sounded in the music of her voice, and deepened the sweet seriousness of her whole gentle nature.

Amy's single year of travel had brought with its culture and experience fresh grace and bloom to the slender girl, who had blossomed suddenly into a lovely woman, frank and generous as ever, but softened and refined by the simple charms of early womanhood.

Gathered in their old places, the sisters, talking cheerfully, waited long for Agnes. But at length she came; slowly and faintly her footsteps sounded on the stair. When she entered, such a change had fallen on her they could scarce believe it was the same bright creature who had left them but a year ago.

Worn and wasted, with dim eyes and pallid cheeks, she came back but a shadow of her former self.

Her sisters knew she had been ill, and guessed she had been unhappy, for a gradual change had taken place in her letters. From being full of overflowing hope and happiness, they had grown sad, desponding, and short. But she had never spoken of the cause, and now, though grieved and startled, they breathed not a word of questioning, but concealing their alarm, tenderly welcomed her and tried to banish her gloom.

Agnes endeavored with forced gaiety to join them, but it

soon deserted her. After the first affectionate greetings, she seemed to sink unconsciously into a deep and painful reverie.

The sisters glanced silently and anxiously at one another as they heard her heavy sighs and saw the feverish color that now burned on her thin cheek as she sat gazing absently into the glowing embers.

None seemed willing to break the silence that had fallen on them till Amy said with a pleasant laugh: "As I probably have the least to tell, I will begin. My life, since we parted, has been one of rich experience and real happiness. With friends and labor that I loved, how could it well be otherwise?

"I have fared better in my trial than I ever hoped to, and have been blessed with health of body and peace of heart to enjoy the many pleasant things about me. A home in Italy more beautiful than I can tell you, a faithful friend in Annie, cultivated minds around me, and time to study and improve myself in the things that I most love—all these I have had, and hope I have improved them well. I have gained courage, strength, and knowledge, and armed with these, I have the will and power to earn with my pencil and brush an honest livelihood and make my own way in this busy world, which has always been a friendly one to me.

"I shall stay with Annie till her marriage with the artist whom we met abroad, about whom I have already told you. Then I shall find some quiet nook and there sit down to live, love, and labor while waiting what the future may bring forth for me."

"May it bring you all the happiness you so well deserve, my cheerful-hearted Amy," said Leonore, looking fondly and proudly at her young sister. "Your cheerful courage is a richer fortune to you than money can ever be, while your contented mind will brighten life with the truest happiness for one who can find sunshine everywhere. Now, Ella, let us know how you have fared and what your future is," continued Leonore.

"The past year has been one of mingled joy and sorrow," answered Ella. "The sorrow was the sudden loss of little Effie, the youngest and the dearest of my pupils. It was a heavy grief to us all, and her father mourned most bitterly till a new love, as strong and pure as that he bore the lost child, came to cheer and comfort him when he most needed it." Here, in the sudden glow on Ella's cheek and the radiant smile that lit her face with a tenderer beauty, the sisters read the secret she had hidden from them until now, as in a low, glad voice she said:

"The joy I spoke of was that this love, so generous and deep, he offered to the humble girl who had tried to be a mother to his little child and sorrowed like one when she went. Freely, gratefully did I receive it; for his silent kindness and the simple beauty of his life had long made him very dear to me, and I felt I had the power to be to him a true and loving friend.

"And now, no longer poor and solitary, I shall journey back to fill the place, not of the humble governess, but of a happy wife and mother in my beautiful southern home. Ah, sisters, this has been a rich and blessed year to me, far more than I have deserved."

And Ella bent her head upon her folded hands, too full of happiness for words.

Agnes had been strongly moved while Ella spoke, and when she ceased, broke into bitter weeping, while her sisters gathered around her, vainly trying to compose and comfort her. But she did not heed them till her sudden grief had wept itself calm. Then, speaking like one in a dream, she said abruptly:

"*My* year has been one of brilliant, bitter sorrow. Such another I could not live through.

"When I first began my new life, all seemed bright and pleasant to me. I studied hard, learned fast, and at last made the wished-for trial, you know how successfully. For a while I was in a dream of joy and triumph and fancied all was smooth and sure before me. I had done much. I would do more, and not content to rise slowly and surely, I longed to be at once what years of patient labor alone can make me. I struggled on through the daily trials that thickened around me, often disheartened and disgusted at the selfishness and injustice of those around me, and the thousand petty annoyances that tried my proud, ambitious spirit.

"It was a hard life, and but for the great love I still cherished for the better part of it, I should have left it long ago. But there were moments, hours, when I forgot my real cares and troubles in the false ones of the fair creations I was called upon to personate. Then I seemed to move in an enchanted world of my own and *was* the creature that I *seemed.* Ah! That was glorious to feel that my power, small as it was, could call forth tears and smiles and fill strange hearts with pity, joy, or fear.

"So time went on, and I was just beginning to feel that at last I was rising from my humble place, lifted by my own power and the kind favor I had won, when between me and my brightening fortune there came a friend who brought me the happiest and bitterest hours of my whole life."

Here Agnes paused and, putting back her fallen hair from her wet cheek, looked wistfully into the anxious faces around her. Then, after a moment's pause, with an effort and in a hurried voice she went on:

"Among the many friends who admired and respected Mrs. Vernon and often visited her pleasant home, none was more welcome than the rich, accomplished Mr. Butler (whose name you may remember in my letters). None came oftener or stayed longer; he was with us at the theater and paid a thousand kind attentions to my good friend and to me, in whom he seemed to take an interest from the first moment we met. Do not think me weak and vain. How could I help discovering it when among many who looked coldly on me or treated me with careless freedom, I found *him* always just, respectful, and ah, how kind? He had read and traveled much, and with his knowledge of the world he taught, encouraged, and advised me, making my hard life beautiful by his generous friendship.

"You know my nature, frank and quick to love, touched by a gentle word or a friendly deed. I was deeply grateful for his many silent acts of kindness and the true regard he seemed to feel for me, and slowly, half unconsciously, my gratitude warmed into love. I never knew how strong and deep until I learned too late that it was all in vain.

"One night (how well I can remember its least circumstance!) I was playing one of my best parts, and never had I played it better, for *he* was there and I thought only of *his* approbation then. Toward the close of the evening I was waiting for my cue when Mr. Butler and friend passed near the spot where I was standing, partially concealed by a deep shadow. I caught the sound of my own name, and then in a low, pained voice, as if replying to some question, Mr. Butler said:

"'I respect, admire, yes, love her far too deeply to willfully destroy her peace, but I am of a proud race and cannot make an *actress* my wife. Therefore, I shall leave tomorrow before she can discover what I have lately learned, and although we shall never meet again, I shall always be her friend.'

"They passed on, and the next moment I was on the stage, laughing merrily with a dizzy brain and an aching heart. Pride nerved me to control my wandering thoughts and to play out mechanically my part in the comedy that had so suddenly become the deepest tragedy to me.

"Actress as I thought myself, it needed all my skill to hide beneath a smiling face the pang that wrung my heart, and but for the many eyes upon us and the false bloom on my cheek, I should have betrayed all when he came to take his leave that night. Little dreaming what I suffered, he kindly, seriously said farewell, and so we parted forever. For days I struggled to conceal the secret grief that preyed upon me until it laid me on a sickbed, from which I rose as you now see me, broken in health and spirit, saddened by the disappointed hopes and dreams that lie in ruins around me, distrustful of myself and weary of life."

With a desponding sigh Agnes laid her head on Leonore's bosom, as if she never cared to lift it up again.

Ella knew why she had wept so sadly while listening to the story of *her* happy love, and bending over her, she spoke gently of the past and cheerfully of the future till the desponding gloom was banished. Agnes looked up with a face brightened by earnest feeling as she said in answer to Leonore's whispered question, "You will stay with us now, dearest?"

"Yes, I shall never tread the stage again, for though I love it with a lingering memory of the many happy hours spent there, the misery of that one night has taught me what a hollow mockery the life I had chosen *may* become. I have neither health nor spirit for it now, and its glare and glitter have lost their charms. I shall find some humble work and, quietly pursuing it, endeavor to become what *he* would have me: not an actress, but a simple woman, trying to play well her part in life's great drama. And though we shall never meet again, he may one day learn that, no longer mistaking the shadow for the substance, I have left the fair, false life and taken up the real and true."

"Thank heaven for this change," cried Leonore. "Dear Agnes, this shall henceforth be your home, and here we will lead a cheerful, busy life, sharing joy and sorrow together as in our childhood and journeying hand in hand through light and darkness to a happy, calm old age."

"Leonore, you must tell us your experiences now, or our histories are not complete," said Amy after a little time.

"I have nothing to relate but what you already know," replied her sister. "My book was well received and made for me a place among those writers who have the power to please and touch the hearts of many. I have earned much with my pen and have a little store laid by for future need. My life has been a quiet, busy one. I have won many friends, whose kindness and affection have cheered my solitude and helped me on. What more can I say but that I heartily rejoice that all has gone so well with us and we have proved that we possess the power to make our own way in the world and need ask charity of none. Our talismans have kept us safe from harm, and God has let us meet again without one gone."

"Leonore," said Agnes, looking earnestly into her sister's face, "you have not told us *all*. Nay, do not turn away; there is some hidden heart-sorrow that you are silent of. I read it in the secret trouble of your eye, the pallor of your cheek, and, most of all, in your quick sympathy for me. We have given you our confidence. Ah, give us yours as freely, dearest Nora."

"I cannot, do not ask me," murmured Leonore, averting her face.

"Let nothing break the sweet ties that now bind you together, and do not be as strangers to each other when you should be closest friends," whispered Ella from the low seat at her knee.

Leonore seemed to struggle with herself, and many contending emotions swept across her face. But she longed for sympathy, and her proud heart melted at the mild echo of her mother's words. So, holding Agnes's hand fast in her own as if their sorrow drew them nearer to each other, she replied with a regretful sigh:

"Yes, I will tell you, for your quick eyes have discovered what I hoped to have hidden from your sight forever. It *is* a heart-sorrow, Agnes, deeper than your own, for you still can reverence and trust the friend you have lost; but I can only feel contempt for what I have so truly loved. You well remember cousin Walter, the frank, generous-hearted boy who was our dearest playmate and companion years ago. Soon after we had separated, he returned from India with his parents, and though *they* took no heed of me, *he* sought me out and simply, naturally took the place of friend and brother to me as of old. I needed help just then; he gave it freely and, by his wise counsel and generous kindness, banished my cares and cheered me when most solitary and forlorn.

"I always loved him, and pleasant memories of the happy past have kept his image fresh within my heart. Through the long years of his absence I have sighed for his return, longing to know if the promise of a noble manhood I remembered in the boy had been fulfilled. He came at last when most I wished him, and with secret pride and joy I found him all I had hoped, brave, generous, and sincere. Ah, I was very happy then, and as our friendship grew, slowly and silently the frank affection of the girl deepened into the woman's earnest love.

"I knew it was returned, for in every look and deed the sweet, protecting tenderness that had guarded me in my childish days now showed itself more plainly still and at length found vent in words, which, few and simple as they were, seemed to fill my life with a strange happiness and beauty.

"Agnes, you have called me cold, but if you knew the deep and fervent passion that has stirred my heart, softening and sweetening my stern nature, you could never wrong me so again. Unhappy as that love has been, its short experience has made me wiser, and when its first sharp disappointment has passed away, the memory of it will linger like the warm glow of a fire whose brightness has departed.

"Two months ago a change came over Walter. He was kind as ever, coming often to cheer my lonely life, filling my home with lovely things and, more than all, with his own dear presence; but a cloud was on him and I could not banish it.

"At length a week passed and he did not come, but in his place a letter from his father, saying that he disapproved of his son's love for me and had persuaded him to relinquish me for a wife more suited to his rank in life; therefore, at his request he wrote to spare us the pain of parting. I cannot tell what more was in that cold, insulting letter, for I burned it, saving only two faintly written words in Walter's well-known hand, 'Farewell, Leonore.' That was enough for me; by what magic the great change was wrought I cared not to discover. All I thought or felt was that he had left me without a word of explanation, breaking his plighted word and, like a coward, fearing to tell me freely and openly that he no longer loved me.

"I have not seen or heard from him since. Though rumors of his approaching marriage, his departure for Europe, and a sudden illness have reached my ears, I believe none of them and, struggling sternly to conceal my sorrow, have passed silently on, leaving him without one word of entreaty or reproach to the keen regret his cruelty will one day cause him."

A proud, indignant light burned in Leonore's eye and flushed her cheek. With a bitter smile she met her sisters' troubled glances, saying:

"You need not pity *me*. *He* wants it most; for money can buy his truth and cast an evil spell on him, and a sordid father has the power to tempt and win him from his duty. None but *you* will ever know the secret sorrow that now bows my spirit, but shall never break it. I shall soon banish the tender memories that haunt me and, hiding the deep wound he has caused me, be again the calm, cold Leonore.

"Oh, Walter! Walter! You have made the patient love that

should have been the blessing of my life its heaviest sorrow. May God forgive you as I try to do."

And as these words broke from her lips, Leonore clasped her hands before her face, and hot tears fell like rain on Ella's head, bent down upon her knee.

Agnes and Amy, blinded by the dimness of their own eyes, had not seen a tall, dark man who had entered silently as Leonore last spoke, and had stood spellbound till she ceased. Then, coming to her side, the stranger said in a low, eager voice:

"Nora, will you hear me?"

With a quick start Leonore dashed away her tears and rose up pale and stately, looking full into the earnest, manly face before her and plainly reading there all she had doubted: truth in the frank, reproachful eyes that freely met her own; tender sorrow in the trembling lips; and, over all, the light of the faithful, generous love which never had deserted her.

Her stern glance softened as she bowed a silent reply, and fell before his own. Standing close beside her and looking steadily into her changing countenance, her cousin Walter laid his thin hand on her own, saying in the friendly voice she had so longed to hear:

"Leonore, from the sickbed where I have lain through these long, weary weeks, I have come to prove my truth, which had your pride allowed you to inquire into, you never would have doubted, knowing me as I fondly hoped you did."

With a sudden motion Leonore drew a little worn and blistered paper from her bosom and laid it in his hand, from which she coldly drew her own, and fixed a keen look on his face, where not a shadow of shame or fear appeared as he read it. He glanced silently from the tearstains to the eyes that looked so proudly on him, with a quiet smile that brought a hot glow to her cheek as she asked quickly:

"Did *you* write those cruel words?"

"I did. Nay, listen patiently before you judge me, Nora," he replied as she turned to leave him. "Two months ago my father questioned me of *you.* I told him freely that I loved you and soon hoped to gladden his home with a daughter's gentle presence. But his anger knew no bounds, and commanding me to beware how I thwarted his wishes, he bade me choose between utter poverty and you, or all his Indian wealth and my cousin Clara. I told him that my choice was already made, but he would not listen to me and bade me consider it well for one whole week and then decide before I saw you again. I yielded to calm his anger and for a week tried to win him to a wiser and kinder course, but all in vain. His will was iron and mine was no less firm; for high above all selfish doubts and fears, all lures of rank and wealth, rose up my faithful love for you, and nothing else could tempt me. That needed no golden fetters to render it more true, no idle show to make it richer, fonder than it is and ever will be.

"It was no virtue in me to resist, for nothing great enough was offered in exchange for that. Poverty was wealth with *you,* and who would waver between a false, vain girl and a truehearted woman?

"Ah, Nora, you will learn to know me now and see how deep a wrong you have done me. But to finish—when at the week's close I told my father that my purpose was unbroken, he bade me leave his house forever and would have cursed me. But his passion choked the sinful words ere they were spoken, and he is saved that sorrow when he thinks more kindly of me hereafter.

"I silently prepared to leave his house, which since my own mother's death has never been like home to me, and should have hastened joyfully to you, had not the fever already burning in my veins, augmented by anxiety and grief, laid me on my bed, from which I am just risen and where through those long nights and days I have been haunted even in delirium by your image and the one longing wish to tell you why I did not come.

"When better, I sent messages and letters, but they were never delivered; for my father, thinking sickness might have changed me, was still at my side to watch my actions and to tempt me to revoke my words. I have since learned that he wrote to you and, guiding my unconscious hand, traced the words that gave you the right to doubt me. But now I am strong again. Nothing can separate us more, and I am here to bury the past and win your pardon for the sorrow I could not spare you. Now, Leonore, I am poor and friendless as yourself, with my fortune to make by the labor of my hands as you have done. You once wished this and said you never would receive the wealth I longed to give you. Your wish is granted. I have nothing now to offer but a hand to work untiringly for you and a heart to love and cherish you most tenderly forever. Will you take them, Nora?"

Leonore's proud head had sunk lower and lower as he spoke, and when he ceased, it rested on his shoulder. Her hand lay with an earnest, loving clasp in his as she whispered in a broken voice:

"Forgive me, Walter, for the wrong I have done you, and teach me to be worthy the great sacrifice you have made for me."

The clock struck twelve, and as its silvery echoes sounded through the quiet room, the old year, with its joys and sorrows, hopes and fears, floated away into the shadowing past, bearing among its many records the simple one of the sisters' trial.

LITTLE GENEVIEVE

In the greenroom of a certain theater stood a group of actors waiting their "calls" and amusing themselves meanwhile by criticizing the Lady Macbeth of the evening, who had just emerged from her dressing room and now stood at a little distance, apparently unconscious of everything but the book in her hand.

Appearing suddenly among them a few weeks before, no one (but Manager Q.) knowing whence Mademoiselle Natalie had come, she awaked great curiosity and interest, both before and behind the curtain, by her beauty and talent and, still more, by the mystery which surrounded her.

Proud, cold, and silent, she faithfully performed her duties and each night won fresh laurels by the energy and fire she threw into whatever part she played. Whenever power and passion were required, there she excelled and seemed to be but acting her own character and history. Words of love fell with strange tenderness from her lips, as if they were but echoes of real ones uttered long ago, still lingering in her memory though their music had departed.

Unconsciously she possessed and exerted a wonderful power over those who saw her, and might have been surrounded by admirers and friends who eagerly predicted a bright future for one so beautiful and gifted. But no sooner was her part played out than she sank back into her cold reserve, shunned all society, and vanished from the excited crowd, who were left to vent their wonder and delight in eager praises and idle conjectures.

Among her many peculiarities was one more mysterious than the rest. She seemed always watching for someone. Each night, however arduous a part she might sustain, this silent scrutiny of the sea of faces before her still went on.

Her keen eye pierced the farthest corner, and if some new or striking countenance stood out from the rest, she darted one brief glance at it and then, as if disappointed, passed on to scan others with the same quick, wistful gaze. So skillfully was this singular search performed that few perceived it except those who watched her closely night after night and studied her more carefully than the idle throng who only wondered and admired.

A darker, more majestic Lady Macbeth had seldom trod that stage than she who stood in the shadow of the great greenroom mirror. Her tall and stately figure supported well the velvet robes that swept from her white shoulders to her sandaled feet. And the golden circlet that bound her hair, black as night, seemed a fitting ornament for the proud head that wore it. Her face was colorless, and a gloomy light burned in the dark eyes bent upon the book as she listened, with a faint, scornful smile upon her lips, to the whispered conversation going on around her.

One criticized her graceful arms, another the jewels glittering on them, while some in lower tones spoke their doubts and wise misgivings as to her mysterious life and character.

Suddenly she heard a timid voice saying softly, as if to itself: "Ah! They be kind to her, not because she is so beautiful and great, but so unhappy and alone."

Startled and annoyed, the proud woman felt her cheek burn, and stealing a quick look from under her long lashes, she saw a little ballet girl gazing at her with a glance of mingled pity, love, and admiration.

She had often seen the pale-faced child before, for she came nightly to dance while her old grandfather who came with her disappeared to unknown regions to perform some needful work. The child now sat in her scanty, cloudlike dress with gossamer wings on her shoulders, mending a little worn slipper. Slight and small, she seemed much younger than in truth she was, but the patient look of sorrow on her tranquil

face showed that she had known care. It touched the coldest
heart, and all in that busy place, however filled with their
own vanities or griefs, still had a friendly word for little
Genevieve.

"Lady Macbeth called," cried a voice, and dropping her
book, Mademoiselle Natalie moved toward the door. Suddenly
she stopped and, with a helpless glance at her heavy robes,
cried anxiously:

"The letter—good heavens, I have forgotten it! Fly, run
somebody! It's on my dressing table. Quick, or I shall be too
late."

Those whom she thus addressed with an imperious gesture
stared stupidly at each other and never stirred, but Genevieve,
flinging down her work, darted away like a flash and came
breathlessly back just in time. Seizing the paper without a
word, Mademoiselle swept out, and the next moment the
sound of her hearty greeting reached the group behind.

"Why, you are hurt, child. Look," said a velvet-clad page,
pointing to a red stain on Genevieve's slipperless foot.

"I struck it on the stairs, but I don't mind the pain much,"
said the child, trying to restrain her tears. She added sorrowfully, "Only I *do* wish she had spoken to me. I admire and love
her so dearly."

"Ungrateful icicle, she might at least have thanked you for
saving her a fall or a fine. There, there, dear, don't sob so bitterly. Come now and let me bathe your foot, and you'll forget
it soon," said the kindhearted page, whose womanly words
and sympathy were oddly suited to her cap and doublet, but
nonetheless comforting and tender.

"Genevieve is very pale. I'm afraid she will hardly get
through. That was a cruel blow for her little foot, though she
will not own it yet," whispered a pretty chambermaid to her
lover as they stood ready for the farce, watching the child as
she flitted like a fairy to and fro, waving her silvery wand and
smiling with tears of suffering in her eyes. As the curtain fell,
she dropped on the stage, fainting with the pain she had so
bravely borne till her duty was done.

"Poor little heart, lift her gently and take her to the greenroom," cried the pretty maid, and as they laid her down, added, "Now some of you take care of her, for I must go and she needs instant help."

"She shall have it," said a musical voice that made them all start. Mademoiselle, followed by her servant, passed through their midst and, kneeling by the child, offered her costly vinaigrette and with a gentle hand smoothed back her scattered hair.

Softened by this unexpected interest and touched by the tender pity which made the hitherto cold face more beautiful than ever, they all stood respectfully back while she, by a few loving words, recalled the child to consciousness. Then, folding her in a large mantle, she bade her maid take her to the carriage, saying in her old haughty voice as she followed:

"Tell her grandfather I will care for her, and remember, deeds, not words, best show true gratitude."

The next moment the three were gone. The spell of her presence was broken, and eager tongues were freely bestowing praise and blame on the strange woman and her stranger conduct.

Through rain and darkness little Genevieve felt herself borne, as if by magic, into a warm, still place, fragrant with flowers and bright with many rare and lovely things that filled her with delight and wonder. Lying on a low couch beside a glowing fire, she watched as in a pleasant dream the scene around her, following with wistful eyes the figure of the stately lady, who now, wrapped in a simple dress, bent over her with such an altered face she hardly could believe it was the same that once had been so dark and stern. Now a soft light shone in her deep eyes, and some gentle memory seemed to send a warm glow from her heart into her cheek and lent a tenderer music to her voice as she talked cheerily to the child and skillfully bound up the wounded foot.

When that was done, she rose and for a moment stood looking down upon the slender figure lying with its white garments torn and soiled, its delicate wings crushed and drooping, and a faint smile glimmering over its wan little face.

As she looked, she pressed her hands tightly on her bosom, murmuring to herself with a bitter sigh: "It is an image of my youth. My childish innocence stained by early knowledge of a sinful world, my purest aspirations that should have borne me up all crushed by hard experience and wrong, and my bruised feet stumbling often on life's rough road. God help me, for *I* had no friend to lift and comfort me."

"I am a very little friend, but I should dearly love to comfort you if I knew how," said Genevieve, with such an affectionate glance that the returning gloom faded from the troubled face above her as Mademoiselle stooped to kiss her with a warmth that filled the child's heart with delight.

"Only love me and I *shall* be comforted" was all she said, but in the close embrace and sudden dimness of her eye, there spoke a tender longing which drew them closer to each other still.

"I cannot sleep till the pain is less, but I will be very still," said Genevieve as her friend laid her on a soft white pillow, bidding her sleep.

"May I look at you, Mademoiselle? It makes me very happy, you are so beautiful and kind," she said, timidly glancing at the drooping head beside her.

For a moment the altered face was turned away, and then it met her gaze without a shadow on it as Natalie bent nearer, saying, "Yes, dear child, in your innocent eyes I shall meet no doubt or coldness, and I need wear no mask to you. Ah, little Genevieve! Your artless trust and admiration are sweeter to me than any flattery the world can give. But call me simply Natalie. I have not heard it spoken so for many years, and it is pleasant from your lips. Now let me sing to you till sleep comes to soothe your pain."

Then, pillowing the weary head upon her arm, Natalie sang the low, simple melodies that mothers sing till, lulled by the mournful music of her voice, Genevieve slept peacefully.

"Ah," sighed her new friend, unfolding the little arm that had been laid about her neck, "the touch of that small hand has wakened all the old pain at my heart and called back all the bitter past. Poor child, she cannot know the trial her loving looks and words will be to me, though I have pined for innocent affection like her own. Oh, my little Marie! My little Marie!"

Tears fell hot and fast as Natalie thus spoke. She drew from a cabinet beside her a broken toy and a baby shoe and kissed, caressed, and wept over these worn relics of some lost blessing with a passionate fondness sorrowful to see, till worn out with her stormy grief, her head sank low on Genevieve's wet pillow. She held fast the little hand that crept unconsciously into her own, and its gentle magic led her on into the blissful land of dreams.

So side by side lay the happy child smiling in her sleep and the sorrow-stricken woman with bitter, hopeless tears still shining on her mournful face.

The next day was a pleasant one to Genevieve, who spent it wandering through the rooms that to her childish fancy seemed almost enchanted—all was so beautiful and new. She watched the skillful needle of the kind old maid as she shaped and ornamented the rich garments of her mistress, who paced to and fro conning a part, stopping often to give a fond word or a silent caress to the happy child, who tried by every simple art to show her gratitude and love.

Word had been sent to her grandfather that she was safe and as yet too lame to leave her new home. So the day wore smoothly on till evening came and Natalie was waiting for her carriage to convey her to the theater.

"It will be fair tonight, for the storm has passed," said Genevieve, lifting the curtain from the window where they stood. "See! Yonder is the moon, and one kind little star has come to meet her that she may not be so lonely in the sky," playfully added the child, hoping to win a smile to her friend's face, which now wore the mask of pride and coldness behind which she hid her true self from the world.

But it vanished as Natalie met the glad look lifted to her own, and with the quiet tenderness which seemed to soften her whole nature when she gave it vent, she looked down at the little figure beside her, saying as she touched its falling hair: "But do you see the black clouds have swallowed up your star, Genevieve, so the poor moon *must* be all alone?"

"But I know that it's still there," replied the child eagerly, "though I cannot see it, and a friendly wind will soon sweep away the clouds. The moon must wait yet longer, and soon the star will shine beside her brighter than before."

"God grant that it may," murmured Natalie, to whom these words had a hidden meaning. "Good night, my darling. You have been a sunbeam in this gloomy house today and a sweet prophet to my restless heart tonight. Sleep quietly and say a little prayer for Natalie, who needs it very much."

With these words she was gone, and Genevieve stood pondering long and watching till the star shone in the cloudless sky, and she knew not why.

That night, as Natalie swept the crowded theater with her keen eye, it paused suddenly at a distant box. A red glow shot across her face and a strange glitter lit her eyes, but nothing more.

Never had she played with half the power she threw into her part that night, until the wild excitement that possessed her seemed to reach her audience, who looked and listened, fascinated by they knew not what, though a dim consciousness stole over them that something stronger than mere art inspired the brilliant woman before them. Among the many bouquets she was called to gather up at the close was one which reached her from the distant box. As if unconsciously she set her foot upon it; and with a smile upon her lips, but a dark, meaning glance in her eyes, she fixed a long look on its giver, a young and handsome man who met it with a start. She saw him flush and pale with sudden recognition and draw hastily back, as if anxious for concealment. Then Natalie knew that her long search was ended, and with a prouder, brighter smile than she had ever worn before, she bowed her thanks and vanished.

"What ill fortune brought her here when I most wished her leagues away?" muttered the stranger fiercely as he left the theater. "If she discovers my attachment to the young heiress (or rather to her wealth), she will ruin all with those cursed letters. I must lure her away at any cost and silence her rash tongue. I must find her out tonight and make some settlement, for there was in her look just now that which told me I cannot escape her longer."

Thinking thus and taking counsel of his evil heart, the stranger paced along the moonlit streets, haunted by the strange menace of the beautiful eyes which had often met his own before, but always tenderly till now.

Natalie sat in her solitary room, still in her costly robes. Jewels shone in her hair and on her stately neck, and never had she seemed lovelier than now, with the glitter still in her eye and the sudden bloom unchanged upon her cheek.

For a long hour she had sat silent and intent, listening with low breathing and a strained ear for a coming step. At length it sounded on the threshold of her door; voices reached her ear, and then a man's tread on the stair. As it approached, she rose up and with folded arms waited his coming, all ice without, all fire within.

The door opened and the handsome stranger entered with an eager smile and outstretched hand. But the one faded and the other fell at his side when the stately woman never changed, but stood there cold and silent like a graceful statue, looking steadily at him with a stern gaze, beneath which his own wavered and fell.

"Natalie, will you not speak to me after this long separation and tell I am forgiven?" he said with well-acted grief and penitence.

"I have waited for this hour seven years," she replied abruptly. "Do not waste it in idle words whose worth I know too well. It is for you to speak. Then *do it,* frankly and truly, I command you."

Her voice was low with suppressed emotion, but her look never faltered nor left his face. He felt its power and with an effort replied in the same humble tone:

"Have you forgotten all the pleasant past, Natalie? All the love I bore you and the home we shared so happily together not long ago?"

"I have not forgotten *what* has changed that pleasant past

into a bitter memory that haunts my life and renders it most miserable," she answered passionately, waving him away as he approached. "I have not forgotten how you came to a friendless child and made her hard life bright with the love she then believed so true. How you *married* her and took her to a quiet home among the hills, where for three years your frequent presence and her little child made an Eden of the earth, before so dreary. How at length you grew weary of her and your neglect roused her spirit till she demanded what you refused to give, a wife's name and an honorable place beside you in the world. How, when she would not yield her right, you took her child, the only living thing that bound you to her, and stole like a thief from the home you had rendered desolate, leaving *proofs,* as you called them, of a false marriage. I have not forgotten how that cruel blow changed the confiding girl into a stern, strong-hearted woman, who locked her griefs in her bosom and from that hour to this has never ceased her silent search for the man who robbed her of the two dearest treasures she possessed, her good name and her child. Both of these you must restore, and *then* I may forget, never before."

As she thus rapidly poured her life's history into her listener's unwilling ear, he felt the shameful truth of her indignant words and saw that no appeal to the love now dead had any power. This failing, he resolved to try a tenderer chord in the proud heart that baffled him. Dropping his humble tone, he looked full in her face, saying seriously:

"I came here tonight to offer you two things, Natalie, and explain what must seem most cruel in my conduct. When my father, through officious friends, discovered our *supposed* marriage (how could it be otherwise, with you a ballet girl, Natalie?), he threatened me with disinheritance and his curse if I did not leave you and return to England. For a long time his entreaties and commands were fruitless. I would not leave you till, maddened by jealousy of the young artist who lay ill under our roof and to whom you were devoted, and rendered desperate by fresh and fiercer letters from my father, I could bear my misery no longer and left you, taking the child, for I would not leave her to be neglected by another. Pardon me for the doubts I soon learned to be false, and tell me why you have never by a single word replied to my many letters. I, too, searched for you and soon heard of you leading the gay, unfettered life of an actress, forgetful of the past and happy in the present. Then, believing all forever at an end between us, I resolved to show an equal pride and henceforth tried to banish your image from my mind. But it is in vain; I love you now as warmly, Natalie, as then. Nay, do not doubt me; on my honor it is true."

Natalie listened to the well-told falsehoods with a look of utter unbelief, but at his last words her flashing eyes told plainly as speech that she saw the lie upon his lips and scorned him for it. But she answered coldly:

"Let all that folly pass. You came to make me offers, generous and noble, doubtless. What are they?"

Stung by her quiet contempt, he longed to vent his passion in words, but dared not, for, seeing her so changed from the fond girl he once could bend so freely to his will, to a woman, resolute and wary as himself, he felt involuntary respect for her courage and a fresh admiration for her ripened beauty.

His old love, selfish as it was, seemed to rise up from the ashes that wasted years of pleasure had cast over it, and so far he spoke truly.

But seeing that the fit moment for tenderness had not yet come, he answered calmly as before: "You *are* not and never *can* be my wife. I own it may be selfish, but I cannot give up wealth, friends, and station for a mere idle form, which is at best a useless tie to those who truly love and a galling fetter to those who tire but cannot part. In your own words, let these follies pass. I see that it must be peace or war between us. *I* would have it peace; therefore, listen and choose which course you will pursue. Will you go on insisting vainly on claiming the rights and title you still fancy yours, thereby making public your most hidden feelings and creating evil rumors which will sting your haughty spirit and prove hard to set at rest? Will you lose all knowledge of your child and never see her more, as I swear you shall not if you bring this history to light? Or," and his voice grew low and winning now as he came nearer, "will you come back to France with me and, in some fairer home even than the last, forget the past and the careless world, whose voice can never reach us there? Will you see your little child again and feel that she is yours forever, to cherish and guard in that secluded home, untroubled by care or sorrow? Which shall it be, Natalie?"

She wavered for a moment at the picture he called up, but her woman's pride and the memory of her wrongs were strong within her. Though the color left her cheek and her white lips trembled as she spoke, her voice was firm as ever as she replied:

"I will *not* consent to live a lie, even for the sake of that which is dearer to me than all but my honor. I *am* your wife— you *know* it, and the world shall know it soon. Till then I will be true to myself and God will guard my little child."

His only answer was to lay silently before her a simply painted miniature of a baby face she knew too well. With a low cry of joy Natalie caught it up and looked long and eagerly upon the little countenance that seemed smiling back at her, till sweet tears dimmed her eyes and glittered on the golden case.

Dear memories came stealing back of happy days when clinging arms were around her, when childish lips called her "Mother" and she held upon her bosom the joy and sunshine of her life. All the long years of lonely sorrow were now swept away like shadows by the warm winds that seemed to come to her from the sunny gardens of the home among the hills, laden with the breath of flowers and the melody of her lost child's loving voice.

Passion and pride were gone, doubt and bitterness forgotten. The sad past grew fair again, the lonely present ceased to be, and nothing but a wild yearning love stirred in Natalie's full heart as she sank slowly down upon the couch and, covering her face, cried brokenly:

"Oh, Louis, do not tempt me. Anything but that I could resist. My little child, how *can* I give her up?"

With a gleam of triumph in his eye, he came to her side, saying gently, "Why wring your heart so uselessly, dear Natalie? Forget your idle fears and come to find and keep her all your own again forever."

Natalie's face was hidden, but her frame shook with the struggle at her heart. He stood by watching her and pouring sweet, false whispers of her child into her ear till she could hear no more. The mother's deep love conquered all. She rose suddenly and, dashing off her tears, said resolutely:

"I will go. Do with me what you please; I cannot lead this miserable life another year. But beware how you deceive me for a second time; if she be dead or lost, you lose the only spell that has the power to win my silence and bind me to the life of falsehood I despise. When shall I see her? Let us go without delay, for I shall not rest until I hold her fast again."

"Wisely chosen, Natalie. You shall not linger long, and I need not fear a change in you, need I? Give me your promise to depart when I have all prepared, and I know you will not fail me," he replied, offering his hand.

For a moment she drew back, but a glance at the pictured face decided her and she advanced to make the promise. But at that moment a white figure flitted through the room, and Genevieve, just risen from her bed, with wet cheeks and tearful eyes, caught her extended hand, sobbing out:

"Oh, do not go. It will end so sadly for us all. Dear friend, stay with me and do not go along that gloomy road."

With a guilty start Natalie looked at the excited child in silence for a moment and then said soothingly, "You have been dreaming, little Genevieve. I am still here and will not leave you yet. Then do not weep so bitterly, but tell me, what has frightened you?"

"*Was* it a dream?" sighed Genevieve, and looking with a shudder at the stranger, she said, "Ah, Natalie, it was so strange. I thought I saw you by a fast-flowing river looking far and wide for something you had lost. Across the stream, among the grass and flowers, stood a little child with a bright star floating over it as it made garlands trying to reach and lead you over the black water while it sang and called your name in its sweet voice. But you never heeded. Soon a person with a dark face like yonder man's came to you, and pointing to a path where the child's shadow faintly fell, he led you away. The gloomy clouds seemed gathering all about you and the child began to weep, but still you never minded. And I tried to call you very loud, but woke and saw you through the open door giving your hand to the dark man of my dream as if you were really going. Why is he here to take you from me? Must you go?" cried Genevieve, seeking to look into her friend's averted face.

"Send the child to her bed again. Our conversation has mingled with her dreams, and a stranger's presence has alarmed her. I have more to tell you, Natalie; therefore, take her away," said the gentleman impatiently.

But Natalie drew Genevieve more closely to her, saying as she knelt to wipe her tears and put away her tangled curls: "Genevieve, I *was* going to find my child. Heaven only knows through what dark ways. Tell me, am I not right to forget all else and follow whoever will lead me soonest to her?"

For a moment the child looked wonderingly in her face. Then, with a vague sense that it was an appeal to her, needing her wisest answer, she said earnestly:

"My mother told me there was always sunshine on the *right* way, and that I must never forget duty even to gain what I most wished, and that conscience was the only guide I ought to follow. Dear Natalie, *I* cannot tell you what is best, but I never saw you half so white and sorrowful before. Is it because you are leaving me, or because the small voice tells you not to go where you most long to be?"

"Your childish words are the echo of my better self. I will listen to them alone, and *you* shall guide me, little Genevieve, for I am very powerless against this great temptation," whispered Natalie, laying her head upon the child's shoulder and holding fast her hand. She said, without looking at the stranger: "Tell him to go and trouble me no further, Genevieve. He knows my weakness and will lead me into deeper gloom than gathered around me in your dream. But now I will not yield. Oh, hold me fast, dear child, and save me from myself."

"Natalie, hear me and cease this childish folly. Think of little Marie pining for you all these years. Think of your lonely future if you reject my offer. Can you—will you—leave the joy and peace I will so gladly give you for a life of solitude and grief? Do not retract your promise, but come away with me."

But she clung more closely, murmuring faintly, "Hold me fast, my Genevieve, and save me from myself."

"Yes, I *will* keep you very safe, dear Natalie," cried the child, stirred by a strange power that made her strong to meet the unfriendly looks bent upon her and to say fearlessly, pointing to the door: "Go, sir, and do not trouble her. She has so many sorrows now. Ah, do not make them more."

Pale with passion, the stranger muttered to himself, "That child must be removed, and then I can lure this foolish woman where I will." Pausing on the threshold, he said coldly, "I shall come again when this weak whim has passed, trusting you may make a wiser choice, Natalie, before it is too late."

She never answered, never raised her head, nor wept nor stirred, and he passed silently out, looking back with a troubled glance at the proud woman clinging fast to the frail child who stood up fair and slender as a spirit in her white garments, with hair thrown back and a strange light shining over her innocent face, while her small hand pointed steadily at him as she whispered to the bowed figure at her side:

"It *will* be bright again, dear friend. Wait yet longer and God will give you back your little child."

"Where is Genevieve?" questioned Natalie, coming wearily home from her irksome duties at the theater three nights later and missing the glad welcome that never failed to greet and comfort her.

"Her grandfather came and took her away, Mademoiselle," replied the servant. "He said he was going on a journey and wanted her with him."

"Did she go willingly?" asked Natalie, for she had learned to love the gentle child with all the warmth of her lonely heart and now longed to win her back.

"Yes, indeed, Mademoiselle" was the reply. "She said it was

gloomy here when you were gone, and leaving her love for you, she went singing away, as if glad to be free."

"Poor child, lonely as it was to her, it will seem doubly desolate to me now that she is gone and the old gloom settles down upon my life again," sighed Natalie. "Heaven bless and keep her wherever she be, for she has been a little comforter to me. I shall not soon forget her."

A mile or more from the city stood a large and handsome countryseat. Snow and ice lay over the fine gardens now, and the untrodden paths and perfect silence gave it a dreary, uninhabited look. But it was not empty; for a thin wreath of smoke rose from one of its many chimneys, and at an upper, curtainless window a little wistful face looked wearily out across the fields of snow toward the distant city, whose lights shone through the evening gloom.

Lured away from her new home by promises of a speedy return, Genevieve, who longed to breathe the air and use her entire feet again, had gladly followed her grandfather, knowing nothing of the supposed journey, being absent when the message was given.

Led by him to the solitary house, she had waited in the gloomy room nearly an hour, wondering what kept him so long away from her.

Tired of the unbroken silence and deepening twilight, she went at length softly out into the passage, and hearing the low murmur of voices not far off, she went toward the half-opened door whence they seemed to come.

Looking timidly in, she saw by the dim light of a newly kindled fire her grandfather and the man of her dream conversing earnestly together. Startled, and trembling with a nameless fear of something wrong, she was gliding away when a few words met her ear that fixed her to the spot, white and still as the image looking from a niche beside her.

"If Genevieve *is* Natalie's child, there is no need of further search," said the stranger's voice, adding with a low laugh, "I little thought when I came to warn you that Mademoiselle's was not a proper home for her, and advise you to remove her instantly, that you would recognize in me the person who seven years ago placed the baby in your daughter's arms. Time has altered you more than it has me, I fancy, for I never knew you."

"Ah, sir, I remember faces well, and yours is not one to fade soon from my memory, though you are a little changed from the pale young gentleman who charged my poor Agatha to love the little one. But there is still the same eye and smile and the same generous hand that made us rich in return for our secrecy," replied the old man, holding fast the roll of bills just given him.

"You say your daughter died two years ago?" asked the gentleman. "And you are sure she never told that well-paid secret to any living soul, are you?"

"Quite, sir, quite," said the old man eagerly. "She was a faithful nurse, almost a mother to the child, who loved her as one, and before she died, Agatha charged me to watch over Genevieve and be silent as the grave until you came to take her back, as you once promised."

"That's well, and now I *will* relieve you from all care of the child. But keep the secret closer than ever, and I will double the sum you hold there." The stranger passed to and fro in silence for a moment, and then, coming to his companion's side, he said, lowering his voice, "I will entrust you with another private matter, for you have proved yourself trustworthy in this. Will you give me your assistance? To be paid for, of course," he added as the bills rustled significantly in the old man's hand.

"Yes, sir," he answered, "if it can bring me into no trouble. I'll do my best for you, for I am poor and sums like these are not often earned by such as I."

The keen eye of the gentleman was fixed upon his downcast face, reading in the pinched features and crafty smile the hidden power that could win the miserly old man to any deed not endangering him nor his hoards. So, placing a well-filled purse carelessly upon the table as a lure, he said boldly, "I am married to this Natalie and would give half my fortune to prove it otherwise, but in my boyish infatuation I was rash enough to do it. One of the witnesses still lives, and Natalie has letters which can do me harm if once she set about the work; and that she would surely do if she suspected that I am about to marry a lady of my own rank here. I fancied her dead or worse; and as I could never own her as my wife without bringing ruin on myself, for my father and friends would never receive her, I naturally forgot this foolish affair until I saw her here and learned that she is resolved to claim her rights. Then, knowing her energy and resolution, I tried to lure her back to France, meaning to substitute some pretty child for the one she lost, and there leave her after securing those letters and the witness, that she may have no power over me.

"But this Genevieve destroyed my plan the first time. That is little matter now, for the knowledge of the true child's existence here so near her will win her easily, I trust.

"Now, what I want of you is this. You desire to return to France—I will supply the means—but in return I wish you to go before us, prepare all for our coming, and secure the silence of the old woman who saw the wedding, that I may not waken Natalie's suspicions by stirring in the affair myself and may escape notice on my own account, for I wish no whisper of this cursed matter to reach America. Do you understand? And do you agree to this?"

"I do," replied the old man, keeping his eyes upon the purse. "When shall I go, sir?"

"Immediately. Get your dismissal from the theater and be off quietly and silently. Leave the child with me. My right as her father allows me to make what use I please of her." (How the little heart in the dim passage beat at that word and sank again, remembering what he was.) "Now go, and take *that* to make all sure."

Tossing the purse into his hand, the young man turned away and began his restless walk again. The old miser crept out and, finding Genevieve in the great empty room, bade her good night, saying he would come and take her home tomorrow.

The child passively submitted, and the darkness hid the

terror, joy, and wonder that blanched her cheek and weighed upon her like a guilty secret.

Long she sat alone trying to collect her scattered thoughts and understand all she had heard. She was naturally quick, and her wandering life and early knowledge of the evils around her had sharpened all her faculties and rendered her intelligent and self-reliant far beyond her years. As she grew calmer, her fear and wonder were forgotten in the great joy that she was the child of beautiful, kind Natalie, for whom she pined so sadly now.

And though Genevieve still thought tenderly and gratefully of the faithful Agatha, to whose simple teaching she owed more than she yet knew, her childish heart had been completely won by the generous and noble nature of her mother, whom she so nearly resembled in character, though not in form or feature, and whom she had loved with her whole soul since the first kind word fell from those lips so cold and silent to all but her.

The clasp of those clinging arms seemed yet about her, the dear head on her shoulder, and the heart she soon would fill with joy beating near her own, as she sat in the darkness whispering the one word "Mother" to herself and weeping silently, so lost to everything but her new happiness that she did not see the approaching light until a voice said anxiously:

"Where are you, child? Come out into a warmer room. I thought you were with Martha till your sobs reached me. Dry your eyes and do not be afraid. Nothing will hurt you here."

Speaking thus, the gentleman led her into the apartment he had just quitted, and seating her beside the fire, stood looking at her with an interest whose meaning she could well divine as she heard him mutter, "Where did she get that sunny face of hers, so utterly unlike us both? Little wonder I did not know her."

She bore this steady scrutiny till her cheeks burned and her full heart throbbed painfully. Then, looking up with eyes brimful of tears, she said imploringly, "Oh, sir, *could* you let me go home? It is so lonely here, and Natalie will miss me very much. Why must I stay with you—?" "Father" was on her lips, but she could not say it with that stern face looking steadily into her own.

"You must ask no questions but wait patiently here till I think it best to send you back. There are books and pictures yonder, and here is a store of trifles such as children like. Amuse yourself with these until I come for you."

As he spoke, her father opened an ivory case upon the table, showing her many curious things, and brought her a store of books and prints. Pleased by his wish to comfort her and the unconscious softening of his manner toward her, Genevieve gratefully accepted them and looked less timidly at him as he threw on his cloak, saying, "I will tell Martha to bring your supper and sit with you if you like it. So good night, Genevieve."

Moved by a sudden impulse, she went to him and, lifting up her tearful face for a farewell kiss, said meekly, "Good night, sir. I will *try* to be good and patient, though it *is* rather dismal here."

Touched by her winning tones, and little dreaming what had worked the sudden change in her manner toward him, her father bent and kissed her forehead while a pang of shame and self-reproach smote him for past and future wrongs to the gentle child, and with a hasty caress he left her happier for knowing that he *could* be kind.

Long after the woman Martha left her, she sat in her solitary bed, watching the black shadows in the room and racking her childish brain to find some means of letting Natalie know all she had learned. "I will get away from this place and travel till I find her, and then we will go away to some quiet place together and never be unhappy anymore," she said to herself, and then, worn out with excitement, she sank into a heavy sleep, broken by restless dreams and haunted by the secret which now burdened her.

When morning came, she rose up unrefreshed, but gathered all her courage and small store of prudence, that no suspicion should be roused as to her purpose. She wandered through the great house, where her light tread echoed through the empty rooms, hoping to find some unseen method of escape. But all the lower doors and windows were heavily barred, and with a sinking heart she saw the only passage out lay through the room where Martha and her husband lived, and where they sat at work, evidently watching all she did. She thought of appealing to them, but after a shy and wistful look into their forbidding faces, she abandoned that idea and sat in the room above, sorrowfully wondering how all would end.

A bright thought came at last, and despairing of escape herself, she gathered up pen and paper and, stealing away into a quiet corner, told her mother all she knew in her simple, childish way, often blotting it with tears and laboring painfully that every line might be legible and clear. And at length, after many trials and trepidations, it was finished, and carefully concealing it in her bosom, she watched eagerly for some means of sending it, hoping some messenger or servant might appear by whom she could dispatch it unseen to the city.

But no one came. Then she turned to the passersby going townward and only separated from her by a low fence and garden plot. She leaned out from the casement, beckoning, and once she ventured to move her little handkerchief at a red-faced farmer's boy, who was whistling as he hurried by, but he only stared and plodded on. No one heeded her, and as the silent winter daylight waned and faded, nothing was accomplished.

"What shall I do? Oh, what shall I do?" the poor girl cried, wringing her hands and pacing to and fro from despair. "Natalie will be deceived, and some great harm will surely come because I cannot go to warn and tell her all I know. Ah, if I were a snowflake, I could flutter to her side and whisper it so safely in her ear," she sighed, watching the white flakes as they fell.

She opened the window to lay the cool snow on her burning forehead, and her eye rested on a trellis where summer vines had grown, now bare and fringed with icicles, but looking firm and strong. With a sudden purpose rising in her mind, she looked at the stormy sky, the far-off city, then at the frail ladder, and silently resolved to put away her fears and try it for her mother's sake. Softly closing the window, she partially undressed and lay down on her bed.

"That's the best place for her, and I'm glad she is disposed of for the night. Of all the strange things Mr. Louis ever did, this, to my fancy, is the strangest," muttered Martha, looking at the child, who lay breathing softly, as if in a deep sleep, though her long lashes quivered and she feared the loud beating of her heart would betray her. But Martha only looked a moment at the flushed face and damp hair of the little sleeper and then, saying something of "evil dreams disturbing her," dropped the curtains carelessly and went away.

Listening till all was still below, Genevieve rose and, wrapping her cloak about her, with the precious letter in her bosom, opened the window and crept softly out.

The wind had risen and the snow fell fast, but she had often, as sylph or spirit, trusted her light weight to a frailer support than that which she now rested on. Though the icicles benumbed her hands and the driving flakes blinded her eyes, she climbed bravely down and glided away like a shadow toward the city, whose lamps were the guiding stars that led her through the storm.

The bitter wind swept fiercely by, the cold grew more intense, and the snow fell faster as evening deepened into night. The clocks struck ten as, faint and anxious, with sinking heart and stiffening limbs, the child came wearily into the city. Though longing for warmth and help, she would not stop lest the drowsy weakness stealing over her should keep her from her mother's side too long.

Conscious of nothing now but the one wish to hear her voice again and sleep in her arms, she struggled on until she reached the long, quiet street where Natalie had made her home. Slowly her frozen feet bore the brave-hearted child along. The dim lights danced before her dizzy eyes, her breath came slowly, and the heavy sleep now seemed to weigh her down. But holding fast the paper, she staggered up the steps. Then, with a feeble knock, she called faintly, "Mother, dear Mother, take me in, for God *has* sent you back your little child," and then sank down, smiling, and the gentle sleep stole over her while the falling snow wrapped her in a soft white shroud.

An hour later Natalie rode homeward through the deserted streets, her secret sorrow lying heavily at her heart. Looking thoughtfully out upon the stormy scene, she now saw small footprints in the newly fallen snow.

"God help the little wanderer in a night like this and send some friend to take it in," she thought, unconsciously following the wavering tracks as she glided on till, with a sudden dim foreboding, she saw they ended at her own door.

Springing hastily out, she raised the slender figure from her threshold and bore it in, calling for help as she went. Laying her light burden on the couch, she lifted the long hair from its face, and there, with frozen tears upon her cheek and a glad smile on her blue lips, lay little Genevieve, dead in her mother's arms.

Every art that love and skill could offer were all tried in vain, and as midnight sounded over the hushed city, Natalie stood colorless and rigid as the quiet form before her, reading the blotted paper found in the little stiffened hand.

As it fluttered to the ground, a cry so sharp and bitter rang through the room that it struck the weeping servant dumb with terror, and Natalie sank, as if smitten by a heavy blow, beside her child, speechless and tearless with her great and sudden grief.

And so till morning dawned, they lay folded in each other's arms, so motionless and still that death seemed kindly to have sent his quiet sleep to both.

All the next day the young mother sat in the hushed chamber where her treasure lay—singing softly to ears that never heard, kissing fondly lips that never answered, caressing the small hands that never pressed her own again, touching each fold of the white garments, and replacing each flower that bloomed around the smiling image of her little child.

She shed no tears till her eye fell on the crumpled paper, forgotten since her first knowledge of her loss. Again she read the lines and now knew whose thoughtful hand had traced them, whose loving tears had stained them; and then, as all grew clear before her, and the simple words, so full of eager love and longing, met her eyes, she wept more wildly and despairingly than she had done when Genevieve first came to her, for now there was no hope. And but for the rebuke of the childish words before her, begging her to pardon all and love the father who had spoken gently and been kind to Genevieve, she would have cursed him for the misery he had brought her in the final ruin he had made. But as she looked at the quiet face upon the pillow, all bitter thoughts of retribution faded like evil shadows in the light of the serene smile shining there.

So, by the bed where the treasure of her life lay dead, the proud woman learned a lesson from the little teacher there that beautified and softened her whole nature, making her sorrow a purifying flame to warm and brighten all her coming years.

Evening came, and with it the stranger, utterly unconscious of all that had passed and eager to renew the tempting offers he had made before.

The outer room was empty, and turning to call Natalie, he saw her standing on the threshold of the inner door, so changed that he felt a thrill steal over him and a sudden fear of he knew not what.

Her black hair had fallen on her shoulders; her face was white as marble; but in her eyes there was a light and on her lips a smile so strange and beautiful that he stood silent and forgetful of all but the apparition looking at him from the gloom beyond.

She did not speak, but beckoned him. Awed by her solemn manner, he followed her into a dim, still room filled with the breath of flowers, and there, standing beside a curtained bed, Natalie said in a voice so calm and passionless it touched her hearer with a deeper sense of shame than her proudest words had ever done:

"You cannot tempt me now, for I have found my child and no power can part us. She is mine forever."

"Found her! How and where?" stammered her companion, shrinking back.

"*Dead* on the threshold of my door, whither she had struggled through the bitter storm to tell me of her father's evil plots to rob and wrong me for a second time. Oh, look there," she cried, sweeping back the white folds suddenly. "Look there, and may God lighten your remorseful sorrow and make you better for the woeful sight."

Pale and motionless, the startled man looked on the little sleeper, while the memory of a patient face uplifted to his own and the echo of a timid voice rose in his heart and wrung it with a keener pang of sorrow than it had ever known before.

Three times had he seen the child, each time coming between him and a sinful deed, as if seeking to warn and win him back. Once with her mother clinging to her for protection against him and her own heart. Again in the lonely chamber overcoming grief and fear, as if unconsciously to lure him by her innocent caress from the new wrong he meditated.

And *now* lying dead through him—and though the white lips were forever silent, there came a mild rebuke and warning from them that sounded through his worldly spirit with strange power and woke his better self from its long sleep.

And it was with eyes that saw but dimly that he read the paper that Natalie placed in his hand, saying in the same untroubled voice: "The magic of my child's pure love has banished every unforgiving thought and evil impulse from my heart. Henceforth I am dead to you and to the world, for convent walls are safe and tranquil as a tomb. And here, beside this quiet bed and in *her* name, I freely pardon you and break the fetter that now binds us."

Drawing from her hand a simple ring, she laid it with a packet of worn letters on the pillow where the bright head lay.

For a moment good and evil struggled in the proud man's heart, but the changed face of the woman he had wronged looked mildly on him. A low voice whispered pleadingly:

"She has had many sorrows. Ah, be generous and do not make them heavier to bear." And obeying that, he folded ring and letters in the paper he still held, and gave them back, saying in the tender voice of long ago:

"I shall never use them, Natalie. Then take them back, and though we separate forever, let me still feel that there is a tie, however slight, to bind me to that little child whose memory, with God's help, shall lead me to atone for a wasted, sinful life. Farewell, your pardon is the noblest revenge and the sight of that dead face the bitterest punishment you could have chosen."

Reverently he bent above the pillow and then went silently away, humbly praying to be made a better and a happier man. And Natalie, kneeling in the quiet chamber, whispered to the child upon her bosom:

"Oh, my Genevieve! Your simple spells have won me back the earthly treasure I had lost. Your love shall be the star that leads me through the gloom into that fairer home where I shall find the dearest one, where my long search will end, and where at last my little child may call me 'Mother.'"

BERTHA

Under a group of fragrant lindens sat a little German maiden singing at her spinning wheel. The morning sun glanced brightly on the distant village spires and on the cottage roof, where white doves softly cooed as they basked in its warm rays. The fresh winds made a pleasant rustling among the leaves, lifted the fair hair of the child, and kissed her blooming cheek. The wayside flowers nodded on their stems and welcomed to their bosoms bright-winged butterflies and murmuring bees, while a cloudless morning sky arched overhead and the summer earth lay smiling in its light.

Here before the cottage door sat little Bertha singing beautiful old ballads to the music of her busy wheel. The doves cooed on the sunny roof, the winds went whispering by, and wild birds caroled merrily among the fragrant boughs. But the sweetest, brightest music there was the clear voice of the happy-hearted child.

A traveler came wandering from the town along the pleasant road, drawn onward by the simple music, which he followed till he beheld the little singer in the shadow of the green old trees. Bertha did not hear his light step on the grass, and standing thus unseen, he listened silently until her song was done. Then, coming to her side, he glanced into her startled face with a friendly smile, saying:

"Thanks for your music, little one. May I sit here and listen longer, till my carriage joins me from yonder town? Do not fear me, but sing again. I like your songs right well."

"Ah, sir," said little Bertha, blushing like the rosebuds in her bodice, "you are pleased to say so. I have little skill in music, but I cannot help singing when the birds are all so merry there above."

The stranger sat upon the mossy stone that lay beside the wheel, and lifting off his broad-brimmed hat, let the cool wind toss his brown locks to and fro and the flickering shadows play upon his beautiful, mild face.

Bertha stopped her work and, looking shyly from among her curls, listened with a strange delight to the low, musical voice that praised her simple songs so kindly.

"Sing me another ballad, little friend," he said. "It mingles so pleasantly with nature's voices. Will you grant this favor to a stranger and forgive him if he asks too much?"

"I will gladly sing to you," replied the child with innocent frankness, "but it is a very little thing to give you pleasure, sir."

Then, folding her hands and fixing her large eyes on his face, she poured forth a plaintive melody in sweet, childish tones, which echoed through the quiet air. The stranger listened with a look of wonder and delight, which deepened more and more as her birdlike voice, changing from sad to gay, told in music the loves and sorrows of the quaint old ballad she was singing.

When she ceased, he drew her to his side and, brushing back the long locks from her cheeks, looked earnestly into the wondering little face, saying in an eager voice, "My child, who taught you this? Tell me freely of yourself, for I am your friend."

Bertha stood confidingly beside his knee and answered with an artless smile: "No one taught me, sir. I must have learned it of the birds, I think, or," she added in a musing tone, with a dreamy glance into the sky, "or of the voices always singing in the air. Music is all about me in my sleep and lingers near me when I wake. I try to sing the lovely songs, but they never sound so beautiful as they do in dreams. But why do you ask, sir? *All* children sing, you know."

"Few sing like you, strange child," he answered earnestly.

"Now tell me of yourself. I must know more of you. What is your name?"

"Bertha," she answered with a quick glance into his face. "I am an orphan, and my home is here with Grandmother. Shall I bid her come and speak with you? She can tell you whatever you may wish to know far better than I. Shall I go, sir?"

"Yes, let me see her, Bertha. I have that to tell her which she will be glad to hear. Hasten and call her, for I have but little time to stay," replied the stranger, and as she tripped away, he watched her, saying half aloud, "I cannot leave this nightingale to sing unheard. She must fulfill the destiny so plainly hers, and heaven grant she never may have cause to reproach me for what I am about to do."

Soon, hastening from the cottage came a cheerful old woman, her gray hair parted smoothly under her white cap and a snowy kerchief folded on her bosom. As she approached, he rose and bent before her with respectful courtesy, saying:

"Pardon my boldness in coming thus unknown before you with a strange request, but I would accomplish much in a short space. Led by your grandchild's music, I wandered hither from the town, and listening, I discovered in her a love of music uncommon in so young a child. She is richly gifted with a rare and lovely voice, which with proper training will in time, I trust, render her well known and loved. Will you let me place her where this may be done soon—very soon? For time is precious, and I long to see her cultivating the rich gift she possesses. Did no one tell you this before, my friend?" he added as a look of joy and wonder brightened the old woman's placid face.

"I knew it, sir," she cried. "I knew my poor Carl's child would one day show the power she inherited from him. I felt it when I heard her singing so gaily all alone, with none to hear her but the birds she loves so well. Her father, sir, was bound up in music, but alas, he lived and died longing for the thing he loved. We were poor, and he would not leave us to seek his fortune in the world while we needed him at home. So, sir, he labored patiently for us until his young wife died;

he soon followed her and left me little Bertha as a precious charge. His last words were a prayer that she might never find the path of duty so hard to tread as he had done, and a prophecy that that passion which had darkened his whole life would be the light and glory of his child's."

"Then you will agree to my proposal, I trust," said the stranger, as the old woman paused to wipe away the tears that fell at the memory of her faithful son.

"Yes, sir," she eagerly replied, "with many thanks I *do* accept your friendly offer, if I may go with Bertha. She is an orphan and I cannot let her leave me. You will not part us, sir, I hope; she is all I care for in the wide world now. I will not be a burden but a help to you if I may go with the child."

"Heaven forbid that I should part you," replied the stranger. "Her home shall be yours, and your only care shall be to love and cheer her on. Now listen, my good friend. In a month I shall return this way. Meanwhile, think of my proposal, talk with Bertha of it, and if on my return you still desire to go with me, it shall be so. If I live, you never shall regret the day you trusted me. Now farewell, for yonder comes the carriage and I must go. Farewell, little Bertha," he added as she came hurrying from the cottage. "Your grandmother will tell you pleasant news, and when I come again, I trust I shall not leave you here behind." And bending down, he kissed her rosy cheek and dropped a purse into her apron, saying, "This is payment for the song. You must not refuse it, and so adieu till we meet again."

Bertha took the generous hand that looked so delicate in both her little sunburned ones, and kissed it, saying timidly, "Ah, dear sir, how can we thank you for your kindness to us? I have only this to show how grateful I am. Will you accept a little flower, sir?" And with childish grace she offered him a rosebud from her bosom.

He took it, smiling kindly, and placed a paper in her hand, saying, "This will tell you who I am and give you greater confidence in me, perhaps, than if I were unknown. Adieu, dame, think of my words and teach the child to love and trust her future friend. God bless you, little one."

A carriage now came rolling down the hill and stopped beneath the lindens at a signal from the stranger, who hurried from the thanks of the grateful old woman and, springing in, was swiftly borne away. But as he vanished, little Bertha saw him wave his hand and saw that he still held her rosebud fast.

"Dear Grandmother, tell me now, what does it mean? When will he come again? And why does he give me all this gold for one poor song?" she eagerly asked when the distant sound of the wheels had died away.

"Come hither, child, and listen, for a great and happy thing has chanced this day," replied the old woman, drawing Bertha to her side and looking tenderly into the earnest face uplifted to her own.

"The stranger," she continued, turning to the paper he had given, "is Ernest Lennartson, the great and good musician, whom your father longed so eagerly to see. He tells me that your voice, dear child, is wonderful and sweet and will one day render you a rich and famous woman if we leave our home and go with him where you may be rightly taught and cared for. This is what he told me, and the gold he so thoughtfully gave is to make us ready to journey away with him when he returns. Do you understand all now? And are you glad to know it, Bertha?"

The child stood with lips apart, the color fading from her cheek and her dark eyes growing larger as she listened with her hands pressed on her bosom, as if to still the little fluttering heart that stirred within. When her grandmother ceased, she threw herself upon the kind old woman's breast and cried out through her joyful tears:

"Oh, can it all be true? And shall I really learn to sing the beautiful, strange songs the voices murmur in my ear? It will seem like a lovely dream to have my life so full of music. What have I ever done that I should be so happy now?"

"Hush! Hush, dear child! And do not weep so passionately, or your joy will harm you," said the fond old woman, smoothing back the long hair from the tearful little face. "I do not wonder at your joy, for my own heart is running over with delight to think that years hence my Carl's child will become a happy and admired woman and never know the poverty and sorrow he so patiently endured. Think, dear heart, how pleasant it will be to live in comfortable homes with wise and loving friends about you and be welcomed wherever you may go, beloved and honored for the sweet gift the good God has given you. Do you think of this? And are you grateful for it, Bertha?"

"I feel nothing but my great joy now," replied the child, lifting her pale face shining with a strange, still happiness. "I can think of nothing but the delight 't will be to me to go singing through the world, feeling that I have the power to gladden others with the music of my simple voice and that I may one day win a quiet home for you, dear Grandmother, where you can rest and let me work for you as you have done for me these twelve long years."

"Heaven bless my generous child and grant her wish if it is best," cried the old woman. "But we will talk of this no more now, for you are trembling with excitement and this busy brain needs rest. Come in and lie upon your bed, dear child. I must hasten to my work, for much is to be done. I have yet to ask the good pastor if I am right in thus early taking you from the quiet of your home into the busy, troubled world."

"I cannot rest, dear Grandmother," replied Bertha, sinking down upon the mossy stone. "Let me sit here and think. It is so dark and close within there. I must be out where I can feel the wind upon my face and hear the birds. I will work soon, but now all seems so like a dream. I fear to move lest I should wake and find it gone."

So with a fond caress the happy grandmother went back to her work within the cottage. But she often left it and stole softly to look with proud smiles and whispered blessings upon the child, who sat with folded hands in the shadow of the green old trees, listening in a happy trance to the sweet voices that seemed to echo through the summer air, whispering pleasant prophecies of the unknown future that now lay before her. The birds sang blithely overhead, the white doves cooed, and the warm winds rustled by. But the spinning wheel stood idle and little Bertha sang no more that day.

II

Five long years had rolled away, and in Ernest Lennartson's pleasant home the child had grown into a maiden.

The dear old grandmother slept in the churchyard near her early home, and Bertha would have been alone in the world had she not found a watchful mother in Ernest's elder sister, a companion and fellow student in his young brother, and a wise, true friend in himself, who taught her patiently the first hard secrets of her art, watched her progress with proud delight, and loved her with the generous affection of a noble heart toward one who looked to it for help and counsel.

Bertha well repaid his care, for the grateful love she bore him grew and deepened with her years; and as the child had freely trusted, so the young girl still looked up to him, told every joy and sorrow, and left her fate to his wise care and guidance.

In the sunny garden that lay around her new home, Bertha sat alone among the flowers. Before her plashed a fountain, making music as its cool waves rose and fell; around her rustled blossoming shrubs and vines, while over all a rosy sunset sky shone down.

Years had wrought a silent change, and the little cottage Bertha had bloomed into a graceful maiden. The child's innocent eyes were deeper and darker now, and the color on her cheek was delicate and warm as the blush of the roses in her hair, the ringlets of which would not be confined, but still lay in bright clusters on her shoulders, free and fetterless as when the winds played with them in the shadow of the lindens long ago.

A book had fallen unheeded from her hands, which now lay idly folded on her knee, as with a thoughtful smile she watched the blue waves sparkle in the evening light and mused of future hopes and joys.

While thus she sat, along the garden paths came the brothers seeking for her. The elder was but little changed since Bertha first beheld him; his locks were thick and brown as then, his face as cheerful and serene, his voice as musical and kind as when he sat beside her little wheel and praised her song.

The younger, a fair-haired, slender youth, leaned upon and looked up to his brother as a loving son might lean and look upon a fond father.

So, arm in arm, the two went wandering through the flowers till they spied Bertha sitting by the fountain all alone.

"Is she not beautiful, Ernest—sitting there so like a smiling statue, bathed in this soft light?" whispered Wilhelm as they paused beneath an overhanging vine to look at her.

"Yes, it is a picture I would gladly keep forever," replied the elder brother with a sigh. "But as that cannot be, it saddens me to look at it, for we may never see her sitting there so calm and beautiful again. W—— has written me that he is ready to admit her now and finish what I have begun. We shall not see her for a long, long time, and then she goes forth to the world, where she may soon forget us. And even if she does not, she will change, and we shall never find her the same frank, happy-hearted child she is now. But, Wilhelm, why is this? Has Gertrude told you nothing of her departure yet?" he asked with anxious tenderness as his brother turned away with a sudden exclamation of surprise and grief, saying in a changed, eager voice:

"Why must she go now when we are all so happy here together? Let W—— come hither, or let us go to Italy with her. I knew she must one day leave us, but now the hour is come, I cannot think of it. All will be so desolate, and I shall miss in her the sunshine of our home."

"Shall I not miss her even more than you, dear Wilhelm?" replied Ernest, looking fondly at the quiet figure half hidden among the flowers. "Will it not be very hard for me to part with the dear child I have loved and taught for five long years? But knowing that it is for her future happiness, I cannot let my selfish sorrow trouble her, but try to forget it that I may increase her joy. Come with me, and let us tell her the glad news generously, without a word of our own grief at parting."

"No, Ernest, go alone. It will seem better tidings from your lips than mine, for you have learned to hide your troubles under a smiling face. I'll go to Gertrude; she will need comforting for the loss of her child, Bertha."

So Wilhelm hastened sorrowfully back while Ernest, banishing all trouble from his countenance, passed on and stood at Bertha's side, saying cheerfully, "Wake, little dreamer, for the time is near when you must up and out into the world to fit yourself for trials and triumphs yet to come. Listen, Bertha, I have glad tidings for your ear."

"Dear master, what have you to tell me? Something new and pleasant? I can see that in your face. Sit here and let me know it soon," cried Bertha as she sprang up and drew him to her seat. She knelt on the green sward at his side and, leaning on his knee, waited with childlike eagerness for what should come.

In cheerful words he told her of the approaching change, touching lightly on the parting and the distance of her new home from the one she loved so well; dwelling long on the pleasant, studious life she soon would lead with her kind old teacher in his fair Italian home; telling of their eager interest in her progress and success and how boundless their delight and pride would be, when at last she was known and loved and winning friends by the magic of her voice, that their little Bertha should possess so great and beautiful a power.

The young girl listened to his words with downcast eyes and deepening color, but when he ceased, she looked up, saying with a radiant face and earnest voice: "And when I *am* so known and loved, *my* greatest joy will be that I owe all to you, dear master. Ah, if you could only be my teacher still, I should learn better than with this old man to whom I'm going, for my heart would then be in my task. But when must I go? Not yet, I hope, for much as I love music, I love this dear home more."

"You must leave us very soon, for we will not keep you when it's best to part. It will seem hard to lose our little Bertha, but she knows it's for her good and that our love goes with her to her distant home and is but strengthened by the parting. Then do not grieve, dear child. All paths, however pleasant, have some thorns concealed among the roses," said

the master, laying his hand tenderly upon the head she had
bowed upon her hands when he first spoke of separation.

"I have felt them," answered Bertha through her tears.
"You have carpeted my way with flowers and made my life so
beautiful and calm that care and sorrow have been strangers
to me until now. How *can* I go so far from all I love? How can
I part from *you,* from Gertrude and dear Wilhelm, never to return, perhaps, or, if I do, to find all changed?"

"*We* shall not change, dear Bertha," said her friend. "Years
may go by before we meet, but you will find us still the same,
for time can never alter love like ours. But *you* will change, I
fear, for in the busy world, amid whose flatteries and fascina-
tions you will soon be dwelling, new duties, cares, and pleasures will arise to make your life a brilliant, happy one. You
will soon forget the past, the quiet years in this old home, and
perhaps even the simple friends you grieve at leaving now," he
added half in jest, half in sad earnest.

"Forget you!" echoed Bertha, rising up before him with an
indignant flush upon her cheek. "Do not fear that I shall ever
cease to cherish above all other passions, thoughts, and feelings a deep love and gratitude for those who gave the orphan
child a happy home. Time, distance, or success can never
change this true affection, for it has grown and strengthened
with my life. I cannot tell it, but a day may come when I *can*
prove its depth and repay the great debt I now owe you. Then
do not wrong me by a single doubt, for you little know the
strength of Bertha's love if you believe she ever *could* forget
you, dearest master, Father, and friend."

As she thus poured out the feelings that had long filled her
grateful heart, Bertha turned away to hide the hot glow on her
cheek, with a timid shame unknown before.

Wondering at the sudden energy and passion which
seemed to change her from a careless child into a woman,
Ernest looked in silence as she stood so beautiful and innocent
before him, and as he looked, he felt how very dear she had
become, and thought with a keen pang of sorrow how desolate his life would seem when he should miss her young face
at his side, the music of her voice in his ear, and the sweet

presence which made his home so beautiful to him. And as he was feeling this, an earnest hope rose in his heart that he might yet win a dearer place in Bertha's love and bind her to him with tenderer tie than that which held them now.

This hope had often haunted him before as he beheld her blooming into womanhood, but fearing lest she should be blinded by her generous affection and in her gratitude should sacrifice her future happiness, he never spoke of his patient love, but waited silently till time should render her a fitting judge of her own heart.

And now, though longing eagerly to tell her this before she went out into the world, he would not bind her by a promise which might prove a fetter to her free spirit, but silently resolved to wait yet longer and trust all to time.

So, banishing each tender look or word that might trouble her, he drew her to his side, saying in his old friendly way, "Forgive me, dearest Bertha, if I wounded you. It was an idle, selfish fear lest others should estrange you from us. Pardon it and forget that it was ever uttered. Now dry these tears and let us talk of the happy years to come, and think no more of partings and farewells. But do not call me master, for you have ceased to be my pupil now; nor Father, for I have neither the years nor wisdom which befit that name. Let me be your *friend* and I shall be content. So call me Ernest, henceforth, Bertha."

"I will call you anything you may desire, for no name can be too beautiful or dear for you," said Bertha warmly. "But call *me* still your child; it sounds so sweet and homelike from your lips."

"You are a child no longer, and I cannot treat you as one, Bertha," he replied, drawing her upon the rustic seat beside him. "You are a fair and gifted woman now. Then do not sit there at my feet as if *I* were the one to be looked up to and beloved, but here at my side as a friend whom I reverence and cherish tenderly and truly, Bertha."

So in the gathering twilight, with the murmur of the fountain mingling with their voices, they sat till the early moon rose up and, glancing through the leaves, shone on the face of

Ernest, brightened by the secret joy which lit his eye and lent a new charm to his cheerful voice that had never sounded half so musical to Bertha's ear as now, when, listening silently, she wondered why her gratitude had never seemed so deep before and why the thought of parting filled her with such bitter sorrow.

"Good night, little Bertha," Ernest said as they heard sister Gertrude calling them to come in from the falling dew. "Give *me* that flower and do not leave it there to fade," he added as she took the roses from her hair and was about to drop them in the fountain. "Do you remember the little bud you gave me once?" he asked. "It was as true an emblem of its child giver as this delicate, half-blown rose is of you now. May I keep it as a symbol of *our* household flower, to look at when she is gone?"

"Dear friend, take all, take anything I own if it can give you pleasure," she answered warmly. "There is nothing I possess I would not freely offer *you,* who have given *me* so much."

"I am content with this and will not ask for more *yet,*" said Ernest, looking down into her upturned face with a strange, wistful gaze. A sudden glow came to his cheek, and words seemed hovering on his lips, but they remained unspoken. And with his evening blessing he left her silently.

And she went wondering away, to dream all night of his kind words and the longing look she had never seen before.

In his darkened chamber Wilhelm sat alone, brooding over the newly wakened hopes and fears that filled his troubled mind, till a hand fell on his bent head and his brother stood beside him, saying anxiously, "What troubles you, dear Wilhelm? Tell me, and if I cannot banish it, then let me share it with you, as I have always done."

Wilhelm looked up. His face was aglow with deep emotion as he replied, "Ernest, I love Bertha—not with a calm affection like your own, but with a love whose strength I never knew till now, when the thought of parting has awakened me to the knowledge that the feeling I have cherished for her is stronger, warmer than the fondest brother ever felt.

"And though this knowledge fills me with a strange delight, yet with it comes a fear that she can never be to me all I so earnestly desire. Tell me, brother (for you know her every thought and feeling), does she, can she ever love me? And if so, will you give her to me, for she is your child?"

The light and glow had vanished from Ernest's face, leaving it colorless and wan as the moonlight stealing into the dim room. But though his happy dream was broken and a shadow had fallen suddenly upon his life, turning his patient love into a secret sorrow heavy to be borne, his generous heart, long used to self-denial, bravely put aside his cherished hopes, that he might gladden his younger brother, even though the cloud he chased from him should darken his own life the more.

Silently the struggle passed, and the sacrifice was made. Then, striving to render his voice calm and kind as ever, he answered:

"Yes, Wilhelm, I *will* give her to you if she loves you. I cannot tell you if it be so. I have never looked into her heart, for it is a sacred place, filled doubtless with all noble thoughts, high aspirations, womanly affections, virtues, and desires—a rich possession, Wilhelm, to whoever is so blessed as to win it.

"She is very young yet, but still there may be tender feelings hidden there, which a word may call forth if the right lips utter it. Then do not fear, but try your fate and bear the joy or disappointment wisely and patiently."

"Then I *may* hope to win her love," cried Wilhelm joyfully, "but how little I shall deserve so great a happiness. You, Ernest, are far worthier to possess so pure and true a heart. I marvel how you can be daily near her, knowing how you are beloved and honored by her, and yet never feel your fatherly affection deepen into something fonder still."

A sudden look of bitter pain and sorrow swept over Ernest's face, but it was calm again when Wilhelm looked with a wondering smile into the kind eyes bent upon him, little dreaming of the struggle it had cost his brother to gain that calmness and to answer without faltering, "The love which I bear Bertha cannot change. It may seem strange to you, but it is better so, Wilhelm. My 'fatherly affection' will never cross your tender passion, and if you (possessing all her love) will spare me a little place in her regard, I shall be content and find a real delight in witnessing the joy of those whose happiness *has* ever been—*will* ever be—the one great object of my life."

"And the one great object of *ours* shall be to make that life most beautiful by our gratitude and love," cried Wilhelm fervently, adding softly as he leaned upon his brother's shoulder: "Teach me, Ernest, to be generous and noble like yourself, that I may be more worthy of Bertha and that she may find in me some trace of those virtues she so reverences in you."

Ernest drew him closer to his side, saying sadly, humbly, "I can teach you very little, Wilhelm; I have many a hard lesson yet to learn. Your own heart will teach you best. Be true to that and Bertha cannot ask for more. In you she will seek for other virtues than the simple ones I may possess, and it is best that we are unlike, for you, I trust, will be her happy lover, while I am still her faithful friend. Now talk no more, but rest, for it is late. Good night, dear Wilhelm. Happy dreams and a bright tomorrow."

So, leaving happiness and hope where he found fear and doubt, Ernest left his brother wrapped in blissful dreams and went silently away into the garden.

All night long the stars looked pityingly down upon the lonely figure pacing to and fro, as if they longed to cheer the troubled heart there seeking in the stillness to grow calm and strong. For Ernest Lennartson was not one to let a selfish sorrow cloud his spirit long and make a discord in the music of his life. But there are moments when the best and wisest mourn the loss of cherished hopes and come forth from the trial purified and strengthened if they bear it rightly.

His love for Bertha had sprung up like a flower. Through the long years they had passed together, her childish trust had nourished it, her fervent gratitude fallen like dew upon it, and her frank affection shone like sunshine, giving it fresh bloom and fragrance till it blossomed forth into a passionflower, filling his life with a beauty he had never known before.

And now, when it was in its fullest prime, he felt it was his duty to uproot and cast it by, lest it should trouble his young brother's peace and prove a fetter to Bertha's grateful heart.

He knew she loved him well, but only as a friend to whom she owed the happiness of her life. He had hoped to have led her slowly onward till this innocent affection should have deepened with her years and come at last to be as warm and tender as his own. But now, learning Wilhelm's secret, he silently put his own hopes away, seeking to forget his bitter disappointment and to gain calmness and courage to think and act wisely and generously for them.

So, heedless of the eager longings that possessed him, and listening only to the low voice of his better self, he wandered in the green solitude, feeling Nature's silent magic in the rustle of leaves that seemed to whisper comfort in the soft kiss of the night wind and in the solemn beauty of the starry sky, till the calm brightness of the summer night filled his restless spirit with a patient courage "to suffer and be strong."

The first red gleams of dawn shone in the east. Standing by the fountain with a few warmer drops upon his cheek than the cold spray scattered there, he looked with the old cheerful smile at Bertha's rose, saying:

"When I took a little bud from her childish hand five years ago, I vowed her happiness should be the first care of my life till she should find a nearer friend to fill my place. That vow, though made only to my own heart, shall be truly kept; and if Wilhelm be that dearer friend, he shall possess her *love* and I will try to be content with *gratitude* and the memory of these few happy years."

Time went on, and Bertha grew slowly conscious of a change in the two brothers. Ernest was but little with her now, though his watchful care and daily acts of thoughtful kindness told her his affection was unchanged. He never spoke of parting as the time for her departure drew near, only of the glad meeting when their separation was over. Nothing seemed to mar his cheerfulness but Bertha's growing gloom, which he bade his brother seek to chase away, while he worked busily, that nothing might be wanting to make her new home welcome to her and her long journey pleasant.

Wilhelm was always at her side, walking in the garden, sitting by her while she worked with Gertrude, pursuing the studies which Ernest had now left him, and seeking in a thousand silent ways to read her heart and find an entrance there.

Bertha, in her deepening wonder and unrest, shrank from the unspoken love in Wilhelm's eyes and longed for the peaceful, happy past, which now seemed so far away, while sister Gertrude, lost in many household cares, hastened busily hither and thither, little dreaming of the unseen struggles going on in the hearts around her—though a passing thought now and then crossed her mind that Ernest was daily growing paler and more silent, while Wilhelm had become restless and gay and strangely unlike his former quiet self.

But other matters soon drove away the fancy, and she thought only of the beloved child and how she might do more for her.

"Madame Mannersted, the sister of your new teacher, with whom you are to travel, Bertha, has arrived at S—— and writes me she is anxious to depart; therefore, you must join her very soon," said Ernest, coming to Bertha as she sat with Gertrude and Wilhelm amid books and packages in her sunny chamber.

"I am ready," replied Bertha, looking quietly up. "But why will you leave me when we must so soon part for years? Come and sit with us, dear master," said she as he seemed about to go. "I have hardly had a quiet hour with you since that evening in the garden weeks ago when you first told me of the coming change. Will you not stay with us, or is there still some weary business to keep us apart?"

Her pleading voice and reproachful eyes smote Ernest's generous heart with a sudden sense of what must seem to her unkind neglect. Though the sight of her young face, so full of love and sorrow, looking wistfully into his own was hard to bear unmoved, and the sound of her voice woke that bitter pain that slept in his breast, he sat beside her and by cheerful words won back the light and bloom to her cheek and eye as she listened eagerly and treasured up his gentle warnings and advices for future need.

"Now I *must* leave you, Bertha," he said at length, "for I have many things to arrange with Madame Mannersted, and shall therefore go before, that all may be ready when you come with Wilhelm in a day or two to join us at S——. Meet me below presently. I will say farewell to you here, for in the bustle and confusion of our parting in the city, I shall have no time for words."

When Ernest joined them, ready to depart, he found them gathered in the shadow of the vines that hung about the old stone porch, and taking his brother aside, whispered earnestly, "Wilhelm, deal generously with my child and do not bind her by any promises that may prove burdensome. I do not doubt *now* that she loves you. I read it in her shy avoidance of you and her silent sadness as the parting draws near. Still, though this be so, leave her free till she has seen the world and learned to know her own heart well. Tell her I approve her choice, and heaven bless you both in your great happiness, dear brother."

Then, drawing Bertha to his side, he laid his hand upon her head, saying, "Dear child, I have no words to tell you how beautiful you have made my life while sharing our home, nor how great is my trust in your strength and purity of heart, how bright my hopes of your future welfare, and how fervent my prayers for your happiness in this troubled world. Be true to yourself and the love we bear you, and come back to us unchanged by your long absence, our own simple, noble-hearted Bertha. God bless and keep you, best-beloved child, and so farewell."

He did not fold her in his arms and lavish fond names upon her, as he longed to do, for Wilhelm's anxious eyes were upon him. But pressing her hands in a strong, earnest clasp, he kissed her forehead, whispering as he stooped: "Be kind to Wilhelm, and I am repaid fourfold for the little I have done for you."

Bertha's colorless face flushed crimson, and her dark eyes fell after one quick glance at the brothers. Then, faltering forth a few broken words of grateful love, she laid her head on Gertrude's breast as if she never cared to lift it up again, and with a pang of bitter sorrow heard his departing steps grow fainter till the clang of the great gates seemed to part them forever.

And Ernest, with a farewell glance, saw Wilhelm at her side, her hand in his, pouring forth eager words whose meaning he well knew. Bertha's face was hidden still, with maiden shame, he fancied, but he could not see how fast the hot tears fell, nor guess how like the idle wind his brother's passionate words swept by her ear.

So with this picture floating ever before his eyes, he went silently away, leaving the heart he had loved for years to be wooed and won by another.

When Bertha met him on the appointed day, his brother, radiant with a happy lover's joy, was still beside her. But a great and sudden change had come upon her; she was no longer bright with smiles and youthful bloom, but silent, pale, and thoughtful, with a secret trouble in her eye and a stern resolve stamped on her face.

With Ernest she exerted all her power to seem unchanged, and in that short, hurried time he only saw in her sweet seriousness the quiet of a heart brooding over its new happiness.

Toward Wilhelm she was doubly kind, timidly seeking to be all he asked and listening to his fond words with a strange, regretful earnestness, as if she had no right to them and knew not how to answer fitly.

And so the parting came at length, and bidding them farewell, she was borne away. But though her last embrace was given to her lover, her last *look* lingered tearfully upon the face which smiled serenely on her now as when she saw it first—a little child beside her cottage door.

III

Years rolled away, and three great sorrows came to Ernest Lennartson. Wilhelm died, and no father ever mourned the death of a beloved son with a deeper grief than he who had been such a faithful friend and who now sorrowed for his young brother. Bertha, from her distant home, sent words of truest sympathy and comfort, seeming to forget her loss in anxiety to lighten his; and thus, though far apart, they seemed drawn nearer to each other by their mutual grief, which, as time went on, softened into a tender memory of the loved and lost.

The second change that took place was the marriage of sister Gertrude, who journeyed away to a home across the sea, where as a happy wife and mother she forgot in her own cares, save by a passing letter, the brother who never told how great his loneliness became when the united household was thus separated and he was left with nothing but his art to render life pleasant to him.

The last trial was the sudden loss of all the hard-earned wealth he had laid up to beautify the lives of Bertha and Wilhelm in the dear old home, which had now passed from him in the wreck made by the fraud of others.

To Ernest this was but another of those lessons so many of which he had already learned. Patiently he accepted it and manfully bore the world's pity and blame while seeking to retrieve the past.

A poor and narrow room, about which the tumult of the city echoed day and night, was now his home. Here poverty and sorrow came to him, but he took them bravely by the hand and went on his solitary way, cheerful and serene in heart, wise and strong in action.

Amid the discords of the world he wove the joys and sorrows of his life into simple melodies and sent them forth to be loved and sung by high and low, whose hearts were won by the hidden magic of the cheerful songs. Friends who had known him in better days felt a warmer interest now and found him pupils, seeking in this and many other ways to show their admiration and respect for his self-denying life.

Thus in daily labor he found peace of mind and happiness in cherishing two secret hopes. The first and strongest was that he might soon see Bertha and find her still unchanged. The glad tidings of her great success had filled him with a proud delight, and as years glided by, there came pleasant rumors from the friends she had met in other lands of the purity and power her voice possessed, of the love and admiration she called forth wherever she went; and, what was better than all else to him, her womanly virtues and quiet deeds of kindness were gratefully whispered by many who had known and loved the generous-hearted singer.

The other strong desire that now possessed him was to purchase back the home he loved so well. For this his solitary heart now longed; for this he labored day and night, cheering himself with visions of a calm old age and a pleasant home wherein to welcome Bertha when she came again.

And at length she *did* return to her native land, and to the city near which she had once dwelt unknown but which was now proud to claim her as its own and welcome her with open heart and hands.

Among the many who crowded her anteroom leaving messages and gifts was one whose face shone with an eager joy as, with the freedom of a well-known friend, he hastened through the throng toward the inner door, where stood a servant receiving and answering inquiries showered upon him.

"Mademoiselle is engaged, sir. You cannot enter," he said as the newcomer would have passed him.

"Not enter!" echoed the stranger, adding with a smile, "My good friend, I am her guardian, and she will be expecting *me* among the first to greet her."

"I am sorry, sir, but she gave strict orders that no one should disturb her after Count Alaric came. Therefore, pardon me, sir, but even *you* cannot pass," replied the servant, glancing somewhat suspiciously at the poor garments of the stranger, whose quiet dignity forbade all rudeness.

Ernest still stood at the door, saying in a low, anxious voice: "Who may this Count be that he is received before her dearest friends? Some member of her company, perhaps—"

"He is the gentleman who will soon make a countess of Mademoiselle, if the world speaks truly, and surely *his* right to enter cannot be questioned, I fancy," answered the servant carelessly, adding more respectfully, as he saw a sudden change fall on the stranger's joyful face: "I will take any message you may choose to leave, sir, and see that she receives it," glancing at a delicate bouquet in his hand.

"I have none. I am like the rest of the world to her now, so give her this if you like," said the stranger, handing a card. "The flowers she will not care for; let them go," and crushing the cluster of carefully gathered roses, he flung them carelessly away and passed slowly out.

"Ernest Lennartson," read the servant as he tossed the card into the heaped-up basket. As he gathered up the scattered leaves, he muttered, "Some old lover of my lady's, doubtless. The handsome young Count will soon win her to fling them all by like these poor things."

Beyond the city gates walked Ernest through the quiet wood paths, saying to himself while the old pain, sharper than before, stirred in his breast: "I will not trouble her, but wait till she comes freely to me as of old to tell her joy. I will believe nothing and judge her by herself alone. She *will* come, and *I* will not doubt my little Bertha yet."

Meanwhile, Bertha had dismissed the Count and, unseen, unattended, had stolen away from welcoming friends and curious strangers to the poor home where, she had learned, her master, as she still called him, dwelt. Through the noisy, narrow streets she hastened on, wondering how he, so fond of light and air, could make his home in such a dreary place.

The half-blind old woman who met her at the door bade her go up and seek for herself, muttering peevishly the while at being roused from her noonday nap. Up the dark stairway Bertha stole with a beating heart and, meeting no answer to her light tap, timidly entered, to find the room deserted. Standing there alone, she looked with pitying eyes at the desolate place so unlike the home she had fancied his. Poor as she knew he had become, she had never dreamed of want like this; and ignorant for what cherished purpose he denied himself so much, she gazed sadly upon the gloomy room so scantily supplied with comforts—its only ornaments the instrument she had first used and a little rose tree from the garden she so well remembered. A single ray of sunlight that stole in fell on the well-worn keys and flickered about the crimson flower, whose fragrance filled the air as it waved in the warm wind. Tears shone on Bertha's cheek as she marked this, and all the dear past rose up freshly to her mind as she whispered softly to herself:

"He still thinks of me and cherishes the things I loved. Ah, dear master, the day is very near when I can show by my gratitude and joy some part of the great debt I have owed so long. I have won the power to fill your life with sunshine, flowers, and music. Wait a little longer, and Bertha will prove that she never forgets."

Long she sat in the lonely room, lost in sweet and bitter musings; still he did not come. So, leaving a few lines of affectionate greeting, speaking of the duties that called her away, and begging him to come to her soon, she left the spot where she longed to linger, and hastened away.

"No note, no message left for me? You are sure, Gretchen?" asked Ernest as at nightfall he came wearily back from his daily task, which never before had seemed so irksome and long.

"No, no, nothing but the music you ordered," mumbled the old woman, in whose memory the sight of Bertha only lingered as a part of the dim dream her visit had disturbed.

"The old master is forgotten, then," he said. "Well, well, I would not have the memory of me a task. Tonight I shall see and hear her and will try to be content with that. Henceforth I must teach myself to think of her no more as 'my little Bertha,' but the Count's betrothed."

Sighing heavily, he entered his room, which now seemed doubly desolate and dark, for the brightest hope that had cheered it was gone. A passing gust had wafted Bertha's loving note to the floor, and it now lay unseen at his feet as he sat in the deepening twilight, softly touching the keys where he had often guided her little hands. The fragrance of the rose tree filled the room, whispering in its sweet voice of the garden fountain where it once looked up and saw the face, so mournful now, lit up with the bright glow of a love which had been the deepest joy and sorrow of his life.

*   *   *

Later that night, in an obscure corner of the brilliant hall, sat Ernest among the hundreds gathered there, his heart beating high with fond and generous pride, his eyes often dim with a joy too deep to find a vent in the noisy acclamations that rang out a welcome to Bertha as she stood pale and silent before them while flowers fell at her feet and merry voices greeted her.

The change her friend foretold had come, and few could see a trace of the young girl in the stately, full-grown woman. A restless light burned in the once calm eyes, her cheek was thinner and more colorless, and when the first faint flush of emotion at her hearty welcome had faded, a look of proud weariness fell upon the beautiful face, which only brightened when she sang.

Then every shadow vanished, and with beaming eyes and a strange glow on her earnest countenance, she sang as birds sing, freely and joyously filling the hearts of those who listened with wonder and delight. But amid the changing notes of her wonderful voice, one ear more delicate than the rest detected a sad strain that came and went like a mournful echo, seeming to breathe some passionate longing or sorrow which a proud heart concealed till it unconsciously found vent in music.

Looking and listening silently, while others saw and applauded only the fair singer, Ernest was seeking to read the woman and to discover the true cause of the weary, restless look that now overshadowed the face he knew and loved so well. Once only it lit up with a sudden smile, and for a moment she stood silent, gazing intently, as it seemed, toward the remote nook where he sat. But hardly had the glad thought flashed through his mind when he caught sight of a young and richly dressed man a short distance before him, who bent eagerly forward, his handsome face beaming with delight, to meet and answer her glance with one as warm and bright as her own.

"This must be the Count. Little wonder she loves so young and ardent a friend," thought Ernest, drawing back with an unconscious sigh as he looked down on his threadbare dress and remembered the silver hairs among the brown locks that fell about his thin and careworn face. He did not know that the gay young lover was unseen and that the sight of him alone called the deep color to her cheek and gave a tenderer melody to her voice as she sang her farewell air; and with a lingering look behind, she vanished from the eager eyes of the excited throng.

"I *must* see her again, if it be but an instant," said Ernest within himself as he hastened through the ebbing crowd while a bitter conflict of sorrow, love, and jealousy went on in his troubled heart. He gained the private entrance where her carriage waited, and mingled with the group of gentlemen who gathered there for a last look as she passed out. Presently she came, closely veiled, leaning on the arm of a gray-headed gentleman. Ernest was pressing forward to say a word to her when the young stranger stepped before him to the carriage door, whispering a few words to the old gentleman, who replied:

"Enter, Alaric. Mademoiselle permits it."

With a grateful bow he sprang in, and they were gone, leaving the wondering group to disperse at will. Ernest stood for a moment with a pale cheek and an unwonted fire in his eye, looking after the departing carriage, which had left nothing but its dust on his cloak to remind him that what had happened was real.

A young friend spied him out and, taking his arm, said gaily, "As our routes are the same, let me walk with you, Lennartson, and offer my congratulations on the success of your fair pupil. When may I offer them upon her bridal?" he added with a meaningful smile.

"Henri, tell me what you know of this Count," replied Ernest, heedless of the question. "I have not seen Bertha alone and should be glad to hear the truth from one whom I can trust."

"All I can tell you is this," said the young man, without looking into his listener's anxious face. "He is a nephew of old Herman's, the gray-headed gentleman we saw tonight, whose daughters are Mademoiselle Bertha's friends, and through them Alaric came to see and love her. I cannot learn whether she returns it, but from his accompanying her hither and the late purchase he has made for her, one may be pretty sure that she will ere long make him happier than he deserves."

"How is that? Is he less noble and worthy than he looks?" asked Ernest quickly.

"He is a generous-hearted man, with high hopes and noble aspirations," returned his friend, "but easily led and too indolent to leave the easy, careless life he leads, to strive and struggle for the honor he might gain in whatever he undertook. Young, rich, and happy, he is content to let the years roll pleasantly away and takes no thought for the future. However, blessed with such a wife as Bertha, he will become both wise and good, that he may be more worthy of her."

"You spoke of some purchase made for her. What is it, Henri?"

His friend hesitated a moment and then said hastily, "I forgot that it might not be a pleasant subject for you, but he has bought your former home; and a welcome gift it would doubtless be if Mademoiselle remembers the beautiful spot as pleasantly as others do. But must you leave me here? Good night, then, and pardon me if I have unwittingly pained you by my thoughtless words."

With a hasty adieu Ernest turned away and through the gay streets went slowly back to his solitary lodgings. There he drew forth the small hoard he had so painfully gathered up and which was now of little value in his eyes. He stood idly watching the gleam of the yellow pile in the faint moonlight that glided in and seemed to dance mockingly over the poor furniture and the thoughtful face of the gray-haired man. Once he had counted his little store with growing pleasure, picturing to himself, as he added sum after sum of his hard earnings, a peaceful future, brightened by Bertha's presence and blessed by her love. Now both home and wife were lost to him, and the long years of patient hope and labor were in vain.

Carelessly pushing the useless gold away, he laid his head upon his folded arms and so sat motionless in the silent room—while the shadow of Bertha's rose tree flickered over him and the night wind, sweeping across the chords of her open instrument, played a soft air, seeming to whisper in fitful music her own words, "I will yet fill his life with sunshine and melody and prove I never can forget." But he saw nothing, heard nothing in the outer world till, from the gray steeple near, midnight sounded over the hushed city.

Roused by the sudden clang of the great bell, he started up, and following the restless longing that led him forth, he threw a cloak upon his shoulders and stole quietly out toward the city gate, beyond which lay the home he went to bid farewell.

On he hastened through the deserted squares, till the sound of sudden laughter and voices reached him as he entered an unfrequented street and saw, just entering a house before him, Count Alaric and a sinister-looking man, who pushed him rudely aside as he passed and closed the door quickly behind them.

"A fit lover for my pure-hearted Bertha," thought Ernest bitterly as he recollected the flushed face, disordered dress, and strange companion of the Count. "I will see yet more of him and judge what has the power to charm away the memory of early friends," he muttered to himself, while pacing to and fro before the gambling house, unwilling to enter, yet led on by a keen desire to watch the person who so deeply interested him.

At length he quietly passed in and glided through the crowded rooms glaring with light, noisy with oaths and the quick rattle of dice. The air was hot and heavy with smoke and wine fumes, and everywhere eager faces—some flushed with triumph, some distorted by varying hopes and fears, others pale and ghastly with despair.

In a distant recess Ernest saw the pair he sought. Short as was the time since they entered, the Count had already lost heavily, judging by the gold that lay before his evil-faced companion, who watched his excited and unwary opponent with a crafty smile, luring or goading him on by false hopes or taunting words.

Standing unseen amid the few spectators, Ernest watched

the game with an intenser interest than any there, forgetting everything for the time except the changing face of the young man playing so recklessly before him.

"He has lost a fortune here during these last few nights, and if he will not be warned, before morning he will be penniless, I fear, for he is no match for the clever villain who has lured him to it and will not quit him till the young man is ruined," whispered one bystander to another.

As the words reached Ernest's ear, a sudden thought darted through his mind, and an evil voice seemed to breathe in his ear: "If he *is* ruined, your home is your own again. If Bertha knew it, she would never be his wife. Let it go on, and the gloom about you will gather about him, while his happiness may yet be yours."

His face flushed and paled, his heart beat loud, and the lights swam before his eyes—for a moment only. Then through the tumult within and without sounded the low voice of his better self, echoing the words he had spoken long ago: "Her happiness shall be the one great object of my life."

The memory of the innocent, trusting child swept over him like a cool wind in a desert place; and scorning himself for his momentary weakness, he thrust the temptation aside and stepped forward, saying as he laid his hand on the young Count's shoulder: "My friend, let me warn you, this is an unequal contest. Quit it before it is too late."

"Who are you that dare to interfere thus? And in whose name do you warn me to stop, sir?" cried the Count, hotly starting up.

Ernest bent and whispered, "In Bertha's name I ask it. I am her friend and, as such, cannot see you wreck her happiness and your own in such a mad hour as this. For her sake, do not thus forget yourself."

Looking full into the noble face before him and reading there the truth and honor of his unknown friend, the Count stood silent for a moment, struggling to collect himself. Then, flinging down his cards, he frankly offered his hand, saying with earnest warmth:

"You have saved me from utter ruin, and I thank you. I

have been mad, infatuated—but the magic of the name you have used is strong enough to stay my reckless folly at its height. I will play no more. Trust me. I will but settle past accounts and then quit this place forever."

"I *do* trust you. Think of her, and evil cannot tempt you," whispered Ernest, and after pressing his hand with a friendly warning, he silently went out.

A burden of bitterness and gloom seemed lifted from his spirit as he passed along the moonlit road he had so often trodden with little Bertha at his side. Now no childish foot tripped over the green pathway, but a beautiful, proud woman seemed to glide before him, looking back with grateful, tender eyes and beckoning him on while she scattered roses at his feet and sang strange melodies that filled him with a new and deep delight.

He reached at last the well-known path that led, through blooming shrubs and trees, to the entrance of his home. But now a closed gate barred the way, and leaning there, he looked long and sadly through the iron bars at the neglected garden, where the fountain babbled softly and the wind stirred among the flowers as pleasantly as when he sat there on a happy night that now seemed very long ago.

As he stood thus, unconscious how the night was passing, a carriage and several horsemen swept suddenly by, and with a quick, foreboding start he caught the sound of the Count's impatient voice saying, "Faster, for God's sake. It must be over before the moon sets."

They were gone and all was still again before he comprehended what had passed. Then, standing in the dusty road, he strained his eyes to follow the distant carriage as it vanished over the brow of a hill. As he stood thus, a man came hastening by with a face pale with anxious terror and fatigue.

"Stay and tell me what this means. Who are those gone before?" said Ernest as the man leaned breathlessly against a tree.

"Don't stop me, sir," he cried when he could speak. "My master had a quarrel at a gambling house in the city, and they are gone to the riverside yonder to settle it. I am hastening to him now, for he bade me follow when I had given his note to the lady in case he never returned."

"Who is your master?" demanded Ernest.

"Count Alaric," answered the man as he darted away.

After a brief pause to collect his thoughts, Ernest sprang over a low hedge and plunged into the wood, through which lay the nearest path to the river.

Thinking of nothing but Bertha and her grief, possessed only by the wild wish to save her lover, on he hurried. Crashing through tangled thickets, heedless of rent garments and torn flesh, dashing through forest pools, leaping from rock to rock, and flinging away hat and cloak that he might speed the faster, on he struggled till at last he gained a little knoll, and paused a moment to see where next to turn. The moon shone dimly, but there just below him on the river's edge stood the Count, pale and resolute, opposite the sinister stranger, who leaned on a low wall with a scornful sneer on his dark face. A group of gentlemen were gathered nearby, and the eager face of the servant was visible as he came hastening from the road beyond.

With a vain effort to call to them, Ernest, faint and breathless, sprang from the knoll as their weapons gleamed in the light, and darting across the narrow dell, stood between them, crying hoarsely, "Stay and hear me." But it was too late. As the first word fell from his lips, a sharp report broke the stillness of the night. The next moment a man rode hastily from the field, and the rest gathered wonderingly about the Count, whose arm was tenderly supporting Ernest as he lay upon the ground, saying faintly with a smile on his colorless lips:

"It is as well so. Be kind to little Bertha, and bid her think sometimes of the old friend who to the last thought of her happiness alone."

Then he fell back, white and still, upon the bloody grass, and no sound broke the silence but the mournful ripple of the stream.

IV

Day after day went heavily by in the darkened room where Ernest Lennartson lay, unconscious that he was again in his own home, which Bertha, through the Count, had purchased back as a gift for him. He never knew the worn, tender face that bent above him with such tireless watchfulness; never heard the low voice singing with a plaintive melody it had not owned before, to soothe his restless fever; never felt hot tears fall like rain on his poor wasted hands when he folded them and blessed his "little Bertha," murmuring brokenly all the secret of his patient love and sorrow that had burdened him so long.

And Bertha listened to these fitful wanderings with the proud head bent very low to catch each feebly uttered word, and with such a glow of wonder, gratitude, and joy upon her face that every trace of weariness and gloom vanished like shadows, leaving it radiant with a deeper beauty than before.

Night and day she sat in that hushed room, watching the pale face on the pillow grow more colorless and thin, the gray locks whiter with long suffering, and heard the low voice daily grow more faint as it tried to murmur the little songs she used to sing when a child beside his knee. And through this long trial, though her cheek faded and her eyes grew dim, her woman's heart grew stronger, and her hidden love burned with a purer flame, while her newfound joy, though often mingled with fear and sorrow, never ceased to cheer and support her through the long vigils, which had now become most blessed hours to her.

At length a deep sleep fell upon him. Through the house there reigned a solemn stillness, as hour after hour went by and his low breathing grew more regular and light, while a healthful dew stood on his brow and the burning fever seemed to leave him.

Bertha was called away, and the old nurse slept at her post when the hollow eyes unclosed. Ernest waked weak as a child, but calm and conscious. A dim mist seemed at first to float before him, and low murmurs filled his ears. But slowly the cloud passed, and he beheld the old familiar objects of his room while voices sounded softly through the twilight around him.

Looking through a half-open door into the sunny apartment beyond, he saw Bertha and Count Alaric standing in the light together in low and earnest conversation.

At first their words fell idly on his ear, but soon he listened like one in a dream, powerless to speak or move. The Count was saying eagerly as he sought to look in Bertha's half-averted face:

"Will you not only let me hope, then? I only ask for that. Months, years will I wait until you learn to love me as I feel you may, unworthy as I am. Will you not grant me this, Bertha?"

"I cannot, Alaric," she replied firmly and kindly. "Listen, and I will tell you why I will not let you cherish a false hope. You have been patient and generous with me and shall be frankly answered, though it is hard to utter what has been so long concealed. But you deserve it. As I cannot give you my love, I will yield my confidence freely, as to a brother."

The Count looked silently into the earnest face uplifted to his and met the frank glance of her eyes, which never changed, though her cheek crimsoned and her voice grew lower as she went on.

"Ten years ago I came into this house a friendless little child, and the same kind hand that led me over yonder threshold then has guided me through all these years to womanhood and happiness.

"Whatever virtue, power, or success I now possess, I owe them all to him who has been, through sorrow, poverty, and absence, a fond and faithful friend to me. Should I not be grateful for all this? And can you blame me that the first thought of my heart should be how best to render his life calm and beautiful, as he has rendered mine?"

"I cannot blame you, Bertha, but forgive me if I grieve that *his* happiness becomes *my* sorrow," murmured the Count with a heavy sigh.

"Hear me out," said Bertha, "and you will not grudge him

any joy, however great, when you have learned how he deserves it, Alaric. His dead brother loved me long ago. *He* bade me gladden Wilhelm's life, and though I only felt a sisterly affection, I obeyed, that through his brother, Ernest might be happy. Ah, I was blind then, and in my eagerness to show my gratitude, I sacrificed his peace and falsely pledged my hand to Wilhelm when my heart and soul belonged to my kind dear master, who, loving me as I in secret pined to be loved, silently smiled upon us while he suffered for our sakes.

"I never dreamed of this, but tried to love poor Wilhelm and bitterly reproached myself when he died thinking me his own. That memory has been my punishment for one false step, well meant but most unwise. My secret passion has been cherished all these years and grown stronger, deeper, till it has become the light and beauty of my life."

"Why have you never told me this before?" questioned the Count bitterly. "How could I guess when you would not listen to my love that he had already won the gift I have been struggling so long to gain? You had not met him since you came until I led you here, where we had laid him, dying, as we thought, on that unhappy night. How, then, can you know that he still thinks of you with unchanged affection after this long separation?"

A smile so radiant and glad lit up her face, and inward joy lent such tender music to her voice, that all her lost bloom seemed restored fourfold as she replied with a fond glance toward the silent room within: "I never knew that. I came to tend him here. Then from his unconscious lips I, for the first time, learned how long and faithfully he too had borne a hidden sorrow and cherished an affection far more unselfish than my own.

"Ah, Alaric, when I think of all his generous and unfailing care, the weary years of self-denial he has suffered for my sake rise up before me, and I can only wonder at my blindness and long more fervently to repay him by the treasured wealth of my deep love."

She bent her head upon her hands, the Count looked out with dim eyes at the distant riverside, and for a moment nothing broke the sunny silence around them. Then, looking up, with pity and affection shining through her tears, Bertha said:

"Forgive me for the pain I cause you, and believe me, were I free, there is no heart I would so freely, gladly take as yours. But this cannot be; therefore, forget the past and give me still what I most truly prize: your friendship."

The young man warmly pressed the hand she offered, saying humbly and seriously, "It is yours forever, dearest Bertha. I can give you up, without one selfish pang, to him who has so well deserved you. Tell him that, and God keep you both to bless each other for these years of constancy. Farewell. When I have learned to love you less, I will return to claim you as my friend and thank *him* for the life he has rendered worth saving by the silent rebuke of his own noble example, which I will henceforth strive to follow."

After kissing passionately the hands he held, with a silent glance into the sweet, approving countenance before him, the Count was gone, and with a sigh Bertha stole back to the inner room and looked with glad wonder at the placid smile on Ernest's pallid face and the healthful sleep that seemed to hover around him like a healing spell.

The magic of a happy heart worked wonders, and the shadow of death passed by, leaving unclouded sunshine in the home of Ernest Lennartson.

Summer flowers were in their fullest beauty when, leaning on Bertha's arm, he walked again among them while the fresh winds brought back color to his wasted cheek and vigor to his feeble limbs.

They came at last to the little fountain, whose bright waters whispered a glad welcome while the flowers nodded on their stems and bird voices echoed overhead.

"Do you remember when we last were here, Bertha?" Ernest asked, looking up from the rustic seat at the fair, thoughtful woman standing in the flickering shadows at his side.

"Yes, I have not forgotten anything that happened in that happy time," she answered musingly.

"And you remember when I asked you for a rose, you bade me take whatever you could give? I did not ask for more *then* and should not venture now, but lying on my bed within there, I dreamed a blessed dream that haunts me still. Shall I tell it, Bertha?"

She started slightly, saying in her low, sweet voice, "Yes, tell me. Do I not enjoy whatever gives you pleasure?"

"I seemed to waken from a heavy sleep filled with sad and troubled visions." Ernest thus went on, watching her changeful face as intently as she watched the dancing waves: "Looking from the gloom around me, I saw you and Alaric in the sunshine near, and from your lips I heard a few warm words I had never thought to hear them utter. Tell me, was it but a blissful fancy conjured up to cheer my sorrow, as it had often done before, or was it real, Bertha?"

Her cheek glowed with womanly shame, then paled with deep emotion, but her frank eyes freely met his own. All her love gushed warmly from her heart into her face and voice as she replied:

"It was no dream, Ernest, but the simple story of a true affection, which always has belonged to you, though unsuspected and unsought."

"Bertha, can you in the bloom and freshness of your womanhood, with such a bright path spread before you, be content to sacrifice the many pleasures you might gain, to beautify and brighten the solitary life of your old master?" Ernest asked with anxious tenderness, adding sorrowfully, "I am poor and cannot even give you a fitting home. I am no longer young and cannot labor as I once could, even for your dear sake. I am broken in health and may become a burden on your generous care. Think of these things and do not let me win my happiness at the cost of yours, my grateful Bertha."

Her only answer was to smooth the gray locks with a fond, light touch and look upon him with a smile so proud and tender that he needed no reply. And coming to her side, while all the glow and buoyant vigor of his youth seemed his again, he whispered fervently:

"God bless you for this hour, Bertha. Years of silent suffering are nothing now, and I am strong and rich again, for you have given me back the sunshine of my life."

"Has Bertha proved forgetful of her early friends, as you foretold?" she asked, leaning in the old childlike way upon his arm, adding softly, "Ah, Ernest, do not doubt the future. The affection that has lived so long in secret will not vanish now when all is told. I have won what is dearer far than anything the world can give, and am content. Fame without love, to a true woman, is a brilliant crown she gladly lays down for Love's simple wreath of flowers. I have a dearer task now than to please a fickle crowd. Loving and serving *you* is henceforth my true happiness and duty. If you are poor, can I not earn enough for both with the gift whose use you taught me? If health deserts you, who will watch and cheer you with such real delight as she for whose sake it was lost? If you are old, am I not here, strong and loving, to support you? The hand by which you led me from obscurity to happiness like this shall minister to every want; the voice you trained with patient skill shall soothe all weariness and pain with its grateful music; and the heart of the poor child you made your own will seek to fill the bloom and sunlight as you have filled the spring of hers."

The low dash of the fountain was the only sound that broke the silence till Ernest laid a worn, stained paper in her hand, bidding her unfold it. Wondering, she did so, and two faded flowers lay before her as he said, smiling:

"The little bud you gave me at the cottage door, the half-blown rose upon the happy night when we sat here together in the summer moonlight—I have kept them all these years as graceful symbols of my little Bertha long ago."

"Say rather of the love which budded in her childish heart when she wept for joy that you accepted her poor gift. The timid passion but half confessed even to herself, and waiting but the one warm word to bid it bloom, is fitly shown in the unfolding blossom given last; but this, with its perfected beauty glowing around its golden heart, is a true emblem now of that same ever-growing love whose warmth, like the flower's perfume, will linger even when its life is gone."

As Bertha spoke, she gathered from a thornless shrub its fairest crimson flower and laid the full-blown rose in Ernest's hand, beside the withered buds.

MABEL'S MAY DAY

"All the valley, Mother, 'll be green and fresh and still,
The cowslip and the crowsfoot is over all the hill,
The rivulet in the flowery vale'll merrily glance and play,
For I'm to be Queen o' the May, Mother, I'm to be Queen o' the
*   May,"*

sang Mabel Heath as she stood in the sunny porch of the old
parsonage on a fair English May morning, looking gaily over
the green slopes starred with buttercups and the hawthorn
hedges white with early flowers.

"It promises a perfect day for your festival, Mabel," said
good Mrs. Heath, bringing out the deep basket her generous
hands had stored with dainties for the rustic feast. "Now stop
that wild singing and listen to me," she added as Mabel went
on with her song, as if her joy could find vent only in the
music of her blithesome voice.

"I have given you to Allan's care, and he has promised to
bring you safely home before the dew falls, so be kind and
gentle to him, Mabel, and let him keep you out of harm for my
sake. You are so rash and willful," said the mother, looking
anxiously into the blooming face beside her.

But Mabel, proud of her rank as village belle and jealous of
the dignity of her sixteen years, only laughed and answered
with a sudden gleam of merry mischief in her eyes: "Poor
Allan, he'll soon tire of his task, for I shall lead him such a
weary life, he will long for night before it is noon. And so I

141

shall be revenged upon him for his promise to lord it over me as if I were a *child.*"

"You *are* little more as yet," said her mother, "and Allan will see no cause to change his manner toward you until you learn to be more gentle and obedient. Why, among all your friends, do you single him out as one on whom to try your wayward freaks of pride and temper? It is not kind, when you know how well he loves you, and this fault will work you sorrow yet if you do not seek to conquer it."

Mabel's heart answered the question very differently from her lips, for the evil spirit of willful pride silenced the tender words of penitence she longed to speak. With a smile she said, "He is so silent and wrapped up in his own wise fancies that he looks on me as a foolish child who cannot understand him, but is only fit to amuse his idle hours. I will make *him* humble before I stoop myself. So never grieve, Mother dear, I must go my own way; I will bear the trouble, when it comes, as lightly as I do the joy. But hark! I hear them coming. Give me my hat and garlands, for I must not keep them waiting for their queen," she cried eagerly as the sound of cheerful voices and laughter was borne to her on the air from the green hill before the parsonage.

Soon there came trooping into the little porch a band of bright-faced girls eager to greet their queen, while their escort of young men and lads stood apart, looking with admiring eyes upon the graceful group and feeling with the true instincts of unspoiled youth that the day was fairer and their own hearts better for the sweet companionship of innocent maidenhood and early flowers.

"How beautiful my crown and scepter are! No real queen could desire a fairer," cried Mabel as her maids of honor laid the garland of violets on her bright hair and placed the scepter, wound with delicate vines, in her hand.

"Yes, Allan made it for you and said it was the best crown you could wear, but I don't know why, except that they are beautiful like you," said little Bessie, eager that her brother should receive due praise.

Mabel's cheek grew red as the daisies on her bosom, and

the proud head bent a little lower, as if she felt the sweet rebuke of the humble flowers lying on it. But she was soon herself again and, nodding carelessly to Allan, said, "Good morning and many thanks, my solemn subject. Let me see if you are out of the clouds and disposed to be agreeable. In that case I shall appoint you my prime minister," she added, peeping under the wide brim of his hat, where such a kind glance met her own that she unconsciously spoke in a gentler tone. "Yes, you are appointed to that high office, and I shall most graciously accept your counsel if it's humbly offered and *I like it.* Now, Harry, as master of ceremonies, lead on."

"To the Cliffs, then. Fall into order and forward," cried the boy, and with a farewell wave of her hand, the young queen put herself at the head of her troops and set forth for their springtide revel.

Merrily they journeyed on—now across broad meadows, seeking cowslips by the brookside and white violets in the damp nooks they brightened with their meek beauty; now through the quiet forest where mayflowers, hidden under withered leaves, were silently betrayed by their sweet breath, and where the lads, eager for daring deeds, swung high up in the treetops, pelting with cones and leaves the fair lookers-on below, who wandered, arm in arm, singing under the green boughs.

Then along breezy hillsides they were led, where daisies nodded at them as they passed and windflowers danced upon their slender stems, till their cheeks were rosy with the kisses of the warm spring air.

So, singing, resting, flower hunting, and talking merrily, they whiled away the hours till the sun shone high above them as they came climbing up the narrow pathway to the summit of the Cliffs.

High up among the gray rocks lay a grass plot, green as if the rain and dew the rough rocks shed from their hard bosoms had been gathered in by the grateful earth till the sunny nook was rendered the one fair spot among the barren Cliffs.

A solitary pine spread its wide branches, hung with fresh garlands, over a new-made mound of verdant moss, while the wind whispered with a pleasant rustle to welcome the coming guests, whose voices woke the echoes far and near.

"Ah! I see the elves have been at work here, that all might be ready for us. How beautiful it is," cried Mabel as she was led to her green throne, and sank smiling down on the soft, mossy seat.

"I know who the elves were," said little Bessie, clapping her hands and pointing at her brother. "That's why you were away so long last night by moonlight and why you were so sadly tired today."

Allan shook his finger at his sister, saying that she must have dreamed all that, and Mabel soon forgot the momentary self-reproach which smote her, in issuing her merry commands and directions for the spreading of the feast, around which they gathered willingly.

"Now, my subjects, I leave you to your own devices till it is time to journey home," said Mabel as they rose from their sylvan table.

Some wandered away among the crags, some lay chatting under the old pine tree, and others, of a housewifely turn, removed all traces of the revel and filled the empty baskets with their flowers.

Allan opened his portfolio and, sitting apart, sketched silently while Mabel and her friend Jennie Gowan tripped to and fro like restless shadows, dancing on the smooth sward or seeking among the rocks for ferns and mosses.

"See that lovely cluster of bluebells just below there," Jennie said. "I wish the fairest flowers would not always grow beyond our reach. What a pity we cannot have them for our garlands!"

"But we *will* have them, Jennie. It's only a step to yonder ledge. Give me your hand and I can gather them quite easily," Mabel answered, peeping over at the flowers growing in a narrow slip of earth on the edge of a steep descent.

"No, Mabel, you can never stand on that bit of rock. Come away, for I will not help you put your life in danger. Allan, bid Mabel stop," cried Jennie as the willful girl prepared to try the dangerous path.

"Mabel, come back," said Allan as he hastened toward them. "How am I to answer it to your mother if I let you play such mad pranks? Come away immediately," he added sternly as he saw her danger.

But the proud, wayward spirit that possessed Mabel was instantly roused by his manner, and with a scornful laugh she turned away, still bent on her foolish venture.

"Dear Mabel, let me get them for you," Allan said more gently as he saw the angry color in her cheek. "Give me your hand and come up from that dangerous place, for the earth is treacherous and the rocks below are very steep. For your *mother's* sake, *obey* me and come back."

But though the changed voice and winning manner almost lured her back, Mabel was proud of her power to draw forth his hidden fondness for her before the group who had gathered near; and so she would not yield, but with a mocking smile waved him away, almost hoping he would still detain her.

But he drew back coldly and let her pass without a word.

Angry at herself and him, Mabel gathered up her courage and climbed lightly down until she stood upon the narrow ledge below.

Then, gathering the coveted flowers, she held them up with a laugh of merry triumph. But it changed suddenly to a sharp cry of terror as the earth slid from beneath her feet, and with a vain effort to reach the arms outstretched to save her, Mabel vanished over the edge of the precipice amid a crash of falling stones and the wild cries of the terrified beholders.

Without a word Allan sprang down the rugged path which led to the valley below, followed by the whole party, who, guided by the echo of his reckless steps, hastened on till they gained an open spot which commanded a view of the cliff over which Mabel had fallen, and there, to their great joy, they saw her lying, apparently unhurt, on a bed of dry leaves which covered a broad shelf of rock not far below the place where she had stood when she fell.

"Mabel, dear Mabel, look up and tell us you are safe," cried Jennie.

Mabel lifted her white face and tried to answer bravely. "I am only bruised and stunned a little. Don't sob so, girls; it makes a coward of me to see you all so pale and frightened."

"Stand back and let me pass," said Allan as he came struggling up through bush and briar, torn and breathless, but with the same stern look upon his face that Mabel had last seen there.

A wide chasm, at the bottom of which a noisy stream went foaming to the dell below, now separated Mabel from her friends. Allan, standing on the edge, looked down into the black and troubled waters and sent one glance across at the trembling girl. Then, putting by the eager lads who tried to hold him back, he flung away his hat and leaped the wide gulf like a deer.

A cheer from the other side and a strong arm around her told Mabel that the peril was over. When she lifted her face from her hands (for she had not dared to look), her eyes met Allan's, looking anxiously and tenderly into her own. She could not speak, but leaning on his arm, stood very white and still while he put away her fallen hair and wound her scarf about her wounded hand, silent as herself, but each mute action full of gentle meaning she well understood.

Meanwhile, the boys came struggling gallantly up from the dell below bearing stout logs and, obeying Allan's rapid orders, soon formed a rude though stable bridge.

"Let me take you over, Mabel. You are still trembling with your fall. Will you not trust me *now?*" said Allan as she drew back with a glance of fear at the deep defile she was to cross.

A flash of her old temper shot into Mabel's eyes at his slight accent of reproach, and with a quick motion she drew her arm from his, saying hastily, "I am not quite child enough for that, though you *will* treat me as one. I shall go alone."

And with a light step she passed over the narrow bridge and into the eager arms of her delighted friends, who embraced her and cried over her with all the warmth of their girlish hearts.

Allan silently followed, with all the sunshine banished from his face, and after a short pause to rest and recover themselves, they turned their steps homeward, warned by the gathering clouds, sobered by Mabel's peril, and anxious to reach some shelter from the coming storm.

"We cannot reach home before the shower," said Allan after they had walked swiftly for a while. "Let us stop at the lodge close by. I know old Rachel, and she will gladly house us till it's clear again."

He led them, as he spoke, to the door of a small cottage standing at the entrance of a wild, neglected park, through whose green vistas glimpses might be caught of a stately but deserted mansion, overgrown with ivy and darkened by the shadow of gloomy trees.

"Mrs. Rachel is up at the hall, but you can rest here. Welcome, sir, if you please," said the child who answered Allan's knock.

Glancing in at the close, small room, Allan said, turning to his companions, "Why not hurry to the hall and wait there? I have often longed to see it, and we shall never have a better chance than now. Shall we go?"

The eager consent of all decided the question, and they hastened away through the lonely park and up the broad stone steps into the dark old hall, where their steps and voices echoed loudly as they passed along looking for old Rachel.

At length they found her high up in a turret chamber, just preparing to descend and hurry home before the storm came on. Allan told her their case and begged leave to shelter and amuse themselves among the empty chambers till they could start for home again without fear of sudden showers.

The kind old woman said she could refuse *him* nothing, and entrusting him with her large bunch of keys, with many warnings and directions to leave all fast and bring them safely to her again, she hurried away and left them to enjoy the gloom and mystery of the storm and the old mansion to their heart's content.

Hardly was Rachel gone when the tempest burst over their heads with peals of thunder and frequent flashes of lightning, which lit up the high chamber with a ghastly glare, while its quaint furniture and somber hangings seemed to fill it with dark shadows and the wind swept through the corridors like mysterious voices wailing and lamenting.

The young girls drew closer and closer together; the gay voices of their companions grew lower and their laughter less frequent till, awed by the violence of the elements without and the deepening gloom within, they ceased entirely and sat in silence. But Mabel, restless as ever and unwilling to listen to the thoughts that troubled her, said suddenly to the quiet, weary group sitting and lying around her:

"Since it is too dark to explore the house as yet and we must stay pent up here an hour or more, let us devise some gay amusement and not sit stupidly silent in the gloom like bats and owls. Someone must sing or tell us a tale. This is just the time and place for a ghost story or a plaintive ballad. As your queen, I command you to do one of the two for our diversion."

"That we will with pleasure, Your Majesty, if anyone will begin," said Jennie. "Allan is the best storyteller; he must make us a fine romantic tale."

"Yes, yes, Allan must begin," cried they all, eager to be relieved of the weariness that was creeping over them.

Allan turned from the old chimneypiece, whose quaint carving he had been examining, and with a glance at the wistful and somewhat frightened faces of the party, he said kindly, "I will do my best to amuse you, and tell the story of this very hall where we are now gathered, for it has a history and a ghost too, though it seldom walks, and never in the daytime, so you need not fear. Old Rachel told me of it long ago and woke my wish to see the place she spoke of. Therefore, as obedience to those appointed to rule over us is a virtue I admire, I will obey our queen and weave the sad history of this place into a tale to while away the hours of our imprisonment."

And with a mock obeisance to Mabel, whose cheek flushed at his words, Allan seated himself in the faded, damask-covered chair and thus began his story, his eyes fixed on Mabel's slender figure as she sat in the deep recess of a window, looking moodily out upon the angry sky.

"Sixty years ago this hall, so solitary now, was a fine and

stately place, filled with gay inmates. These rooms, so dark and empty, were noisy with happy voices, and light feet sounded through these silent galleries. Children played in the neglected gardens; fair ladies and blithesome gentlemen wandered through the porch and sat upon the terrace there below. It was a cheerful, splendid place in those old days.

"Rachel's mother was the nurse of Lord Ashley's only child, the Lady Maud, a proud, handsome, willful girl with a generous heart and a noble nature, ruined by neglect and wayward passions, as in time you shall hear.

"This very room where we now sit was hers. She liked to be alone, and here she came to work or sing the strange songs she loved so well. By that window where *Mabel* is now sitting, *she* too sat and watched the tossing treetops, the gray crags piled up far away, and the changeful clouds that swept athwart the sky, often less wild and dark than her own troubled thoughts.

"Young Maud lived here alone for years, her mother being dead, her father long abroad. So the lonely child grew up wayward and imperious, pining for love and suffering for a mother's wise and watchful care. Indulged and idolized by her old nurse, she ruled her small dominions like a little queen, feared and loved too by all about her, for when she chose, her winsome ways could lure the coldest to be kind and tender with her.

"Thus time went on, and she grew up a fair and stately girl, restless and strange as ever, but more cheerful now; for tidings of her father's return filled her with a deep delight, and many were the visions of a beautiful, bright future which she conjured up when thinking of her father and his love. Day after day she watched and waited for his coming. There was no ornament or comfort that her fancy could devise that was not carefully prepared. The whole house was opened and hung with garlands for his welcome, and on the appointed day she stood hour after hour on the terrace, straining her eyes to catch a glimpse of him whom she could just remember as the young and handsome man she once had called 'Father.'

"She had put on her dead mother's ornaments, that she

might seem more beautiful and dear to him, and there she stood with the sunshine falling on her proud young head and on her face, all lit up with a glow of happiness never seen there after that sad day.

"At length he came, and with a cry of joy so fond and eager that it should have touched and won his heart, she sprang to greet him as he came out from the carriage. But suddenly she stood white and still as marble, for a tall, dark lady, very fair and haughty, followed him and, leaning on his arm, came up the wide stone steps.

"Maud's nurse, who saw it all, held her breath, expecting some outbreak of wild grief or anger from the young girl whose long-cherished hopes were thus blighted. But the sudden shock passed quickly, silently. With a powerful effort she banished every trace of sorrow and, drawing herself proudly up, stood there pale, cold, and stately, with a strange smile on her lips, more dreadful to those who knew her heart than if she had fallen dead upon the stones.

"Her father looked up at her as he came on, with a glance of wonder, admiration, and almost dismay at the womanly beauty of the child he had left and seemed expecting to behold unchanged.

"Maud saw it, and the smile upon her lips grew darker as she read the faces looking up at hers. But she never mourned or spoke till, leading the strange lady to her, he said with a cold kiss on her forehead: 'My daughter, receive and welcome your mother.'

"The lady offered her hand and murmured a few words of greeting. But Maud never touched it and, only bending haughtily, replied, looking straight into her father's lowering face: 'Your wife, sir, coming as an unexpected guest, can hardly look for the welcome she might have met had I known before whose place she came to fill. Allow me to conduct you in to some refreshments after your long journey.'

"And she swept before them through the hall with as firm a step and calm a pace as if her heart were not burning with the bitterest grief and disappointment.

"She ordered all the garlands she had hung with so much

care to be torn down. She removed every trace of the gifts her thoughtful love had so happily prepared, and then took no further heed of anything around her done in honor of their coming.

"All that day she was unchanged, replying to her father in the same cold manner, treating her stepmother with an outward courtesy through which her inward dislike was plainly visible. For with her quick eye she read the character of the wife who had taken her mother's place, and saw in her a heartless and ambitious woman who had married without love for the rank and wealth her father could confer upon her.

"Deceived by her feigned fondness and devotion, the old man lavished on her all the affection his stern nature could bestow, thus robbing his daughter of the love she pined for and shutting his heart against her when a fond word might have drawn her to him and made *his* life a better and *hers* a happier one.

"That night, passing through the gallery to this room, Maud met her father, and with a gush of the long-treasured love that had been thrust so rudely back, she went to him and would have put her arms about his neck, praying him to give her but a little place in his heart, for she was very lonely without any friend to love and guide her.

"But he put her coldly aside, saying she was a foolish girl and that her proud behavior had displeased and disappointed him, adding, as he left her, with an angry glance at the ornaments she wore: 'Those jewels, Maud, belong now to your mother. I desire that no one else should wear them.'

"'No one shall hereafter, sir,' she replied, with all the old bitterness and passionate despair coming back more heavily than ever to her empty heart, whose gentlest, noblest feelings were repulsed till, instead of sweetening and purifying her wild nature, they became sad memories to haunt and darken her whole life.

"That night everything that had been her mother's was laid out on *this* hearth and burned while Maud's hot tears fell on them like rain, though she never paused or faltered till all the little relics she had cherished from a child lay there before her but gray ashes. Then she placed the few jewels in a heavy box and, gliding through the porch, flung them far into the deep, dark lake that lies beyond the lodge.

"A stormy scene ensued when her father learned what she had done, but all his angry reproaches only brought the strange, disdainful smile to his daughter's face, though not a word of penitence or sign of fear. After that, Maud never asked for love again, and her father never tried to bend the haughty spirit that rose up against his will.

"Lady Ashley seemed unmoved by anything that passed, and treated Maud with coldness equal to her own, seeking by secret means to alienate her father still more from her and win a stronger power over him for her own ends.

"So the year rolled miserably on, Maud growing paler and more gloomy day by day, but hiding all her suffering with jealous care beneath a cold, hard manner, sad and strange to see in one so young.

"Suddenly her father seemed to wake to the knowledge of her imperfect education and utter want of those accomplishments befitting her age and rank, and at length, to her great surprise and secret joy, invited the rector's son to read and sketch with her till they should go to London.

"Arthur had been the friend and playmate of her lonely childhood, and she found with him the only happiness her sad life now possessed.

"At first Maud feared Lady Ashley had some scheme to forward by this pleasant change; but her evident dislike to the young man and her increased coldness soon quieted her fears, and she gave herself freely up to the first real pleasure she had known since her father's return.

"So the two studied daily together and daily grew more eager for each other's society. Maud found in her new companion what she most needed and desired, a *friend,* frank, generous, and sincere, and Arthur found a strange charm in the noble-hearted but impulsive girl and tried most earnestly to banish the faults which had been fostered by her neglected childhood.

"And wondering at herself, half doubting, half afraid, Maud yielded to the gentle hand that led her on, and listened to the kind voice that cheered while it reproved, till with Arthur all the beauty and true tenderness of her warm nature blossomed freely in the light of that love which shone upon her from his face, his words, and his silent actions, making her a new and happy being.

"Each knew how well they loved and were beloved, but they felt that words could never bring them nearer, and few were uttered. Happy in the happy present, they thought of nothing but how to enjoy that more fully, and so the summer glided peacefully away.

"Early in autumn Maud's cousin Lord Effingham came for a brief visit, but lingered week after week, to her great wonder and annoyance. He was a grave, silent man, much older than herself, but not too old to feel the charm of her beauty and long to make her his.

"Lady Ashley was courteous and friendly in an unusual degree, which rendered Maud's dislike more deep. For Maud had been wronged by the estrangement of her father's affection and stung by a hundred little slights and unseen cruelties, and her pent-up grief grew silently more bitter till she looked upon the artful woman as her greatest enemy and hated her with the intensity of a proud and passionate nature.

"Lord Effingham had not been long at the hall when Arthur was suddenly dismissed without thanks or explanations, and Maud was left alone again, though the house was filled with gaiety and she the fairest and most sought after there.

"She pined for Arthur, but he never came. Weeks went by so wearily that though she wore a smile upon her face and joined the merriment around her, it was like one in a troubled dream; and life seemed very dark and burdensome.

"One day she was summoned to her father's presence and there told with more kindness than he had ever shown before that Lord Effingham had asked her hand and that it was her father's earnest wish she should accept it, as he had long desired a union of the estates and families.

"Though startled and dismayed, Maud was touched by his unusual kindness and gently implored to be spared a marriage with one for whom she never could feel anything but cousinly affection and respect.

"But sternly putting her away, Lord Ashley replied that he knew of Arthur's love and, for that, had banished him, adding as he saw the quick, defiant light flash into Maud's dark eyes: 'Remember, if you wed with my consent, you are an heiress—without it, a beggar. Accept your cousin, and rank, wealth, and happiness are yours. Leave this for love and Arthur, and all I possess shall pass to one whose real devotion I can ill repay.'

"As he spoke thus, with a meaning glance at Lady Ashley, who had sat silently regarding them, a sudden thought darted through Maud's quick mind, and in an instant many things were clear that seemed very dark before.

"The truth floated dimly through her troubled brain. Not content with gaining all the father's love, Lady Ashley coveted his wealth and had thus schemed to win it. He had been failing slowly through the years, and a time might soon come when all would be hers, or Maud's if the old man's anger was not roused against his daughter.

"The keen-eyed woman had seen the girl's innocent affection for the rector's son and, by a feigned interest in the girl's welfare, had brought about his entrance there and watched the progress of the love which would accomplish her evil ends, for she well knew Lord Ashley would never consent to Maud's union with so humble a lover. Lord Effingham's arrival was most fortunate, and by well-timed hints her father's eyes were opened; the one suitor was banished, the other welcomed and encouraged.

"The rest was clear. Knowing Maud's resolute will and generous love, Lady Ashley felt sure that she would cling to Arthur, come what may, thus forfeiting her father's wealth and disappointing his most eager hopes.

"But well as she plotted, Lady Ashley had forgotten one strong power, which now rose up to thwart her. She little knew the hatred she had roused in the young girl's breast, nor the wounded pride which, scorning complaint, grew stronger and more eager to repay the insults against which it rebelled in silence.

"All these thoughts swept swiftly and confusedly through Maud's brain as she stood before her father, trying to crush down the longing of her heart for liberty and rest with Arthur. But the task seemed too hard, too cruel to them both, and she was lifting up her head to answer that her choice was made when in a mirror near her she caught a glimpse of Lady Ashley bending eagerly forward, watching her with a triumphant smile upon her scornful face.

"That sight roused every evil passion in Maud's heart, swept away every tender feeling, and left no wish, no thought, but the memory of her wrongs and the reckless resolution to defeat her enemy, whatever it might cost.

"So, listening only to the voice of her passionate pride, she laid her hand within her father's, saying as she fixed her dark eyes full upon Lady Ashley: "I *will* obey you, sir, and be my cousin's wife."

"If Maud had hoped to baffle and dismay, her wish was gratified, for—in spite of her efforts—wonder, rage, and bitter disappointment struggled in Lady Ashley's face and left it pale with suppressed passion.

"With a warmth he had never shown before, her father thanked Maud for her meek compliance with his will and hastened away to tell the anxious lover his good fortune.

"As he left them, the eyes of the two women met. For a moment they gazed silently, and in that glance many things were said. Maud spoke first, with a mocking smile: 'You played your game secretly and well, madam, but you have *lost*.'

"Lady Ashley made a sudden motion as if she would have risen up and silenced her forever, but controlling herself, she answered calmly, though her lips were white and her voice unnaturally low: 'I have—but my loss is small compared to the utter wreck you have made of your whole life's happiness and peace. *You* will suffer most and, in the long, miserable years to come, sigh vainly for all you have sacrificed in this rash hour and wish from the depths of your empty, aching heart that you had *lost,* not won. I am content and can dance at your bridal with a gayer heart than your own, conqueror though you are.'

"Maud thanked her with mock courtesy for her kind wishes and, with the same defiant smile, left her and fled away to her own room to weep wildly and despairingly over the gloomy future she had made by her own rash will.

"A month rolled away, and Maud never faltered in the path she had chosen. With false bloom on her colorless cheek and gay apparel concealing the rapid wasting of her form, she mingled with fitful gaiety in the festivities around her, finding in the growing kindness of her father the only happiness she knew.

"Arthur she never saw, though these walls could tell sad tales of tender letters blistered with tears and of sleepless nights and hours of bitter struggle wearing the poor girl's life away.

"She might—nay, doubtless *would*—have listened to her better self if, like an evil spirit, Lady Ashley had not been ever before her, by silent looks and actions taunting her with her misery and goading her on by false sympathy and cruel pity.

"Lord Effingham was serenely happy. Proud of his beautiful bride, he never dreamed of looking into the heart so soon to be given into his keeping. A world of suffering and sorrow would have been spared them all if he had.

"The wedding day was fixed, and with the same resolute calmness Maud went through the preparations usually so full of interest and excitement. It was a sad mockery to her, poor girl.

"The night before her marriage, after playing well her part below, Maud came wearily into her quiet chamber, longing to lie down and sleep forever.

"Worn out with her long struggle, oppressed with mournful memories and forebodings, she sat in the deep recess yonder, looking out upon the lowering sky, where a fierce storm was gathering.

"As she sat thus, a low voice whispering her name caught her ear, and looking down upon the lonely terrace, she saw by the moonlight that shone fitfully thro' the clouds the uplifted face of Arthur, who stood there fervently imploring her to free herself before it was too late.

"'Maud,' he said solemnly and earnestly, 'soon there *can* be no turning back from the sinful path you have chosen. Pride and passion blind you now. Put them away and look upon the deep wrong you are doing to yourself, to the man you wed to-morrow, and to me. Oh, listen to the voice of your nobler self which bids you scorn the falsehood which will darken three lives if you are not strong enough to triumph over the dark passions that control you now. Here upon the terrace, where we have so often pictured a bright future, I await your final answer. Call me if it be what I would have it. If not, be silent and I will go away forever, with a blessing for your past love and a prayer for your future peace.'

"Maud could not speak, but flinging down the flowers she had worn, turned away. And then began the conflict between love and pride, both passions so strong and deep and the heart they strove to win so weak and sorely tempted.

"Meanwhile, the storm came on with gusts of wind and thunder like that echoing about us now. But through all this tumult Maud still heard the patient footsteps pacing slowly to and fro, unchecked by wind or rain, and each echo seemed to call her loudly to the side of the true friend who watched and waited there for her.

"But as if conjured up by an evil spirit, every cruel deed or word, every scornful look or gesture, of the woman she hated seemed to haunt her now. As often as she struggled to forget the past, to think of Arthur and a happy future, between her and the peaceful fancy seemed to glide the dark, haughty face of Lady Ashley with a smile of triumph on her scornful lips, rousing all the passions she would banish and rendering vain her efforts to think calmly and decide as heart and conscience counseled.

"So the storm within and without raged on, but as midnight approached, both tempests lulled. The rain fell more gently and the thunder died away. Maud's tears ceased to flow, and kneeling before the picture of the mother she had never known, the friendless girl prayed humbly to be delivered from the temptations of her own ungoverned heart.

"A calm fell on her as she listened in silence to the voice of her good angel, and she was rising up to give a welcome answer to the patient watcher there below when suddenly her door was softly opened and Lady Ashley entered.

"All Maud's newfound strength was needed to sustain her then. She dared not speak or listen, but hiding her face within her hands, she waited silently, all her thoughts and energies bent on keeping down the rising passion that would overthrow her hard-won peace and lure her from the true path she had chosen.

"Lady Ashley had come on this last night to make an effort to dissuade her from the marriage with her cousin, whereby she would lose her own happiness and freedom from a revengeful motive. She talked long and earnestly, for the young girl's indomitable will and silent suffering had won her secret admiration and wakened some pity in her heart, cold and unfeeling though it was.

"Maud heard her warnings like one in a dream, but would not tell her that they were useless now. From other lips than hers the welcome words should come when she was far away, where no sight of her triumph should meet her eyes. So, silent as an image, she sat heedless of all about her till Lady Ashley, finding her efforts vain, turned to leave her. The rustle of her dress seemed to rouse Maud, for with a quick start she raised her head and glanced eagerly at the clock which stood in yonder empty niche. The hour had passed unheeded, and Arthur had gone unanswered.

"With a cry that long rung in her listener's ear, she sprang to the casement, flung herself half out, stretching her arms into the empty air and calling in a voice of passionate entreaty: 'Arthur! Arthur! Oh, come back! You shall not go alone—wait for me! Wait for me!'

"But no footstep sounded on the terrace, no face was uplifted to her own, no glad voice answered her. The rain beat on her uncovered head like chilling tears, the wind swept wailing by her like a sorrowful farewell, the echo of her own imploring cry came whispering from the hills—and that was all.

"Lady Ashley, startled and dismayed by the sudden change, and fearing lest the house would be alarmed by Maud's wild cries, went to her and with a gentle force tried to draw her from the window where she clung. But Maud turned on her with a face so altered that she fell back trembling beneath the fierce light of her eyes as Maud burst into a strange, bitter laugh, saying:

"'You have lost again, and now the game is ended. No more doubt nor wavering for me. Arthur is lost, your schemes thwarted, my heart broken, and tomorrow I will end the conflict by this marriage, which completes the *disappointment* of *your* life and the *misery* of my *own*.

"'Another hour and all would have been yours. Arthur was waiting there below for my last reply, and I had battled down my pride and hatred. I had put away all poor revenge for many wrongs and gladly made the sacrifice of all for his dear sake. The words you burned to hear me speak were trembling on my lips when you came hither to destroy my hard-won victory and to defeat by your own evil presence all your cherished hopes forever. Now leave me; for the hour that might have saved me has gone by, and nothing is now left but this gay bridal, for which we are a fitting mother and daughter, happy, tender, and true!'

"As she ceased, the wild laugh echoed through the room again and smote heavily on Lady Ashley's heart as she essayed some hurried words of comfort. But Maud bade her go with a stern gesture and leave her to such peace as she could find upon her wretched bridal night.

"Awed and bewildered, Lady Ashley left her, but stole often to her door, haunted by the fear that the unhappy girl might end her sorrows violently. But all night long the muffled sound of her ceaseless tread, as she paced to and fro, came to the listener's ear, but not a sigh, a word, or sign of grief was heard, only the footfalls, regular and slow, coming and going in the silent room.

"Toward the end of dawn they ceased, and fancying that,

worn out with her weary night, Maud at last was sleeping, Lady Ashley crept away to her own apartment. But no sleep came to her eyelids, no rest to her mind, for one by one those distant footsteps seemed drawing nearer and nearer to her door and then pacing slowly back again along the gloomy corridor.

"Each time as they came, the listening woman hid her face upon her pillow, fearing to see before her the pale figure of the motherless girl to whom she should have been a mother— fearing to read in the wan face mute reproaches which her own heart whispered, of the evil she had done in goading a rash, misguided spirit on to sorrow and despair, when it might have been made most beautiful and noble by a little love.

"So hour after hour the haunting fancy came and went till day dawned and she rose up, worn and haggard with the scenes of that unhappy night.

"When the old nurse came late that morning to call Maud, she found her lying on the cushioned recess of the window, her head pillowed on her arm, the fresh wind playing idly with her long hair, heavy with the rain which had fallen unheeded on her half-covered shoulders and on her face so colorless and cold that but for the restless eyes, Janet would have fancied her young mistress dead.

"She roused herself when spoken to, and bade the nurse put on her bridal dress and then leave her undisturbed till the appointed hour arrived.

"Full of grief and wonder, old Janet obeyed, knowing well her strange ways and fearing to question or advise. When Maud joined the friends and guests in the great hall below, a murmur of surprise and admiration rose among them, for a fairer, stranger bride had never stood beneath the old roof that had witnessed many weddings. White as her veil, her eyes shining with a fitful light, her lips moving unconsciously, and her hands clasped tightly together, she passed among them as if she saw nothing, heard nothing, felt nothing but the one desire to have all over and past help.

"As, leaning on Lord Effingham and following her parents, Maud and her bridal train passed to the chapel over the broad terrace, now carpeted with garlands, her eye fell on the knot of crushed and faded flowers she had given Arthur, lying beside the statue he had leaned upon when last she saw him in the dark and stormy night.

"All the past seemed to rush back upon her at the sight. She stopped abruptly, pressed her hands before her wandering eyes, and said wearily, 'Arthur is waiting for me. It will soon be over and then I can go to him.' She gathered up the flowers and stood playing fondly with them, utterly unconscious of the wonder and dismay around her.

"Lady Ashley came anxiously towards her, saying, 'You are ill, my child. Let us turn back till you are yourself again.'

"At the sound of her voice, the color rushed into Maud's face, her eye kindled, and she drew herself proudly up, saying in her old haughty way as she motioned Lady Ashley back: 'He said there was no turning back for me, and there is none. I *must* go on till all is over, and then you may lead me to my grave and I will follow meekly as a child.'

"She smiled, and her voice rang out clear and loud as with the old queenly gesture she waved them on and took one step forward. But there the long struggle ended, and she fell at her father's feet, cold and white as the marble where she lay.

"For many days and nights Maud lay unconscious. When at length she woke, it was far worse than if she had died in the long sleep; for now her high heart was subdued, her pride brought very low, her wayward spirit broken, and her reason gone forever.

"Lord Effingham went abroad and never married; Arthur had vanished like a shadow, no one knew where; and old Lord Ashley died soon after Maud's sad fate was told him, bequeathing his whole fortune and his most unhappy daughter as a sacred charge to his wife.

"But though Lady Ashley was mistress of all she coveted, a curse seemed to rest upon it, and it was a mockery to think of happiness with such a living reproach ever before her as the frail shadow of the once bright Maud.

"She tried to drown memory in pleasure. She put seas and lands between her and this mournful home, but all in vain.

She could not win forgetfulness nor rest, and at length, brought low with sickness and remorse, she came to look upon it as her just punishment and humbly accepted it, coming back to watch and guard the darkened spirit of poor Maud, now when it was too late to help or brighten it.

"So for three long years the two dwelt here together in the lonely hall. Lady Ashley sat day after day in the gloomy rooms below, her dark hair growing gray and her proud head bent very low, as Maud's feeble steps went gliding by or sounded from the sunny terrace, where she walked for hours, singing plaintive songs, or calling in a voice that wrung one hearer's heart most bitterly—'Arthur, come back and listen to me.'

"Here in this room she sat in her old place, stretching her arms imploringly to some phantom in the air, or watching the dial with placid patience pitiful to see, fearful lest the hour that never came should pass unheeded.

"So those weary years rolled on, and slowly wasting away, Maud at last lay down upon her bed and never left it till the night she died. The watcher in her room saw her rise up and, like a spirit, glide away through the deserted rooms till she went in at Lady Ashley's door.

"What passed there never has been known, but it is whispered that the listening watcher heard meek prayers for pardon and saw the gray-haired woman kneeling very low before the dying girl, in whose wasted arms she lay forgiving and forgiven.

"If this be true or but a dream of the fond old nurse, who now can tell, but out of that still room Maud glided back with a light upon her wan face which shone more radiantly there than the morning sunbeams which fell on her when they found her smiling in the dreamless sleep that set her free at last.

"Lady Ashley lived here till her death. Since then the old hall has been deserted, for its owner will not occupy it, being a gay young lord who has no fancy for a gloomy, haunted mansion—for it is still believed that steps are heard at midnight on the terrace and a frail white figure flits through the empty rooms, wringing its hands and calling mournfully to some phantom that never comes to answer it.

"This is the story of the haunted hall, clothed in simple words and colored with some fancies of my own."

As Allan ceased, some of his eager auditors glanced timidly about the shadowy room, some wiped away their tears, and others examined with new interest the faded hangings and quaint furniture of the apartment where poor Maud had lived and died. But Mabel still sat in the window with her averted head upon her hand, looking out upon the brightening sky and trying to conceal all traces of emotion, for the tale had deeply moved her. She felt such an earnest sympathy for Maud, whose proud, rash nature she so well could understand, whose faults and feelings seemed so like her own, and whose mournful end filled her with strange compassion, fear, and sorrow.

Meanwhile, as the clouds broke away and the sun glanced brightly over tower and tree, the young party recovered their lost gaiety and one by one left the room to explore new mysteries in the lonely house, bidding Mabel follow when she had dreamed enough.

But Mabel did not move. She sat in the quiet chamber lost in thoughts both sweet and bitter, for tears and smiles passed like an April day across her face. Some struggle seemed to stir within her and some victory seemed won, for suddenly she rose as if to leave the room. Her eye fell on the portfolio Allan had left when he stole out last of all and left her to the silent thought which he hoped would work a happy change in the warm but willful heart he loved.

The withered bluebells she had risked his life and her own to get were drooping from the half-closed cover. With a self-reproachful sigh she opened the book to replace them, when she saw the sketch Allan had been making while he told the tale.

It was of the turret window and, leaning from it, the figure of Maud, but the face uplifted to the stormy sky was her own, with the proud look it so often wore. Below, leaning on the broken image, with the streak of moonlight on his face, stood Allan and not Arthur.

Mabel's cheek burned and her eyes filled with shame and sorrow, but the resolution she had taken rose up rasher and stronger than before. Hastily replacing sketch and flowers, she hurried to the window, as if fearing her gentle mood would pass too soon, and putting aside the vines, looked down.

As she had fancied from the sound of steps, Allan was walking there with folded arms and the shadow which his countenance had worn all day long still lingering there.

Suddenly a low voice called him. With a start he raised his head, and there above him, looking through the fluttering leaves, with sunshine glancing over her bright hair, he saw the smiling, tender face of little Mabel as she whispered, "It is not too late to call *you* back, dear Allan. I have put away my sinful pride and waywardness. I will try very hard to be your gentle, happy-hearted Mabel for the future. Will you come back?"

Clouds and shadows vanished like mist before the sun, and with one glance of fond approval Allan sprang into the hall and up the long oaken stairs that echoed to his eager tread, and stood before Mabel with a face as bright and joyful as her own. She went to him, offering her hand with earnest frankness, saying softly, humbly, "Will you pardon all my past unkindness and help me to conquer those faults you know so well, lest, like poor Maud's, they darken my whole life and take from me your friendship, Allan?"

What need to tell his answer or the boon he asked of her that night in the moonlit porch of the quiet parsonage.

THE LADY AND THE WOMAN

"What style of woman *do* you admire, then, since your dislike for the 'strong-minded' is so great, Mr. Windsor?"

"That I can hardly tell you, Miss Kate, for I am not sure that I know myself. But I fancy that, like most men, I admire such as claim our protection and support, giving us in return affection and obedience. Beautiful and tender creatures, submissive to our will, confident in our judgment, and lenient to our faults—to be cherished in sunshine and sheltered in storms. I have given little thought to the subject in my busy life, but that's a hasty sketch. Does it meet your approbation?"

"Not at all. You have given your idol a heart, but no head. An affectionate or accomplished idiot is not my ideal of a woman. I would have her strong enough to stand alone and give, not ask, support. Brave enough to think and act, as well as feel. Keen-eyed enough to see her own and others' faults and wise enough to find a cure for them. I would have her humble, though self-reliant; gentle, though strong; man's companion, not his plaything; able and willing to face storm as well as sunshine and share life's burdens as they come."

"Such a character, Miss Kate, would be hard to find and might perhaps, though beautiful in thought, prove repulsive and unwomanly in reality. If these 'strong-minded' ladies who are clamoring so fiercely for their rights are samples, however bad, of the style you desire, I can never hope or wish to see it perfected. A masculine woman is both unnatural and unlovely, and you surely cannot admire such?"

"You are right; they are as utterly disagreeable as the effeminate men who are a disgrace to manhood. Ah, Mr. Windsor, there are two sides to the question and much to be set right on both. Give the brothers and sisters of our great family an equal share of the pleasures, duties, benefits, and rewards of life, and in time you will see the beautiful result. With a truer knowledge of each other, there will come a nobler justice for all, and what are now discordant fragments will become a harmonious whole.

> *'As unto the bow the cord is,*
> *So unto the man is woman,*
> *Though she bends him, she obeys him,*
> *Though she draws him, yet she follows,*
> *Useless each without the other.'*

And Hiawatha's Indian philosophy was a very true one, to *my* thinking."

"What is your opinion upon the subject, Miss Amelia?" asked the gentleman, addressing a handsome, languid lady who with veils, shawls, fans, and smelling bottles filled one corner of the carriage.

"Oh, I agree with you entirely, Mr. Windsor, and nothing would induce me to adopt Kate's ideas. They are so dreadfully peculiar. I am willing to be led, and quite content with my share of good gifts. Somebody says, 'Man is the head and woman the heart,' and it's quite true, I daresay."

"It is like putting to sea without a rudder, Amelia," said her energetic friend. "Hearts are often shipwrecked, passions and feelings are an unruly crew. So let me advise you to take head as pilot, for you may find, as I have done, that the voyage of life is not quite a pleasure trip."

"Be that as it may, I shall float comfortably along till a stronger hand than mine comes to hold the helm for me, for I'm no sailor and never mean to be if I must become one of those odious creatures Kate thinks so fine. I never saw one yet that was not unutterably disagreeable." And the lady's fine eyes rested thoughtfully upon the gentleman before her, as if considering his fitness for the post of pilot to the *Amelia*.

"*I* have seen a woman fill a father's as well as a mother's place and guide four willful boys with a firm though gentle hand, and yet no one ever thought *her* unwomanly, or breathed a word against a character as beautiful as it was uncommon," said the pale-faced lad at Mr. Windsor's side, with a glance of grateful affection at his sister Kate.

The elder gentleman did not see the look, but said musingly, "I should like to know such a woman."

"Perhaps you may," replied the boy significantly; and then they rode on in silence for a while, each lost in thought.

The young party journeying together had met at a certain country place much frequented by city visitors and were now making a two-day pilgrimage to a distant mountain, which no summer sojourner at L—— could leave unseen.

Edward Windsor, the leader of the excursion, was a young gentleman of family and fortune, handsome, generous-hearted, and agreeable, a favorite wherever he went, and nowhere more so than at L——, where quite a rivalry existed among the young ladies, each anxious to find favor in his eyes—some from real admiration for the many good and noble qualities he possessed, some from a lower regard for his wealth and position, and others from mere love of conquest. So, had the young gentleman possessed much vanity, this universal favor might have done him harm.

Careless of the honors he unconsciously won, he laughed good-naturedly at the amiable sirens by whom he was surrounded, and though courteous and kind to all, distinguished none above the rest. But as the pleasant circle was about to separate early in autumn, he found himself regretting secretly the departure of one friend whose society he had enjoyed so much that he almost decided to secure it, if possible, not for the winter, but for life.

This desire grew stronger as he thought of it, but a certain beautiful face smiled so bewitchingly upon him when he came, and grew so sorrowful when he departed, that he sometimes fancied his happiness would be best secured by obtaining the heart belonging to the handsome face.

Kate Loring, though with no pretensions to beauty, possessed a certain life and vigor which gave a fresh and peculiar charm to her intelligent face, and contrasted pleasantly with the inanimate countenances about her.

She had read and thought much on many subjects sadly unfashionable, and though enjoying the various amusements of her young companions with the zest of a gay and cheerful nature, yet when they were over, she could find in conversation, books, or her own thoughts pleasant and profitable occupation for the hours which others spent in idleness or frivolous gossip.

Left at eighteen with four younger brothers, she had filled the double place of parents and sister as few girls could have done, and was rewarded for many anxieties and sacrifices by the love and admiration of the lads, who looked upon "sister Kate" as unsurpassable in beauty, worth, or wisdom.

Her early trials had strengthened an originally strong character till she possessed a decision and energy seldom seen in so young a woman. Her straightforward truthfulness and independence won the confidence of the most timid, while her womanly tenderness and the softer virtues she possessed, though unobtrusively displayed, made many warm and faithful friends wherever she went.

Coming to L—— with her invalid brother for country air and exercise, she straightaway set to work to accomplish her purpose, never stopping to ask what people might think or if anyone else did the like. So while others were wasting the summer days by lounging on sofas, flirting in shaded parlors, driving out in state, or on the sultry nights dancing in crowded rooms, she was up at dawn, walking or riding miles away among the hills, getting a healthy bloom upon her cheek and fresh vigor of body and soul.

People stared, wondered, laughed, and then admired her. Some contented themselves with that, but others followed her example and found in her a companion whose friendship grew in value as they learned to know her worth.

Alfred, Kate's brother, was a quiet lad, still feeble from a long illness, busy with his studies, and devoted to "sister Kate," his nurse and dearest friend.

Miss Amelia Langdon, the languid lady, was a beauty and a

belle, accomplished in all the graceful arts of fascination and coquetry, but with little else to interest or charm.

She had set her heart upon the captivation of Mr. Windsor; and few thought there was any doubt of her success, for he admired her beauty and had paid her many kind attentions, though some said it was only since she had conceived such a warm attachment for Kate Loring. However, be that as it might, the two young ladies and the gentleman were great friends.

Toward sunset the party of travelers reached the village where they intended to pass the night. But the innkeeper, with many regrets, told them that his house was filled already with parties going and returning from the mountain and therefore they must go further on to a certain farmhouse two miles or more away, where they might be comfortably accommodated. So on they went, and were most hospitably received by the young farmer's wife, who was accustomed to entertaining stray travelers to the mountain.

"Maybe you'd like to go a piece up the ravine. It's quite famous hereabouts and well worth seeing if you're fond of rocks and water, ladies and gentlemen," said their hostess as they rose from her bountifully spread table.

Thanking her, the party strolled out to while away the twilight in a voyage of discovery. They climbed up the rocky way, following the babbling brook that dashed foaming down the deep ravine, whose sides were fringed with pines and carpeted with delicate ferns and moss. The higher they went, the wilder it grew, and when they reached the rustic bridge which spanned the waterfall, the rocky glen, the broad green meadows, and the distant mountains lay before them, beautiful with evening lights and shadows.

"This stream reminds me of *your* style of woman, Miss Kate," said Mr. Windsor as, leaning on the rude railing of the bridge, he glanced from Miss Amelia, who was reclining gracefully upon a mossy bank, gently swaying a green brake to and fro while gazing dreamily upon the scene before her, to Kate, who stood erect on a projecting crag, with folded arms and the red light streaming full upon her thoughtful face and gleaming eyes. There was something in her attitude and smile which made her beautiful as she looked down and answered, pointing to a little pool below them in a meadow:

"And that reminds me of yours, Mr. Windsor. See how placidly it lies, reflecting whatever shape may fall upon it, but with no life, no motion of its own. It may be clear and pleasant for a while, but summer heats will dry its shallow waters and winter frosts will freeze them. Winds may ruffle it and weeds may choke whatever secret spring it possesses, and soon it will be gone, or changed to a dark and stagnant pool, unlovely and unhealthful."

"Dear me, Kate, what strange ideas and tastes you have. I am sure the pretty pond in that nice meadow is far preferable to this noisy stream and these rough rocks. Don't you agree with me, Mr. Windsor?" Miss Amelia asked, grouping herself and her rustic parasol in a still more graceful attitude.

"Let me hear the other side, and then perhaps I can answer you better," he replied, looking up at the slender figure standing out in bold relief against the darkening sky.

Kate laughed a merry laugh that echoed musically among the rocks, and said, glancing from the dell to the faces lifted to her own: "Ah, you may smile and think me a romantic girl, but I'll defend my beautiful, bright stream and prove its great superiority to any shallow pool, however clear. If my brook is strong and rapid, it is kind and gentle too, for see how it stays to bathe the little mosses and the maidenhair that fringe the basins, where it lingers for a while and then flows on, leaving all greener and more lovely than before. Like the generous deeds that beautify a noble life, trees, flowers, and ferns all bend and gather around it as toward a friend. Listen to its cheerful voice and see with what bloom and freshness it fills this dell, so gloomy and so silent but for my lighthearted brook."

"Spring rains and melting snows may render it a terrible and a destructive thing, Miss Kate. How then?"

"Like all strong natures, if it be not well and wisely governed, it will carry rain in its reckless course, but if controlled and turned to worthy purposes, the torrent grows more quiet, but not less deep and strong, and turns the mill wheel yonder, filling whole meadows with its music and its verdure, and, quietly surmounting every obstacle, leads a useful and a happy life till, changing slowly to a noble river, it rolls serenely to the sea."

Kate's clear voice ceased, and for a moment nothing broke the silence but the dash of water, as if the stream leaped up to thank her for her sympathy and praise and then flowed singing on with one more happy memory to swell the music of its cheerful voice.

"If I were sure that I possessed the power of governing as well as loving and admiring, then, like you, I should prefer the free mountain stream, Miss Kate," Mr. Windsor said, with a glance that deepened the color in her cheek.

"Shall we go now? The dew is falling, and we must be off betimes tomorrow. Let me assist you down," he added, offering his hand.

But she sprang lightly from her perch, saying gaily, "No, thank you, waterfalls need no help in tumbling over rocks. Devote yourself to the placid lake, for the least jar ruffles its tranquility, you know," and with her brother on her arm, Kate's active figure vanished down the winding path.

"What a dear, strange creature she is, isn't she?" asked Miss Amelia as she rose with a charming sigh of pity for her friend's oddity.

"She is a very fine one, I think," answered Mr. Windsor, taking her parasol and shawl with a queer smile lurking about his mouth.

"Well, yes, not beautiful, you know, but striking perhaps, and she might be very agreeable if she were not so sadly masculine," Miss Amelia said, while a smile spread over her companion's face; and he laughed quietly to himself under cover of the deepening twilight as she clung to his arm in affected terror at the steep descent, shrieking at toads, half fainting at a snake, and bewailing stones, dirt, and dew till they reached the house; and she sank utterly exhausted into the large cushioned chair prepared for Alfred.

Kate silently pillowed her head upon her shoulder and

filled the quiet room with the music of her cheerful voice as she chatted, laughed, and sang, exerting herself as much to entertain her brother as she had ever done to please a group of gay, admiring friends.

"Well, I must say, 'Lisha," said Mrs. Mills, as she came from the parlor where she had been to carry lights, "I must say, though the little lady is a sight the prettiest and the smartest dressed, the tall one is worth a heap of such, for while the pretty one is dozing in the big chair where she ain't no right to be, the other one is chirping away in there like a bird to cheer up her brother's spirits while she's dropping with sleep herself, I know. I declare it does a body's heart good to hear her say 'Thank you, ma'am' or look into her nice, bright face, and I shouldn't wonder if the young gentleman thought so too."

Kate was just leaving the room to make Alfred comfortable for the night, so Mrs. Mills's outburst was plainly heard. The "young gentleman" nodded approvingly and looked into the "nice, bright face," which grew nicer and brighter with a blush and a smile as it went hastily away.

When she came down again to wake her friend, Kate found Mr. Windsor leaning over the great chair, chatting in a low voice with Amelia, who looked as if sleep was one of the lost arts.

As he looked up, Mr. Windsor saw a troubled, anxious expression flit across Kate's face. It was gone again instantly, and though Amelia wondered how anyone could be tired when she felt so fresh herself, Kate never alluded, in self-defense, to their different modes of spending the evening, but waited till the young lady had settled her flounces and collected the various articles without which she never moved; and then with a quiet "good night" Kate went away.

Mr. Windsor sat a while meditating on the blush, smile, and look without coming to any very satisfactory conclusion; for the truth was, he found his regard for Kate increasing very rapidly. He had been first attracted by her faithfulness to her brother and the intelligent vivacity of her conversation, but he soon felt the real nobility of her character and loved her in spite of himself.

For, like the best of mortals, he had his prejudices and weaknesses, and one of them was a great dislike for anything peculiar or in the slightest degree unfeminine, according to his notion of the word. So, though Kate was always graceful and refined in word and manner, her blunt sincerity, her quiet disregard for the false and foolish opinions of the world, and her peculiar ideas on many subjects kept him in constant fear lest by some rash action or unwomanly sentiment she should dispel the charm which he now found in her society.

He often wished that she possessed some of Amelia's beauty, the fascination of which he daily felt, though at the same time he was obliged to confess that there was a great lack of something in the young lady which he never found in Kate. So, wavering often in purpose, though always true at heart, he watched and waited, hoping to find in Kate that union of gentleness and strength which makes a true womanly character.

His meditation ended just where it began, and he strolled away to bed, leaving Mrs. Mills in a state of great curiosity to discover which of the ladies caused his thoughtful mood. As he leaned from his chamber window, looking anxiously at the cloudy sky, Amelia's voice sounded from the room adjoining his, saying with a drowsy laugh:

"I suppose you don't care to know what Mr. Windsor was saying me when you came in?"

"Yes, I do, if you choose to tell me," Kate answered with her usual straightforwardness.

"Ah, but I don't choose. Only if you hear someday that we are engaged, you need not contradict it. But don't ask any questions, for I shall say no more, so good night to you," and one of the young ladies laughed and the other sighed.

The listener longed to know which did the latter, but having so far verified the old proverb in hearing no good of himself, he hastily withdrew, muttering something which sounded very like "baggage," which epithet, as there was only a carpet bag in the party, must have applied to the truthful Miss Amelia, whose voice went murmuring on, though he knocked his boots about to warn them of his neighborhood.

Presently it ceased, and giving a last look at the sky, he

was about to close the window when the sound of quiet weeping caught his ear. The wind had risen and rain began to fall, but through these sounds the low sobs came distinctly every now and then, as of someone trying vainly to stifle their emotion.

Mr. Windsor stood motionless, longing to speak but feeling that he had no right to offer sympathy unasked or venture to intrude upon a private grief. But which could it be? he thought. Not Kate; she never wept, they said. Amelia often did, and he had seen her water the grave of a dead bird with copious showers, but not with such tears as were falling now. Yet what could either have to weep for? He longed to know that it was Kate, selfish as it seemed, and so sat listening till it ceased and a light step passed his door and entered Alfred's room beyond his own. He heard the murmur of voices and soon the continuous sound as of someone reading.

"Alf must be ill," he thought, and remembering Kate's weariness, he hastily assumed his coat and went to offer his services as nurse or watcher.

The boy's door was open, and pausing in the gloom of the low passage, the young man looked at the group within with an interest that held him there in silence for several minutes. Kate sat at her brother's bedside reading in a low tone, hoping thus to soothe him to sleep. One arm lay over the pillow, gently caressing the restless head that tossed to and fro; the other hand shaded her eyes, whose lids drooped heavily. Her black hair, loosened from its bands, lay on her shoulders, making her pale face paler, and over her whole countenance there was an air of patient weariness and sorrow that touched the watcher's heart and made the quiet, drooping figure in the dimly lighted room more beautiful than the animated one, bright with sunset radiance, which had been before him until now. The boy's eyes never wandered from her long, and a look of grateful love shone over his thin face as the music of her voice fell soothingly upon his ear till restlessness and pain seemed chased away by the simple magic of her presence.

A tap disturbed them, and Mr. Windsor begged to share or lighten her long watch.

"The fatigue of the long ride and the sultriness of the night have made Alf restless, and I am reading him to sleep, that is all. Many thanks, but I need no help," Kate said. But in the unconscious tremor of her voice and the downcast eyes that never met his own, Mr. Windsor read all he desired to know, and gently taking the book from her hand, he led her to the door, simply saying she must rest, for he had taken possession and would not be refused.

"Did you ever have a sister, Mr. Windsor?" Alfred asked abruptly as Kate's door closed.

"No, Alf, neither brother nor sister."

"Then I pity you, that's all. Brothers are well enough, but a sister like our Kate is a blessing worth having, sir."

"I hope you are grateful for it," said Mr. Windsor, laying down the book, seeing that the lad seemed disposed to talk and feeling no inclination to check him, the subject being what it was.

"I should be a brute if I were not, remembering all she has done for us. Did she ever tell you about our life at home, sir?"

"No, but I should like to hear of it," answered Mr. Windsor with great animation.

"Of course she didn't. I might have known that, for she couldn't speak of it without telling some of her own good deeds; and that she never does," said the boy, pleased with the other's interest and eager to sound his sister's praises.

"Why, you see, sir," he went on, "when Father died, we found ourselves poorer than we ever dreamed of being. Ned and Harry thought they must give up going to college. That made them cross enough to wear out the patience of a saint, but it didn't Kate's. She just took the little fortune Aunt Mary left her, sent the boys off happy, put Will and me to school, and settled things in the old house, that we might always have a home to come to. Then, when all was done, we found that in making our happiness she had destroyed her own; for Mr. Elliott, when he found she was no longer rich, left her like a villain and nearly broke her heart. I suppose I ought not to mention this, but my blood is up whenever I think of it. Kate never speaks of it, so I must free my mind and vent my rage now and then. Yes, sir, he left her, and how many girls of eighteen, I wonder, would have borne it as she did? Her 'contempt killed her love,' she said; and though she altered very much, she never spoke of it, but went straight on, thinking, planning, working for us good-for-nothing boys when she needed help herself. That's nearly seven years ago, and now, instead of being a rich, happy wife, she is only our dear sister Kate. And people may call her poor and plain as much as they like. I know her worth, and by Jove, sir, if ever I get on my legs again, if I don't make other people know it too and don't pay part of the debt I owe her, I don't deserve to have any legs, and hope I shan't," cried the boy, thumping his pillow energetically to hide the tears in his eyes.

"Never think her poor or plain, for she is rendered beautiful and rich by her own virtue," Mr. Windsor said earnestly, with an averted face—adding more quietly, "I thank you for this, Alf, and now let me see you asleep, and then I shall have kept my promise to your sister."

And utterly unconscious of a single line, he read on till the boy slept soundly and nothing broke the midnight silence but the patter of the rain upon the roof. Then he stole away to dream of the quiet figure until dawn.

All night the rain fell heavily, and in the morning, instead of continuing their pilgrimage, the young party were forced to wait patiently till the storm should cease. After many consultations and observations of the sky, whose sullen appearance gave no hope, they settled down to spend the time as best they might.

Miss Amelia, after great lamentation, made herself comfortable on her cushioned throne, amusing herself and displaying her white jeweled hands to advantage among the beads and many colored silks of which she was crocheting some dainty article while holding gracious audiences with Mr. Windsor and Alfred and laughing at Kate, who had completed her conquest of Mrs. Mills by relieving her of the children, whose wants, mishaps, and uproar seriously impeded the progress of her household duties.

But though Miss Amelia laughed, Mr. Windsor thought

Kate had never looked so well as he watched the gentle wiles she used to win the friendship of the little ones and saw her sitting on the floor building block houses with the baby cooing in her lap or the other three hopping merrily about her, shouting at the splendid towers she raised so patiently for them to demolish, putting their chubby faces close to hers, and showing by every artless look and word their love and admiration for the "nice, kind lady," who possessed the power to make a rainy day such a festival of fun for them.

Miss Amelia looked quite disagreeable, in spite of all her beauty, when she pushed away an admiring urchin who ventured to lay hands upon the trinkets at her side, saying with a sharpness quite astonishing: "Oh, go away, child, your hands are shockingly dirty. Go to Miss Loring, for mercy sake. One victim is enough, I'm sure."

And as the rebuffed young gentleman indignantly went back to his old friend, the lady's voice sank into its usual musical drawl and with her sweetest smile she renewed the conversation. But Mr. Windsor soon deserted and, joining the noisy group in the corner, found himself so comfortable that he stayed till dinnertime.

As the afternoon wore on and still the rain poured down, Miss Amelia's patience was exhausted, and after a few fretful exclamations she retired to her room, where in a nap and a novel she found some relief from her ennui.

Kate begged some sewing of Mrs. Mills as a favor, but her quick eye discovered that, like many farmers' wives, the poor young woman was so burdened with work that her health was giving way and her children suffering for the care she could not give them.

So, leaving her hostess to a few hours' rest, with her little ones about her, Kate sat stitching pinafores with an energy and dispatch that showed her zeal. Alfred worked on an unfinished sketch, Mr. Windsor read aloud, and the time slipped so pleasantly away that it was dusk before they had thought of weariness.

"Hark!" said Kate, suddenly dropping her work. "What is that?"

They listened, and a loud, continuous roar like distant thunder was plainly heard.

"It is the brook, but it sounds very near," said Mr. Windsor, going to the window. A sudden exclamation brought his companions to his side, and they saw a dark flood rushing by where an hour ago there had been a grassy road.

"This is a wild freak of your undine's, Miss Kate. See how it washes away that bank opposite. I'm afraid the bridge will go, and then we are prisoners here unless a boat can be found. How do you like this adventure, Alf?" said Mr. Windsor.

"Would you be so kind as to step out a minute, sir? I'd like a word with you, if you please," said the farmer, at this moment showing his anxious face at the door.

Mr. Windsor followed him to a back door, and there a wild and somewhat alarming sight presented itself. The old house stood upon a little mound. On one side flowed the stream; on the other a green lane wound over a bridge from the road below. The brook now came foaming down from the fall, bearing with it stones, trees, and the ruins of the rustic bridge. At a narrow bend close to the house, a mass of rubbish had collected, half choking up the stream, which had risen higher and higher till it overflowed and poured along the lane, forcing its passage through every obstacle till the barn was separated from them by the deep gully the water had worn in the sandy soil.

"You see, sir, if the dam above the fall should give way, we ain't as safe as might be," said the farmer as they stood watching the furious stream and listening to its increasing roar. But it's pretty firm, and if the 'spilins' don't give way, we shall do. I jest would say that if it does, the barn may go; so if you'll lend a hand, I'll get the horses over here into the shed. I'll wade across and fetch 'em over if you'll take 'em on this side, for they may give trouble—and it's got to be done quick, for the water is deepening every minute."

Mr. Windsor was ready instantly and, standing on the bank, watched the farmer make his way across. The rain poured down in sheets, and the roar of the fall grew every moment louder while the black stream whirled swiftly by carrying all before it.

Mr. Mills had just descended into the water, leading one of the horses, when a large timber shot down the current with such velocity that before a warning cry could be uttered, the farmer was carried away by it and the terrified horse was careering wildly from the stream to the barn.

A loud shout brought the anxious faces at the windows in a crowd to the door, and Kate, putting back her brother, sprang down the bank to find Mr. Windsor, pale and dripping, with the young farmer lying senseless across his knee, with blood flowing from a deep cut on the forehead and one leg doubled under him in a strange, unnatural way that made her sick to see.

Never stopping to scream, faint, or cry, Kate, without a word, supported the wounded head on her shoulder while Mr. Windsor, with the strength of excitement, lifted the man in his arms and carried him through the trembling group into the house and laid him on his bed.

"Amelia, take these children and quiet them while Mrs. Mills and I attend to her husband," Kate said, trying to make herself heard through the screams of the babies and the poor woman's loud cries for 'Lisha to speak one word to her.

But Amelia was preparing to faint on Alfred's shoulder and would have done so if Kate had not gone to her, saying in her decided voice, with a slight shake to rouse the young lady's faculties: "Listen to me, Amelia, this is no time to faint. Be a woman and keep these children quietly out of the way for their mother's sake. Mind me and forget yourself; there is no danger yet."

Amelia obeyed like a child and, receiving the little ones as if she were afraid of them, administered a few vague pats and scraps of comfort. But the children refused to be consoled by such means and roared louder than ever till, at a signal from his sister, Alfred carried them off to another room and peace was restored.

"Can you hold the basin while I bathe his forehead,

Amelia? Mrs. Mills is trembling so, she cannot stand," Kate said as her friend showed her frightened face at the door.

"Oh, I couldn't. The sight of blood makes me so faint. Do come away, Kate. How can you do it?" whimpered Miss Amelia, hastily retreating.

"Let me help you if I can," said Mr. Windsor, coming to the bed instead of following the weeping lady to console and comfort her, as she hoped he would.

Kate's hands were as cold as ice, but firmer than those that met her own. Though her lips and cheek were white, she never trembled nor turned away from the ghastly sight before her, but with a light, skillful touch bound up the wound and soon brought back the life and color to the poor man's face. He muttered feebly as he looked into the pitying countenance above him:

"You're very good, miss, and I don't know what we'd have done without you. Don't cry, Jane, it's all right now. She'll bring me round again in a minute."

"You must have a doctor, sir, directly. I'll saddle one of the horses and go for him," said Mr. Windsor as he hurried away. But as he came struggling up the bank with the first one, Kate stood there and simply said:

"I will help you, for no time must be lost and it's dangerous work alone." She took the bridle from his hand, led the animal into the shed, and was back again in time to receive the others as one by one he led them over.

When all were safe, they paused a moment to take breath, for the wind blew fiercely and the rain fell faster than ever. As they stood thus, a sudden rush far up the dell warned them that the dam the farmer spoke of had probably given way. Their fear proved true, for before the young man could cross, the swollen torrent came thundering down, bringing destruction and dismay. For as it swept by, the opposite bank gave way, and the old barn fell with a crash into the stream, turning its course most dangerously toward the house.

One after the other, Mr. Windsor led the horses to the water's edge, but none would venture in, and the treacherous bottom, the swift current, and the logs constantly dashing by added to the gloom. The wind and rain might have deterred even braver swimmers.

"I must go on foot, then," he said, "but I dislike leaving you all here in such apparent danger, for another turn might take the house. This accident to Mills is most unfortunate; however, it's no time to talk. I'll get a lantern and be off."

But when the group within the doors learned of his decision, they opposed it with so many arguments and lamentations that he was thoroughly perplexed as to what was best. Even Mr. Mills called faintly from his bed:

"Don't leave the women, sir, for me. I'll get on somehow till morning, or till the danger's over, for the storm can't last much longer. Stand by 'em, sir, for heaven's sake and let the boy go if anyone does."

Kate had stood listening silently, but now said decidedly as she drew near them: "Alf must not stir. It would be going to his death, but *I* can and will. Say no more, but let me set out instantly."

"You, Miss Kate? It's perfectly impossible," cried Mr. Windsor and the rest in an astonished chorus.

"Listen a moment," she answered quietly, "and you will see the plan is a reasonable one. Mr. Mills must have a doctor and we must have help. You, Mr. Windsor, ought not to leave them. Alf is out of the question, and Mrs. Mills must stay to comfort her husband and her children. Who, then, remains to go but Amelia or me? One of us must. I leave it to you to say which it shall be."

The person addressed glanced from the breathless beauty sitting in her disordered finery, speechless with amazement and terror, to the energetic figure before him, standing calm and collected amid the tumult within and without, courage in her eye and the glow of her generous purpose shining in her face, inspiring confidence and hope at a single glance.

He caught the smile that lingered on her lips as she watched him, and divining its meaning, he answered with a frank laugh, "You are right, Miss Kate, the strong-minded wins the day, so if any safe means can be found by which to cross the stream, I suppose we must let you go, rash as it seems."

"But, my dear miss, the rain and the dreadful roads!"

"Oh, Kate! Alone at night, how dare you!"

"Let *me* go, sister. I can stand it."

"You're a brave girl, and we shan't forget it, miss" were a few of the exclamations that went on around her as Kate wrapped herself up in the hooded cloak Mrs. Mills gave her and, bidding them be of good cheer, lit her lantern and went out into the storm.

Mr. Windsor followed her with a singularly bright and earnest face, considering the time and place, and after some search found a heavy beam wedged between the banks and firm enough to bear her weight.

"Miss Kate, I fear I am doing wrong in permitting this," he said, as she paused a moment looking over the wild stream into the gloom beyond. "It is two lonely miles, and the storm does not abate. Have you no fear? Can I not dissuade you from it?"

"Fear is one of the soft, ladylike qualities I am so unfortunate as not to possess," Kate answered with a little bitterness in her tone. But it was gone as she bent to take the lantern, with the old smile on her lips, though something glistened softly in her eye as she said cheerfully, "Do not try to keep me, for I ought to go. Only take care of Alfred, and put some courage in poor Amelia. Now, each to our work—you to watch and I to wander. So good-bye."

And with a wave of her hand she set out lonely upon her journey. When halfway across the perilous bridge, she paused suddenly and nearly fell, startled by a loud scream from Amelia, who was watching from the porch.

Alfred unceremoniously pushed her in and shut the door in her face while Mr. Windsor sprang forward as he saw the dark figure waver for a moment.

But a cheery voice cried all was well, and in silence they watched the light flicker over the black water and glide swiftly away till it was lost in the windings of the road.

And now, when it was too late to call her back, both the young men wondered how they had ever let her go, and fancied every possible and impossible accident which could befall her. The two long miles through lonely wood, the overflowed roads and broken bridges, the rain, the darkness, and the hour all haunted them till they would have followed but for their promise to stand by the helpless creatures left to their protection.

Restless and anxious, they went to and fro, often looking with a cheering word into the room where Amelia sobbed and dozed upon the sofa, or visited the quiet chamber where the wounded man lay suffering while his wife, surrounded by the sleeping children, tended him with every comfort her loving heart could offer.

Then they wandered out again to look for Kate, long before she could return, to quiet the restless horses, to listen to the whistling of the wind and watch the dangerous eddies of the stream. The banks were washing rapidly away, and the little mound on which the house stood seemed hourly to contract and bring the stream still nearer to the walls.

With logs and stones they strove to turn its course, but little could be done. So hour after hour dragged on and no help came. The darkness and the storm increased, and as they sat together in the little shed anxiously waiting, each followed silently in thought the lonely figure with the flickering light, wondering where it might be then, pushing bravely on or resting by the way. Or was the light extinguished and the face which had so lately smiled on them turned unavailingly to them for help, bewildered in some gloomy spot? Or was it lifted calmly to the pitiless sky as black waves bore it on, lifeless and still, after the treacherous fall and the brief struggle were past?

As they thought thus, they unconsciously looked into each other's faces for some cheering hope, but found none, and sat pale and silent, listening to the tumult around them.

"It is nearly eleven, Alfred, and she must be lost. But hark, what's that?" Mr. Windsor said, as the sudden surge of water sounded under them and the shed shook violently. "Out with the horses, quick! The bank below has gone, and we shall have it over our heads in an instant," he shouted through the crash of falling stones and earth.

The shed stood a few rods from the house, and as they watched it settling to its fall, Alfred said with a hopeless glance toward the distant town: "If she is not here soon, it will be too late. A few stout arms on the other side could turn the flood and save poor Mills from further damage. I wonder no one thinks of him. What shall we do, sir? Where can Kate have lost herself?"

His only answer was the noise of the shed as it went down, and standing on the doorstep, they looked upon the conflict that went on below as the stream tossed and tumbled foaming over the ruins, coming nearer and nearer as the bank gave way.

"We must warn them within there, and devise some way to get them safely over to the rocks if the house begins to go," Mr. Windsor said with a last despairing look into the gloom.

But as he turned away, a dozen lights came flashing up the hill, voices echoed cheerily, and figures were seen hastening to their aid. With one shout of welcome the two stood watching with eager eyes and hurried breath the movements of the approaching party. One light came swiftly on before the rest and passed just opposite the dangerous curve that widened every moment, and Kate's voice sounded loud and clear above the din, saying:

"The house is in danger. Dig just here and turn the current from the bank. Bend to it heartily and all will be safe in an hour."

"The bridge you spoke of, miss, is gone."

"How are we to cross?" another voice inquired as the clash of shovels and the quick rattle of earth told how well Kate was obeyed.

"Down with that tree, then; we can cross on that," she said. "Here is the ax, doctor. I will hold the lantern for you. Alfred, Mr. Windsor, are you there? Keep at a distance, and we will be with you soon."

"By Jove, sir, my sister is splendid tonight. Look at her work!" cried Alfred, pale with excitement, as he held fast by his friend's shoulder and leaned forward eagerly.

Mr. Windsor did not answer, but his eyes never moved

from the dark figure near the tree with the dull light of the lantern shining on it, showing glimpses of a face as resolute if not as calm as when he saw it last.

The shovels clattered and the ax rang till the rocks echoed back the sound, and soon the tree fell crashing down across the stream. The young men sprang to clear the boughs away, and presently, with a last word of encouragement to the men who worked as if for a wager, Kate came slowly over the rough bridge into her brother's arms.

"Nay, Alf, dear, don't stop to kiss me now. I'm safe, and much must be done before you all are too. So come in from the rain and let us see to Mr. Mills," she said after one embrace, as close and warm as it was brief; and then, followed by the village doctor and her friend, she hastened in.

With a face glowing with exercise, eyes brilliant with excitement, garments dripping, and hair fluttering in the wind, Kate came into the full glare of the lights lit up to guide her home. Amelia, with a little scream of rapture, ran into her arms, crying out:

"Oh, Kate, my dear brave girl, *have* you come back at last, and neither drowned nor murdered by the way? How glad, how grateful we all are for this, and how I wish I were like you."

The long hours spent in danger and alone had not been without some good to one head and heart, both better than they seemed when once roused to action. So Miss Amelia clung to Kate and sobbed out her admiration, gratitude, and excitement on her bosom.

Kate looked down upon her friend with a smile half merry and half sad, wondering, while she soothed, if this pale-faced, disheveled creature, so woebegone and weak, could be the beautiful and graceful Amelia she had sometimes envied when certain eyes looked admiringly upon her. She did not see the glance now shining on herself from those same eyes; for suddenly the lights and faces danced before her, and she knew nothing more until she found herself laying on the sofa with someone gently chafing her cold hand.

"Do not let him know I was so foolish as to faint, Alfred,

for he would only laugh at me. I tried so hard to keep up for you all, so do not tell him," she said, half unconsciously expressing her first thought.

"Tell who, dear Kate?" asked Mr. Windsor, pressing the hands he held and bending nearer to look earnestly into her face.

She looked up at him with a startled glance, and her cheek grew crimson as the cushion where it lay. But after a brief pause she answered frankly:

"You, Mr. Windsor."

"And why think so unkindly of me, Kate?"

"Forgive me if it seemed so, but I would not have you think me weak, both because I value your opinion and desire to *be* all that I may *seem.*"

"I never thought you weak and never can, for the beautiful, strong nature, womanly and true, which you so well described and I so longed to see, I have found tonight in *you,* dear Kate."

And as he spoke, the young man kissed the hands that lay so passively in his, and Kate sat erect with all her lost bloom glowing in her face. But she did not speak, for Alfred now came hurrying in with a cordial and a mandate from the doctor for her instant retirement and rest if she would escape the consequences of her long exposure to the storm.

She quietly submitted, and leaning on her brother, whose pride and tenderness were beautiful to see, she went away to dream as she had never done before, leaving Mr. Windsor standing with the wet cloak on his arm, but in thoughts so pleasant that he never stirred till his reverie was broken by the sudden exit of Miss Amelia and the entrance of the doctor, who, having dressed the wounds, had some preparation to make before attending to the broken leg.

"How is the young lady, sir?" he asked, unrolling his bandages. "A pretty wild night's work for her, though not so bad a one as poor Mills has had."

"She has retired according to your advice, doctor, but I hope no serious consequences need be apprehended, sir."

"Oh, no, a good night's rest will set her up. But I tell you what, sir, there ain't many ladies who would have done what she did," said the old man with great animation. "Why, do you know she got lost and went a mile into the woods and found her way out again? And what's more, come all the way back without a word of complaint or sign of fear, though it's not an easy walk, I can tell you, such a night as this."

"Where did she find you? And how did you collect so many men to help us?" asked Mr. Windsor, with an eagerness that far outdid the doctor's.

"Well, this was the way, sir," the doctor answered willingly. "We were assembled as usual around the tavern fire, as we always do stormy nights, and were talking over matters and things when the door opened and in came the young lady, white as a ghost and dripping like a mermaid, but as calm and cool as the best of us; and in half a dozen words she told us your fix. At first nobody stirred, being kind of dumbfoundered-like at the sight of her and the suddenness of the whole thing. Besides, between you and me, Elisha Mills ain't liked over and above well hereabouts. So, thinking the woman had been scared about nothing, we were rather slow in moving.

"When she saw that, her eyes flashed and the color came, and looking straight at me, she said, 'If you are a man, sir, you will come instantly, for Mr. Mills is suffering for your help. As for the rest, let it be said of them that a woman, and a stranger, came miles alone through such a storm as this to ask in vain their aid for an unfortunate neighbor who was powerless to save his wife and children from the flood that threatened to lay his house in ruins. Let them stay. I do not ask their help unless, remembering their own homes, they can give it freely and like men.'

"By George, sir, there wasn't one of us that didn't grow as red as that pillar, and turned out with a will. And when they heard what she had left and come through, there was a regular stir, and each was trying to do and offer most. But she wouldn't rest or ride or be carried, and kept ahead the whole way through thick and thin. She's a fine girl, sir, and you've a good right to be proud of such a sister." And the enthusiastic old doctor wiped his hot face and shook hands heartily with the young gentleman, who answered, smiling:

"She is not my sister, sir, but I'm prouder of her than if she were."

"Oh, your wife, is she? Lord bless me, I never thought of that, but what on earth possessed you to let her go?"

"Neither wife nor sister, doctor, so I had no right to keep her, though I tried. She was the only one who had the courage and could be spared, and I was compelled to stay, you see."

"Oh, ho! I see, I see! It's all right. You'll weather most any storm with her at the helm, and I give you joy, sir," said the doctor, with a knowing nod and an approving smile as he looked into his companion's telltale face, and then he hurried away with a merry twinkle in his eye.

At midnight the storm began to abate, and in the morning the sun came cheerily up, looking through his veil of mist upon the scene which had lately been so terrible and wild. The stream flowed more quietly, and the ravine looked green and sparkling as the sunshine fell on leaves and mosses bright with raindrops.

"Has Miss Loring appeared yet?" Mr. Windsor inquired of Mrs. Mills, as he came down from his chamber with as light a step and gay a face as if the past night had been one of great festivity and pleasure.

Mrs. Mills, comforted by her husband's quiet sleep and the doctor's kind assurances of a speedy recovery, was moving busily about, that all should be in order for her guests, and looking up from her work, said eagerly, with tears in her eyes: "Yes, sir, she is out somewhere with the folks, and oh, sir, would you tell her how grateful 'Lisha and I are for all her goodness to us? We are to you all, sir, but specially to her who has done so much and now won't let me thank her for it."

"I'll tell her with *all my heart,* Mrs. Mills," said her guest as he hurried away, leaving her, with a suddenly enlightened face, to nod her head wisely at the fire as she put the teakettle on.

Mr. Windsor found Kate standing on the temporary bridge the men had constructed, watching them as they worked sturdily, as if her words were still ringing in their ears and they were bound to prove them false.

*   *   *

The men had all shouldered their shovels and gone home. Alfred and Amelia were waiting and Mrs. Mills was in despair about her cooling breakfast before the two figures, which had been seen going slowly into the ravine, came as slowly back, wondering at the hour and penitent for their forgetfulness.

Miss Amelia looked eagerly for any suspicious symptoms in either of the faces, which seemed utterly unconscious of her scrutiny. But Kate was calm and cheerful as usual, and Mr. Windsor, though a little absent, so like himself that she felt assured nothing had happened to overthrow her hopes and was content.

At noon the carriage and horses were conveyed across the quietest part of the stream, and with many kind wishes on both sides, the young party took leave. Mr. Windsor was detained a moment behind the rest by Mrs. Mills, who insisted on restoring the little roll he had left in her hand at parting, saying as she looked after Kate:

"I couldn't take it, sir, for she, the excellent young lady, left some under 'Lisha's pillar because she knew I wouldn't take it. And I shouldn't now; but he said she seemed so pleased with her little trick, not knowing he was awake and watching her, and we don't wish to spoil her pleasure. Just tell her that, and don't ask me to take another mite. I'm heartily obliged, but I couldn't do it. So good-bye and a pleasant journey, sir."

He shook her rough hand warmly and went away, but the roll came back in little Jenny's pocket when she had watched the carriage out of sight.

"What an eventful pilgrimage ours has been," said Alfred, as they drew near their journey's end and the mountain rose up close before them.

"I shall soon set out upon a still more eventful one," replied Mr. Windsor, with a glance at Miss Amelia, who was apparently sleeping peacefully behind her veil.

"I wish we were going with you, for I like this style of traveling, amazingly. Are you going alone?" asked Alfred.

"No, your sister Kate has promised to go with me."

"My sister Kate!" began the boy in great surprise, but a single glance explained the mystery. With a face of perfect satisfaction and delight, he gave a hand to sister and friend, saying, "I thought you'd find the woman you so much desired to see close at your side if you only chose to look, Mr. Windsor, and I give my consent most heartily."

"The lady says she has decided not to go, sir, as she has met some friends here and prefers to stay with them," said a waiter, coming to them as they stood waiting for Miss Amelia at the foot of the mountain.

"I don't believe she was asleep, and so heard all we said in the carriage. That's a good joke," cried Alfred. "And that accounts for her willingness to stay behind with the Morgans, whom she hates. I'm glad of it, for I don't fancy dragging up the mountain with her on my arm."

"Poor Amelia!" said Kate with a sigh of generous pity for her friend's disappointment.

"Kate, was the falsehood she told you the cause of your tears last night?" said Mr. Windsor, smiling at the look of wonder and confusion in the face before him as he heard the low assent which Kate's truthful tongue could not refuse to utter.

"And now I hope you are satisfied, for I have proved myself womanly and weak on two occasions. But if we are going, let us hasten. Come, Edward, I am waiting for you."

Kate stood above them on the first green slope of the mountainside, and as she spoke the name that never seemed so musical to its owner's ears before, she stretched her hand to him. And from the figure bathed in light and the earnest face turned toward the distant peak there seemed to come a voice softly saying, "Come up higher."

It touched the heart not yet grown cold and worldly, and looking up at her with mingled reverence and love, her friend answered half playfully, half seriously, "You are standing now where I would have you, dearest Kate, above me in the sunshine, leading me by your gentle hand, out of the shadows here below, along the narrow path that winds through light and darkness, like our lives, up to the purer air and sunlight of the distant mountaintop."

"No, this is not my place. I would not be above you as I now am, nor yet below, like poor Amelia in the garden. But *here,* where every woman should be, at her husband's side, walking together through life's light and shadow," Kate replied, as she came and laid her hand in his with a smile as serene and beautiful as the mellow autumn sunshine glowing on her face.

He held it fast in both of his, and so they journeyed upward side by side.

RUTH'S SECRET

Miss Barbara sat in her easy chair dozing over her knitting, occasionally rousing to pick up a stitch or glance at the clock. Mr. Robert, her brother, a grave, studious man, sat reading opposite, and Ruth, on a low seat between them, bent over the laces she was mending, never lifting her head nor speaking as the long winter evening went slowly on.

The crackle of the fire on the wide hearth was the only sound that broke the silence. The cheery blaze shone brightly on the dark mirror, the polished oaken furniture, and the three still faces. It just touched Miss Barbara's silver hair and twinkled for a moment on her spectacles. It lingered longer around her brother, as if it found some kindred light and warmth in that countenance so serious and benign. But its brightest glow fell on little Ruth, giving a rosy hue to her pale cheek, glancing from the waves of her brown hair, peeping into her downcast eyes, and flickering about her quiet figure, as if it loved to touch and brighten that young face, innocent as a child's but thoughtful as an anxious woman's.

The clock struck ten. Miss Barbara woke up and bade Ruth put away her work, see that the house was safe, and bring the keys to her.

"Your old habits are unchanged, I see, sister Barbara," said Mr. Robert, looking up from his book as the door closed on Ruth.

"Yes, I never change, and during your long absence I have been obliged to be more punctual and particular than ever, or the house would be in a fine state of confusion. Even now I never should manage to keep things straight, lame and helpless as I am, if I had not taught Ruth all my ways and trained her to fill the place of housekeeper as well as companion."

"Where did she come from?" asked the gentleman, kindly continuing the conversation, as his sister seemed inclined to talk.

"Bless me! Didn't I tell you? Well, you see, when I found that my lameness prevented my stirring about and overseeing things myself, I advertised for a respectable young woman to read, sew, wait upon me, and see that my orders were obeyed. After trying a dozen, I was giving up in despair when Ruth came to me. Though she had no recommendation, she looked so sensible and tidy that I took her and was perfectly satisfied, and here she has been now over a year. I haven't a fault to find with her, for she is quiet, industrious, and obedient, and that can be said of very few young women nowadays." And Miss Barbara rolled up her work with a flourish, as if challenging the world to contradict her.

"I am very glad you are so comfortable, and hope my return will add but little to your cares," said her brother, turning to his book again as Ruth came back with Miss Barbara's crutches.

After sundry orders and a deal of fuss, the old lady with great dignity began her tedious journey bedward. Mr. Robert rose with old-fashioned courtesy to open the door for them, saying, "Good night, sister Barbara. Good night, Miss Ruth."

The girl glanced up with a look of pleased surprise, for the kind voice had not varied its respectful tone in uttering her name. And every fear she had felt before the gentleman's return was banished by that simple act, as unexpected as it was pleasant to her.

She only dropped a little curtsy as she went out, but a grateful smile lit up her face and made it beautiful.

Mr. Robert found himself recalling that glad, wistful look as he sat alone over the dying embers arranging books and papers till the great hall clock striking twelve echoed through the silent house. As he passed along the passage to his chamber, a streak of light from a half-opened door near his sister's room arrested his steps. Fearing she might be ill, he put down his candle and, looking in, saw Ruth sitting there alone.

Though it was after midnight, she was sewing still, but not on Miss Barbara's laces. Some plain, coarse work lay on her knee, and she bent steadily over her swift needle with such an altered face that the retreating watcher paused in wonder as he caught a glimpse of it.

Flushed and agitated it looked now, and tears fell often on her work, though she never stopped except to dash them off, as if she had no time for grief. But as the last stitch was taken, the pent-up sorrow could no longer be restrained, and dropping her weary head upon her hands, Ruth broke into a passion of such bitter weeping that the kindhearted gentleman was on the point of entering to comfort her when her light, flickering in the draft, suddenly went out. Then, fearful of startling her, Mr. Robert, full of pitying wonder, stole silently away.

The next morning, when he met his sister, at her side was the same tranquil face which he had seen the day before, and which now looked so cheerful and serene that but for the heavy eyes he would have fancied the bowed, weeping figure was some dream of the past night.

So, thinking it was but some girlish trouble, Mr. Robert was relieved, and though night after night the light shone out beneath the door, he never watched the girl again nor asked why she was there.

"Ruth, you are ill," said Miss Barbara abruptly a few weeks later, after studying the unconscious face before her for a while. "You are ill; you know you are, so don't deny it. You are losing flesh and color; your eyes are bloodshot at this very minute; and your hands trembled like a leaf when you tied my cap this morning."

"Indeed, indeed, Miss Barbara, I'm not—only a little nervous, perhaps," stammered Ruth, startled at the sudden accusation, glancing timidly as she spoke toward the recess where Mr. Robert sat. But he seemed not to hear, and his sister, lowering her voice, went on with increased asperity:

"Now, don't contradict me, for I have proofs that you are overworking yourself, though not in my service, thank heaven. What do you say to that?" And the old lady triumphantly laid a part of the mysterious needlework upon Ruth's lap, adding, "Jane found it in your room and says, moreover, that she has discovered you often sitting up till nearly morning sewing on these things. Now, I insist on knowing what it means, immediately."

But Ruth sat silent with bent head and folded hands, as if prepared for anything but a confession. Miss Barbara's temper lasted through a long storm of impatient expectation, but receiving no reply, it gave out. With an emphatic rap on the floor with her crutch, she said angrily:

"So I'm to be treated in this disrespectful manner, am I, with never a word of explanation or excuse? But let me tell you, I'll have none of this mysterious nonsense. I'll have no shirking of proper work, no secret sittings up, nor any underhand doings in my house without knowing why. So answer me at once."

The color flushed into Ruth's face, but she met the old lady's suspicious eye with a glance so open and affectionate that it unconsciously grew milder as she said in her low voice, as firm as it was respectful: "Dear Miss Barbara, do not wrong me by such words. I never have neglected any duty or disobeyed any command, but have tried to be as faithful, diligent, and cheerful as you desired to have me. Did I ever displease or give you cause to suspect me before?"

"No, I can't say you did," muttered Miss Barbara.

"Then do not doubt me now. I will tell all I can, for Jane was right. I *have* worked many nights when you imagined me asleep. But even in this I have been careful to obey your orders, for, knowing you desired no lights in the servant's rooms after ten, I have always used the night lamp in your dressing room and found my way up in the dark when I had done. Can you not forgive me this?"

"Yes, child, I can. But I'm not satisfied yet and want to know what all this work is for," said Miss Barbara, much mollified but still curious.

Ruth did not speak.

"Then I'm to understand you won't explain," cried the old lady sharply.

"I *cannot,* Miss Barbara."

"But you *must,* Ruth; otherwise, how am I to know that what you are doing is right and proper?"

"I think you will trust me."

"But if I do not and, disliking mysteries, should tell you to confess or go away—what then?"

"I should thank you heartily for all kindness and should go away."

Miss Barbara put on her spectacles and looked long into Ruth's face. Something there disarmed her anger, for she took them off again, saying kindly, "No, you wouldn't, for I can't spare you, child. But it's wrong in me to let you go on killing yourself in this way. Lord bless me, what shall I do for you?"

"Respect her secret, trust her freely, and lighten her duties, that she may have time for rest and exercise," said Mr. Robert's voice from the recess, though he neither turned nor looked up from his paper.

"Oh, thank you, sir! I may be trusted in this thing, indeed I may, though it grieves me to seem so willful and unkind," and Ruth's tearful eyes turned gratefully towards the distant corner.

"Yes, that I'll do, and I'll raise your wages, Ruth. I wonder I didn't think of it before; it will prevent all this late work," said Miss Barbara with a relieved expression, which, however, changed to one of disappointment and wonder as Ruth answered earnestly:

"You are very generous and kind, dear madam, but it will do no good. I have money laid by now, which I never use, and your whole fortune could not help me. I *must* work as I have done a little longer. So please have confidence in me and let me go on as before. Soon, very soon, there will be no need of secrecy or labor."

As she spoke, a shadow fell on Ruth's face, and in her voice there was a mournful cadence that touched Miss Barbara's heart.

So nothing more was said; and henceforth Ruth had many

hours to herself, for gradually Mr. Robert took her place beside his sister, reading to and amusing her so pleasantly that she declared she had never been so comfortable before.

Ruth saw and was very thankful for all this. She was doubly cheerful and industrious, performing every duty with a faithfulness that proved her gratitude, while her returning health and bloom wrought such a change that Mr. Robert felt repaid for any sacrifice of time or comfort he had made.

Still Miss Barbara pondered over the secret, often dropping hints that troubled Ruth. The servants watched and wondered, taking no pains to conceal their suspicions and distrust. But though tried and harassed by these things and the unknown sorrow that oppressed her, she still labored on and gently, uncomplainingly bore all.

"I haven't many weaknesses," began Miss Barbara (and to judge from her rigid figure and stern face, she was right), "but being a woman, I have my share of curiosity and naturally feel a strong desire to know what Ruth is about, for she grows more and more mysterious every week. Robert, do put down that paper and listen to me a moment, for I really think it is my duty to demand an explanation when things get to such a pass as this."

"As what?" asked her brother with more interest than she expected.

"Why, the sewing goes on more steadily than ever, and for the last three days she has come in from walking with such a weary, miserable face, I was really alarmed. But as she said nothing, I asked no questions and let her go on as she pleased, according to your advice; and now, here it is past ten o'clock and she is not in yet. I don't know what *you* call propriety, but such doings as this are not according to *my* notions of it," and the energetic nods of Miss Barbara's head expressed more than a torrent of words.

"Where can she be?" asked Mr. Robert anxiously.

"As I am not to ask questions, I can't inform you. She has very likely got into mischief and run away for want of proper looking after. She never can blame me for it, thank heaven."

The rigidity of Miss Barbara's attitude increased alarmingly as she spoke, for, having followed her brother's advice in leaving Ruth free, she now felt that whatever happened, all blame belonged to him, and determined he should have it.

"Come, come, sister Barbara," cried Mr. Robert pleasantly, "trust my judgment a little longer, and if I am deceived in this case, never follow my advice again. Ruth has been detained somewhere and will be back tomorrow to explain it. Have patience with her a little longer, for some real trouble must be weighing on her mind; and if she cannot confide in us, we have no right to reprove her while she performs all her duties so faithfully and well."

"Oh, I can wait as long as you please and say nothing, but I am not to be deceived. Now, ring for Jane and see that all is safe below, for I'm not going to wait any longer for young women who have so little regard for the proprieties of life."

And the old lady indignantly retired, venting her anger in chidings to Jane and remarks upon the falsehood of the world during her progress upstairs.

Mr. Robert stood a moment where she left him. Then, saying to himself, "She must be there," he threw on a cloak and said a few words to the servant, and as Miss Barbara's chamber door closed behind her, the house door opened to her brother.

Through street after street he went till, entering the poorer quarter of the city, he knocked at a small house and was admitted by a tidy old woman, who cried out in great astonishment, "Lord bless us, Mr. Norton, what on earth brought you here at this time o' night? Miss Barbara ain't ill again, I hope?"

"No, Betsy, all is right with her, but I want to know if Ruth, her young woman, is here," said Mr. Robert, glancing around the small room.

"Dear me, no, sir. And what's more, I don't know where she is. But don't be troubled. My Ben is with her, and he'll see she comes to no harm. If you'll sit down and listen a bit, I'll tell you how it is, for indeed I think you ought to know, so don't stop me as you did before."

Mr. Robert sat down and listened intently to the old woman's story.

"You see, sir, having worked for your sister so long, I take an interest in all concerning her, and so am anxious to tell you about the matter. The other day, you know, when coming here with my rent from Miss Barbara, Lord bless her, you heard the young woman's voice in the next room and were a deal surprised; but when I wanted to tell you about her, you desired me never to do it, not even to yourself, and so I haven't. Now I really ought to, for she needs help."

"Thank you for your obedience, Betsy. You may speak now, if I cannot assist her without. When did she first come here?" said the gentleman.

"The first I ever saw of her was months ago when she came about your sister's work and, happening to find out that I had a room to let, hired it, for a friend, she said. This friend was a poor lost creature, sir, worn out with trouble and sin, who looked half dead when she came but under the girl's care soon grew better. She had been handsome once and was ladylike and well behaved at first. She did a little plain work, but the girl paid her board and kept a kind of watch over her all the time, coming every day, rain or shine, to see that all was right. I soon knew why, for sitting here alone brooding over her troubles seemed to make the woman crazy-like; and then she drank and, wandering away again, was worse than before."

"And Ruth, what did she do?" said Mr. Robert, with such pity in his voice and look that the woman's unconsciously softened as she went on.

"Do, sir? She looked for the poor soul and brought her back as kindly as a lost child. I would not have taken her in, but the girl begged so hard, I hadn't the heart to refuse her.

"And so it has gone on all winter—the woman growing feebler and feebler, wandering away oftener and staying longer; the girl always finding and bringing her back, never blaming, never neglecting, always patient, kind, and faithful, wearing herself out with work and care till it quite breaks my heart to see her."

"Poor Ruth, poor little Ruth," sighed Mr. Robert softly to himself, adding aloud, "But Betsy, why did you never let us know? We could have done some good in a quiet way without disturbing her."

"Ah, sir, I did make bold to mention it; but the girl said it could not be and made me promise not to speak of it, for you were all so good to her, she could not ask for more. As for the woman, she fell into a dreadful passion when I said how glad Miss Barbara would be to make her comfortable."

"Strange pride in one so low. Ruth is too grateful for the little we have done."

"I don't understand it at all, sir. But I hope the girl won't come to harm, for she's a good young thing and I'd be glad to see her happy."

"Who is this woman she supports so secretly? Did she never tell you, Betsy?"

"No, sir, never. I didn't like to ask outright, though I tried to find out by talking of her sisters. But she said she had none, and when I hinted, was she an orphan? she gave a bitter sigh and said there were few sadder orphans than herself, so I can't make it out why she should be so fond and faithful to the miserable thing."

"But where is Ruth now? You have not told me, Betsy."

"She is out looking for the woman again, sir, who went off three days ago.

"I made the girl take my Ben with her, she looked so ill and weak, besides being too young and pretty to go about alone. Heaven knows where they'll find her, but Ruth will look till she does. I never saw such patience and such courage as this poor young thing has shown. Hark! There's Ben's knock, I declare."

Old Betsy hurried to the door and soon came back followed by a lad, who breathlessly told his errand—how they had found the woman in a miserable place, too ill to be brought home; how Ruth would stay, and had sent him home to get some comforts for the night.

"I'm going back to take care of her, for though she says she's not afraid, I know it's no place for her, with men playing cards on the one side and women fighting on the other. So hurry, Mother, for I must be off," said the boy, drawing his sleeve across his face.

"I shall go with you," said Mr. Robert, rising when the bundle was ready.

Down among the squalid lanes and alleys, where night was made hideous by evil sights and sounds, went the grave gentleman, saying often to himself, "What scenes for gentle little Ruth." His young guide ran on without pausing till he went in at a low, dark door.

The air was heavy with foul odors and filled with the discord of many voices. Drunken oaths and shrill cries sounded through the passages, and half-open doors showed many a wretched sight.

Quietly the two glided up till the boy stopped at a room whence a low moaning issued, broken by fierce exclamations and the murmuring of a gentle voice.

"Go in and ask her if Mr. Robert can be of any use," said the gentleman as they paused to listen. The lad soon came out, saying, "Come in, sir. She said no one could be more welcome than yourself."

The one dim candle burning in the squalid room showed little Ruth, pale and worn with her long search and anxious vigil, kneeling by a bed where lay a miserable woman raving in the fierce delirium of the fever fast hurrying her life away. Ruth's cloak was spread over her to conceal her ragged garments; Ruth's arms were folded about her, and Ruth's bosom pillowed the restless head as Mr. Robert entered. Before Ruth could speak to him, the woman rose up in her bed and, pushing away the black hair streaming around her haggard face, cried out fiercely as she waved him back:

"I know you! I know you! But why are you here? After making my life wretched, can you not let me die in peace?"

"Hush, dear, hush, it is a good, kind friend. Be calm and trust him as I do," whispered Ruth after one glance of grateful welcome as he came and stood beside her with no wonder or contempt in his mild face, only pity and an earnest wish to serve or comfort her.

The woman fixed her hollow eyes upon him, muttering with a bitter laugh, "I'll not believe it, for I know the face. It may look kind, but there's a cruel heart beneath, child," and she clutched Ruth's arm. "Remember, never trust a friend.

Looks are deceitful, words empty air, and promises made to be broken. Put faith in none of them. They are all false, all false."

"Lie down and let me bathe your poor hot head. There, try to sleep, dear. Oh, sir, what shall I do to ease and calm her?" Ruth asked, her white face looking up imploringly into the friendly one beside her.

"You must have a doctor instantly. I will find one while Ben brings his mother. Keep up a good heart, my child. I'll not be long away." And before she could thank him, Mr. Robert was gone.

When he returned, accompanied by a physician, the woman lay in a deep stupor. The doctor, after looking at her a few moments, whispered to the gentleman that the poor soul would soon be out of pain, and so departed with a few words to Ruth.

She scarcely heeded him, but holding the wasted hand fast in her own, said quietly, "Will she be better soon?"

"Yes, Ruth, very soon."

And then they sat together silently as hour after hour went by, watching the red fever-flush fade to ashy pallor, the restless limbs grow still, and the wild muttering sink to feeble breathing, growing fainter every hour.

"Ruth, where are you?"

"Here, dear, close beside you always."

"Where is the face, Ruth? I want to see it again," and the dying woman's dim eyes wandered eagerly about the room till they met Mr. Robert's pitying gaze.

"I see it, but it is younger, gentler than hers. There is no pride, no hatred there. This is a good, true face. Bring it to me, Ruth."

It came and, bending over her with no contempt for present degradation, no rebuke for past sin, and its benign compassion shining through the darkness of that hour, brought back a blessed gleam of faith and penitence to the poor soul lying there.

"Ruth," she whispered, "say some prayer for me. I am going now. God bless and reward you, good and faithful child, for I have been a bitter shame and sorrow to you all these years."

"Never that, ah, never that. How could it be, while I remembered what you were?" cried Ruth, and gathered the drooping head close to her bosom with such a rain of tender tears that every stain seemed washed away from that unhappy life.

And Mr. Robert, standing by the poor bed, repeated solemnly and reverently that best prayer for every human suffering or sin.

The dying woman listened silently, and when he ceased, they saw her try to fold her feeble hands, saying brokenly, "Forgive our sins as we forgive those who sin against us. That is a good prayer for us both, Barbara." And then, groping blindly for the faithful hand that had led her from many great temptations, upheld her in many trials, and did not shrink through the last sharp struggle, she went down into the valley of the shadow, clinging to it still.

"Quiet at last, and safe from a world that has few hearts like yours to take her in. Let that comfort you, dear Ruth," said Mr. Robert, as he laid the heavy burden from her arms upon the pillow.

"I cannot wish her back, and who, sir, should have taken her in if not I? She was my mother."

As Ruth spoke, she covered the dead face and laid her arm about the miserable figure, as if to shield it from even a cold look. And as she stood there, with no shame mingling with the sorrow shining in her quiet eyes, her friend felt the beauty and the strength of that pure love, which clung unaltered to the mournful wreck of womanhood and sanctified what it now was by the memory of what it had been.

He laid his hand on Ruth's bent head, repeating softly, "God bless and reward you, good and faithful child," and then left her alone while he gave Ben and his mother directions that all should be done as quietly and simply as Ruth would like it.

In the gray light of the morning, he took her home, listening to the story she confided to him and wondering more and more at the constancy and strength of the little creature leaning on his arm.

Miss Barbara asked no questions, but sat grimly silent

while her brother told her that Ruth had lost a friend and must be undisturbed. But when she saw Mr. Robert drive away next day with Ruth to the funeral, her pride was roused, and she resolved to punish the girl for her want of confidence and discover the secret kept carefully from her. And she kept her word.

Ruth's gratitude could find no vent in words when she saw the mournful figure she had left in the poor room now lying in old Betsy's home so changed and quiet that she scarce knew it. Kind hands had removed the rags and clothed it decently, had smoothed the wild hair and laid the tranquil face on its last pillow with no trace of past misery to grieve the one true heart that sorrowed over it, with no thought of the heavy burden death had removed from her young life.

So, not alone and comfortless as she had thought to be, but with the friendly old woman to console her and Mr. Robert to take kind thought for all her needs, little Ruth stood at her mother's grave with half the sorrow of the hour removed and, with the fervor of her innocent heart, prayed God to bless those who had been friends to her when she was most unhappy and alone.

The summer air stirred freshly in the room, and the sunshine flickered on Ruth's quiet face while the rustle of green leaves mingled pleasantly with her low voice as she read, "'Dear little Dorrit, you may love someone; and if it be so, tell me, my child, and I will try, with all the loving friendship and respect I feel for you, to do you lasting service.' Oh, if he had known, if he had known the sharpness of the pain he caused that patient heart in speaking thus."

"You are reading very badly, Ruth. Turn this way and go on louder," and Miss Barbara went on with her work while Ruth, steadying her voice, continued:

"'No, ah, no,' sighed little Dorrit with an air of quiet desolation that he remembered long afterward. But now he saw her clear, true eyes and the quickened bosom which would so freely have thrown itself before him to receive a wound directed at his breast, with the dying cry 'I love him!' and no suspicion of the truth dawned on his mind. The light of her domestic story made all dark to him!"

"Why, child, you are crying! What on earth is that for?" cried the old lady as the reader's voice faltered and failed.

"It is so sorrowful, and oh, so real to me," sobbed Ruth, forgetting for a moment what she said.

Miss Barbara sat looking at her for a moment with an angry thought rising in her mind, a thought that had haunted her before but which now took form and purpose, for with a sudden movement she leaned forward and, looking into the girl's eyes, said sternly, "Ruth, you love my brother."

There was no answer, for with her hands clasped before her face, Ruth sat silent while the wind fluttered idly to and fro the pages whose tender secret had revealed her own.

Miss Barbara's harsh voice broke the silence. "I have watched you for some time, never thinking to learn a thing like this, and have discovered something of your mystery; and I am sorry to find that the 'friend' for whom you have worked so hard was a creature whom no honest girl would for a moment countenance."

"Oh, speak gently of her. She was much sinned against. Leave her in peace," cried Ruth, always brave for others though so timid for herself.

"Well, let that pass. I'm glad it's all done with," continued the old lady. "While trying to discover one thing, I have learned another. This is very wrong in you, Ruth, very, after my indulgence and my brother's many kindnesses (ill-advised as I always said they were). He must never know this folly; therefore, for his sake and your own you must go away at once."

Ruth brushed away her tears and answered meekly, "I will go. But oh, Miss Barbara, believe me, I never meant to be ungrateful, never meant to disobey you even in thought. But I could not help it. He was so kind and I so very sorrowful and lonely. I never knew how much I had dared to love him till a little while ago. I struggled with it, but it was too strong to be put down. Then I felt that I must go away. But my heart clung so closely to this home, the only happy one I ever knew, that I have weakly lingered until now. Forgive me, and good-bye."

Ruth's face, so full of truth through all its innocent humility and grief, touched Miss Barbara, but believing it to be her duty, she went on more coldly than before lest some gentle word should betray the sympathy she felt.

"Go to old Betsy's till I can provide for you. It is best that you should be where nothing can betray your weakness to my brother. Good-bye, child, you have been very faithful to me, and I shall not forget you."

Ruth kissed the hand that motioned her away, and with one wistful look around the pleasant room, turned to leave it, saying half aloud, "I have been very happy here, and it seems hard to go."

"Where, Ruth?" and Mr. Robert took in both of his the trembling hands that were groping blindly for the door.

"To find another home, sir. Let me go," she faltered.

"No farther, for it is already found. *Here,* dear Ruth," and she was gathered closely, tenderly within his arms while, with a smile as genial as the sunshine, he looked down upon the little drooping figure, saying, "Lie lightly, confidently here, my child, for, knowing all, I gladly offer you the first place in my heart and home. Will you not take it, dearest Ruth?"

"Oh, sir, I am not fit. I could not fill it worthily. Remember what has passed, remember what I am," she humbly began, distrustful of herself in all her great bewilderment of joy.

"I do remember, and that memory makes you dearer still. The dying voice that blessed you, Ruth, unconsciously assured me that the good and faithful daughter would make a good and faithful wife. I heard your innocent confession and was glad to know I had the power to make you happy. But what is this? Do not leave me, Ruth."

She drew herself away, and the glow of timid joy faded from her face, leaving it resolute and pale, as she said steadily, "I cannot stand between you and your sister, sir. She has been kind to me, and I am very grateful."

"Then prove it by going away instantly, and Robert, don't

let your good nature make a fool of you," said Miss Barbara
sharply, angry and excited at the discovery of her brother's
love for Ruth.

Mr. Robert stood looking at her with no trace of anger in
his face, only reproach and pity, which strangely troubled her,
as he said gravely, "Sister Barbara, will you listen to me for a
few moments, and then if you still desire Ruth to go, I will not
oppose it."

Miss Barbara moved uneasily; but something in her
brother's eye compelled her to consent, and she sat listening
without a word while he went on.

"Thirty years ago two friends, both young, proud, and
beautiful, loved the same man. He chose the younger of the
two and privately married her. The elder, in her bitter disappointment, passionately vowed to be revenged for what she
called their falsehood, and she kept her word. For instead of
softening, she increased the anger of the young wife's father
till he cursed and disowned her and, dying, left his fortune to
a stranger.

"The unhappy pair disappeared, and then the creator of
their misery was left to a long and bitter repentance. She
never married, but led a solitary life and, locking her remorse
in her own bosom, sought by secret charities to expiate her
fault. Sickness and age came to her, softening her heart till it
longed to be forgiven. But the lost friend never came, and
never can again.

"After years of poverty and trouble, death took the husband and the children, leaving only one, the youngest of the
flock. And this young daughter clung to her through many trials and became the guardian angel of the mother's most unhappy life. Seeking for honest labor whereby to support
herself and her mother, the young girl came by chance to
the lonely woman's home and made it pleasant by her cheerful presence.

"Learning soon whose roof covered her, she would have
brought the alienated friends together, but a sadder shadow
than poverty had fallen on the injured one. Remembering the
cruel pride that had so wronged her, she would not listen to

her daughter's prayer, nor touch the money earned in the service of her enemy, as she still looked upon her.

"The daughter, taught by hard experience, feared to leave the safe home she had found, and hoping still to reunite them, she bore her secret sorrow bravely and labored patiently to guard and brighten the last hours of the life of that mother, who died praying to be forgiven as she forgave.

"Oh, sister Barbara, you may well bow down your head and ask pardon of this noble girl, for that false friend was *you;* that woman wrecked by your hand, the playmate of your youth; and that good daughter, little Ruth."

Miss Barbara had listened with a changing countenance, but as her brother ceased, she averted it and sat silent, though the white kerchief rose and fell upon her bosom, stirred by the emotion she was too proud to show.

Ruth came and knelt upon the cushion at her feet, whispering softly, "Shall I go away, or stay and be a loving child to you?"

Miss Barbara turned, and two great tears rolled down her faded cheeks as she drew the girl close to her, saying in a voice so changed and humble that it was musical with feeling: "God forgive me for a sinful, passionate old woman and make my age better than my youth. Stay, Ruth, and make my brother happy. He deserves you, my good child."

Ruth suddenly recalled Miss Barbara's angry words and rose up, saying sorrowfully, "I will not have him make my happiness at the cost of his own. No, I will be a faithful child to you both, and there shall be no sacrifice for me."

But Mr. Robert stood beside her with all his generous affection shining in his truthful face as he said seriously and tenderly, "Dear Ruth, I am not young and ardent, but in this heart of mine there is a love for you honest and true as man ever felt.

"It has grown up silently like your own and had its hopes and doubts and fears. See, Ruth, how fond and simple it has been. This little pansy, dropped long ago by you, has been cherished here because its sunny face seemed to look up from among these sad-colored leaves as yours looks through the cares and troubles of your life, my cheerful Ruth. Ah, you see, we grave and silent men have fancies foolish as a boy's, yet tender as a woman's. Will you not believe me now and let me give you the dear name of wife?"

And radiant with perfect confidence and joy, little Ruth went gladly home to the shelter of his love.

THE CROSS ON THE CHURCH TOWER

Up the dark stairs that led to his poor home strode a gloomy-faced young man with despair in his heart and these words on his lips: "I will struggle and suffer no longer. My last hope has failed, and life become a burden I will rid myself of at once."

As he muttered his stern purpose, he flung wide the door and was about to enter, but paused upon the threshold, for a glance told him that he had unconsciously passed his own apartment and come up higher till he found himself in a room poorer but more cheerful than his own.

Sunshine streamed in through the one small window, where a caged bird was blithely singing and a few flowers blossomed in the light. But blither than the bird's song and sweeter than the flowers were the little voice and wan face of a child who lay upon a bed placed where the warmest sunbeams fell.

The face turned smiling on the pillow, and the voice said pleasantly, "Come in, sir. Nell will soon be back if you will wait."

"I want nothing of Nell. Who is she? And who are you?" asked the intruder, pausing as he was about to go.

"Nell is my sister, sir, and I'm 'poor Jamie,' as they call me. But indeed I am not to be pitied, for I am a happy child, though it may not seem so."

"Why do you lie there? Are you sick?"

"No, I am not sick, though I shall never leave my bed

again. See, this is why." Folding back the covering, the child showed his little withered limbs.

"How long have you lain here, my poor boy?" asked the stranger, touched and interested in spite of himself.

"Three years, sir."

"And yet you are happy! What in heaven's name have you to render you contented, child?"

"Come sit beside me and I'll tell you, sir. That is, if you please. I should love to talk with you, for it's lonely here when Nell is gone."

Something in the child's winning voice and the influence of the cheerful room calmed the young man's troubled spirit and seemed to lighten his despair. He sat down at the bedside looking gloomily upon the child, who lay smiling placidly as with skillful hands he carved small figures from the bits of wood scattered around him on the coverlet.

"What have you to make you happy, Jamie? Tell me your secret, for I need the knowledge very much," said his new friend earnestly.

"First of all, I have dear Nell," said the child, his voice lingering lovingly upon the name. "She is so good, so very good to me. No one can tell how much we love each other. All day she sits beside my bed singing to ease my pain or reading while I work. She gives me flowers and birds and all the sunshine that comes in to us, and sits there in the shadow that I may be warm and glad. She waits on me all day, but when I wake at night, I always see her working busily and know it is for me, my good, kind Nell. Then I have my work, sir, to amuse me. And it helps a little too, for kind children always buy my toys when Nell tells them of the little boy who carved them lying here at home while they play out among the grass and flowers, where he can never be."

"What else, Jamie?" and the listener's face grew softer as the cheerful voice went on.

"I have my bird, sir, and my roses. I have books, and best of all, I have the cross on the old church tower. I can see it from my pillow, and it shines there all day long so bright and beautiful, while the white doves coo upon the roof below. I love it dearly."

The young man looked out through the narrow window and saw, rising high above the housetops, like a finger pointing heavenward, the old gray tower and the gleaming cross. The city's din was far below, and through the summer air the faint coo of the doves and the flutter of their wings came down like peaceful country sounds.

"Why do you love it, Jamie?" he asked, looking at the thoughtful face that lit up eagerly as the boy replied:

"Because it does me so much good, sir. Nell told me long ago about the blessed Jesus who bore so much for us, and I longed to be as like him as a little child could grow. So when my pain was very sharp, I looked up there and, thinking of the things He suffered, tried so hard to bear it that I often could. But sometimes, when it was too bad, instead of fretting Nell I'd cry softly, looking up there all the time and asking Him to help me be a patient child. I think He did, and now it seems so like a friend to me, I love it better every day. I watch the sun climb up along the roofs in the morning, creeping higher and higher till it shines upon the cross and turns it into gold. Then through the day I watch the sunshine fade away till all the red goes from the sky, and for a little while I cannot see it through the dark. But the moon comes, and I love it better then. For, lying awake through the long nights, I see the cross so high and bright with stars all shining around it, and I feel still and happy in my heart as when Nell sings to me in the twilight."

"But when there is no moon, or clouds hide it from you, what then, Jamie?" asked the young man, wondering if there were no clouds to darken the cheerful child's content.

"I wait till it is clear again, and feel that it is there, although I cannot see it, sir. I hope it never will be taken down, for the light upon the cross seems like that which I see in dear Nell's eyes when she holds me in her arms and calls me her 'patient Jamie.' She never knows I try to bear my troubles for her sake as she bears hunger and cold for mine. So you see, sir, how many things I have to make me a happy child."

"I would gladly lie down on your pillow to be half as light of heart as you are, little Jamie, for I have lost my faith in everything and with it all my happiness." The heavy shadow which had lifted for a while fell back darker than before upon the anxious face beside the bed.

"If I were well and strong like you, sir, I think I should be so thankful that nothing could trouble me." With a sigh the boy glanced at the vigorous frame and energetic countenance of his new friend, wondering at the despondent look he wore.

"If you were poor, so poor you had no means whereby to get a crust of bread nor a shelter for the night—if you were worn out with suffering and labor, soured by disappointment, and haunted by ambitious hopes never to be realized, what would you do, Jamie?" asked the young man suddenly, prompted by the desire that every human heart has felt for sympathy and counsel, even from the little creature before him, ignorant and inexperienced as he was.

But the child, wiser in his innocence than many an older counselor, pointed upward, saying with a look of perfect trust: "I should look up to the cross upon the tower and think of what Nell told me about God, who feeds the birds and clothes the flowers. And I should wait patiently, feeling sure He would remember me."

The young man leaned his head upon his folded arms, and nothing stirred in the still room but the wind that stole in through the roses to fan the placid face upon the pillow.

"Are you weary waiting for me, Jamie dear? I could not come before." As her eager voice broke the silence, sister Nell came hastening in.

The stranger, looking up, saw a young girl regarding him from Jamie's close embrace, with a face whose only beauty was the light her brother spoke of, which beamed warm and bright from her mild countenance and made the poor room poorer for its presence.

"This is Nell, my Nell, sir," cried the boy, "and she will thank you for your kindness in sitting here so long with me."

"I am the person who lodges just below you. I mistook this room for my own. Pardon me and let me come again, for

Jamie has already done me good," replied the stranger as he rose to go.

"Nell dear, will you bring me a cup of water?" Jamie said. As she hastened away, he beckoned his friend nearer, saying with a timid, wistful look: "Forgive me if it's wrong, but I wish you would let me give you this. It's very little, but it may help some. I think you'll take it to please 'poor Jamie.' Won't you, sir?" As he spoke, the child offered a bright coin, the proceeds of his work.

Tears sprang into the proud man's eyes. He held the little wasted hand fast in his own a moment, saying seriously, "I *will* take it, Jamie, as a loan wherewith to begin anew the life I was about to fling away as readily as I do this." With a quick motion he sent a vial whirling down into the street. "I'll try the world once more in a humbler spirit and have faith in *you* at least, my little Providence."

With an altered purpose in his heart and a brave smile on his lips, the young man went away, leaving the child with another happy memory, to watch the cross upon the old church tower.

It was midwinter, and in the gloomy house reigned suffering and want. Sister Nell worked steadily to earn the dear daily bread so many pray for and so many need. Jamie lay upon his bed, carving with feeble hands the toys which would have found far readier purchasers could they have told the touching story of the frail boy lying meekly in the shadow of the solemn change which daily drew more near.

He remained cheerful and patient; and poverty and pain seemed to have no power to darken his bright spirit, for God's blessed charity had gifted him with that inward strength and peace it so often brings to those who seem to human eyes most heavily afflicted.

Secret tears fell sometimes on his pillow and whispered prayers went up, but Nell never knew it. Like a ray of sunshine, the boy's tranquil presence lit up that poor home, and amid the darkest hours of their adversity, the little rushlight of his childish faith never wavered nor went out.

Below them dwelled the young man, no stranger now, but a true friend, whose generous pity would not let them suffer any want he could supply. Hunger and cold were hard teachers, but he learned their lessons bravely. Though his frame grew gaunt and his eye hollow, yet at heart he felt himself to be a better, happier man for the stern discipline that taught him the beauty of self-denial and the blessedness of loving his neighbor *better* than himself.

The child's influence remained unchanged, and when anxiety or disappointment burdened him, the young man sat at Jamie's bedside, listening to the boy's unconscious teaching and receiving fresh hope and courage from the childish words and the wan face, always cheerful and serene.

With this example constantly before him, he struggled on, feeling that if the world were cold and dark, he had within himself one true affection to warm and brighten his hard life.

"Give me joy, Jamie! Give me joy, Nell! The book sells well, and we shall yet be rich and famous," cried the young author as he burst into the quiet room one wintry night, with snowflakes glittering in his black locks and his face aglow with the keen air, which had no chill in it to him now.

Nell looked up to smile a glad welcome. Jamie tried to cry "hurrah," but the feeble voice faltered and failed. He could only wave his hand and cling fast to his friend, whispering brotherly:

"I'm glad, oh, very glad, for now you need not rob yourself for us. I know you have, Walter. I have seen it in your poor thin face and these old clothes. It never would have been so but for Nell and me."

"Hush, Jamie, and lie here upon my arm and rest, for you are very tired with your work—I know by this hot hand and shortened breath. Are you easy now? Then listen, for I've brave news to tell you; and never say again I do too much for you, the cause of my success."

"I, Walter?" cried the boy. "What do you mean?"

Looking down upon the wondering face uplifted to his own, the young man answered with deep feeling: "Six months ago I came into this room a desperate and despairing man, weary of life because I knew not how to use it, and eager to quit the struggle because I had not learned to conquer fortune by energy and patience. You kept me, Jamie, till the reckless mood was past, and by the beauty of your life, showed me what mine should be. Your courage shamed my cowardice; your faith rebuked my fears; your lot made my own seem bright again. I, a man with youth, health, and the world before him, was about to fling away the life which you, a helpless little child, made useful, good, and happy by the power of your own brave will. I felt how weak, how wicked I had been, and was not ashamed to learn of you the lesson you so unconsciously were teaching. God bless you, Jamie, for the work you did that day."

"Did I do so much?" asked the boy with innocent wonder. "I never knew it, and always thought you had grown happier and kinder because I had learned to love you more. I'm very glad if I did anything for you, who do so much for us. But tell me of the book; you never would before."

With a kindling eye Walter replied, "I would not tell you till all was sure. Now listen. I wrote a story, Jamie, a story of our lives, weaving in few fancies of my own and leaving you unchanged, the little counselor and good angel of the ambitious man's hard life. I painted no fictitious sorrows. What I had seen and keenly felt I could truly tell—your cheerful patience, Nell's faithful love, my struggles, hopes, and fears. This book, unlike the others, was not rejected, for the simple truth told by an earnest pen touched and interested. It was accepted and has been kindly welcomed, thanks to you, Jamie, for many buy it to learn more of you and weep and smile over artless words of yours and forget their pity in their reverence and love for the child who taught the man to be not what he is, but what with God's help he will yet become."

"They are very kind, and so are you, Walter. I shall be proud to have you rich and great—though I may not be here to see it."

"You will, Jamie—you must, for it will be nothing without you." As he spoke, the young man held the thin hand closer in his own and looked more tenderly into the face upon his arm.

The boy's eyes shone with a feverish light, a scarlet color burned on his hollow cheek, and the breath came slowly from his pouted lips. But over his whole countenance there lay a beautiful serenity, which filled his friend with hope and fear.

"Walter, bid Nell put away that tiresome work. She has sat at it all day long, never stirring but to wait on me." As he spoke, a troubled look flitted across the boy's calm face.

"I shall soon be done, Jamie," said Nell. "I must not think of rest till then, for there is neither food nor fuel for the morrow. Sleep yourself, dear, and dream of pleasant things. I am not very tired." And she bent closer to her work, trying to sing a little song, that they might not guess how near the tears were to her aching eyes.

From beneath his pillow Jamie drew a bit of bread, whispering to his friend as he displayed it: "Give it to Nell. I saved it for her till you came, for she will not take it from me and she has eaten nothing all this day."

"And you, Jamie?" asked Walter, struck by the sharpened features of the boy and the hungry look which for a moment glistened in his eye.

"I don't need much, you know, for I don't work like Nell. But yet she gives me all. Oh, how can I bear to see her working so hard for me and I lying idle here!"

As he spoke, Jamie clasped his hands before his face, and through his slender fingers streamed such tears as children seldom shed.

It was so rare a thing for him to weep that it filled Walter with dismay and a keener sense of his own powerlessness. He could bear any privation for himself alone, but he could not see them suffer. He had nothing to offer them, for though there was seeming wealth in store for him, he was now miserably poor. He stood for a moment looking from brother to sister—both so dear to him and both so plainly showing how hard a struggle life had been to them.

With a bitter exclamation the young man turned away and went out into the night, muttering to himself, "They shall not suffer—I will beg or steal first!"

And with some vague purpose stirring within him, he went

swiftly on until he reached a great thoroughfare, nearly deserted now, but echoing occasionally to a quick step as someone hurried home to his warm fireside.

"A little money, sir, for a sick child and a starving woman," and with outstretched hand Walter arrested an old man. But the latter only wrapped his furs still closer and passed on, saying sternly:

"I have nothing for vagrants. Go to work, young man."

A woman poorly clad in widow's weeds passed at that moment, and as the beggar fell back from the rich man's path, she dropped a bit of silver in his hand, saying with true womanly compassion: "Heaven help you! It is all I have to give."

"I'll beg no more," muttered Walter as he turned away, burning with shame and indignation. "I'll *take* from the rich what the poor so freely *give*, God pardon me. I see no other way, and they must not starve."

With a vague sense of guilt already upon him, he stole into a less frequented street and slunk into the shadow of a doorway to wait for coming steps and nerve himself for his first evil deed.

Glancing up to chide the moonlight for betraying him, he started—for there above the snow-clad roofs rose the cross upon the tower. Hastily he averted his eyes, as if they had rested on the mild, reproachful countenance of a friend.

Far up in the deep wintry sky the bright symbol shone, and from it seemed to fall a radiance warmer than the moonlight, clearer than the starlight, showing to that tempted heart the darkness of the yet uncommitted wrong.

That familiar sight recalled the past. He thought of Jamie and seemed to hear again the childish words uttered long ago, "God will remember us."

Steps came and went along the lonely street. The dark figure in the shadow never stirred, but only stood there with bent head, accepting the silent rebuke that shone down upon it and murmuring softly, "God, remember little Jamie and forgive me that my love for him led me astray."

As Walter raised his hand to dash away the drops that rose at the memory of the boy, his eyes fell on the simple ring he always wore for his dead mother's sake. He had hoped to see it one day on Nell's hand, but now a generous thought banished all others. With the energy of an honest purpose, he hastened to sell the ring and purchase a little food and fuel, and borrowing a warm covering of a kindly neighbor, he went back to dispense these comforts with a satisfaction he had little thought to feel.

The one lamp burned low, a few dying embers lay upon the hearth, and no sound broke the silence but the steady rustle of Nell's needle and the echo of Jamie's hollow cough.

"Wrap it around Nell. She has given me her cloak and needs it more than I. These coverings do very well." As he spoke, Jamie put away the blanket Walter offered, and suppressing a shiver, hid his purple hands beneath the old, thin cloak.

"Here is bread, Jamie. Eat, for heaven's sake. No need to save it now." Walter pressed it on the boy, but he only took a little, saying he had not much need of food and loved to see them eat far better.

So in the cheery blaze of the rekindled fire, Nell and Walter broke their long fast, and never saw how eagerly Jamie gathered up the scattered crumbs, nor heard him murmur softly as he watched them with loving eyes: "There will be no cold nor hunger up in heaven, but enough for all, enough for all."

"Walter, you'll be kind to Nell when I am not here?" he whispered earnestly as his friend came to draw his bed within the ruddy circle of the firelight gleaming on the floor.

"I will, Jamie, kinder than a brother" was the quick reply. "But why ask me that with such a wistful face?"

The boy did not answer, but turned on his pillow and kissed Nell's shadow as it flitted by.

Gray dawn was in the sky before they spoke again. Nell slept the deep, dreamless sleep of utter weariness, her head pillowed on her arms. Walter sat beside the bed, lost in sweet and bitter musings, silent and motionless, fancying the boy slept. But a low voice broke the silence, whispering feebly:

"Walter, will you take me in your strong arms and lay me

on my little couch beside the window? I should love to see the cross again, and it is nearly day."

So light, so very light the burden seemed, Walter turned his face aside lest the boy should see the sorrowful emotion painted there. With a close embrace he laid him tenderly down to watch the first ray climbing up the old gray tower.

"The frost lies so thickly on the windowpanes that you cannot see it even when the light comes, Jamie," said his friend, vainly trying to gratify the boy's wish.

"The sun will melt it soon, and I can wait. I can wait, Walter. It's but a little while." Jamie, with a patient smile, turned his face to the dim window and lay silent.

Higher and higher crept the sunshine till it shone through the frostwork, on the boy's bright head. His bird awoke and caroled blithely, but he never stirred.

"Asleep at last, poor, timid little Jamie. I'll not wake him till the day is warmer." Walter, folding the coverings closer over the quiet figure, sat beside it waiting till it should awake.

"Jamie dear, look up and see how beautifully your last rose has blossomed in the night, when least we looked for it," said sister Nell as she came smiling in with the one white rose, so fragrant but so frail.

Jamie did not turn to greet her; for all frost had melted from the boy's life now, another flower had bloomed in the early dawn, and though the patient face upon the pillow was bathed in sunshine, little Jamie was not there to see it gleaming on the cross. God had remembered him.

Spring showers had made the small mound green and scattered flowers in the churchyard. Sister Nell sat in the silent room alone, working still, but pausing often to wipe away the tears that fell upon a letter on her knee.

Steps came springing up the narrow stairs, and Walter entered with a beaming face to show the first rich earnings of his pen and ask her to rest from her long labor in the shelter of his love.

"Dear Nell, what troubles you? Let me share your sorrow and try to lighten it," he cried with anxious tenderness, sitting beside her on the little couch where Jamie fell asleep.

In the frank face smiling on her, Nell's innocent eyes read nothing but the friendly interest of a brother, and remembering his watchful care and kindness, she forgot her womanly timidity in her great longing for sympathy and feeling, and freely told him all.

She told him of the lover she left years ago to cling to Jamie and how this lover went across the sea, hoping to increase his little fortune that the helpless brother might be sheltered for love of the sister. How misfortune followed him, and when she looked to welcome back a prosperous man, there came a letter saying that all was lost and he must begin the world anew and win a home to offer her before he claimed the heart so faithful to him all these years.

"He writes so tenderly and bears his disappointment bravely for my sake, but it is very hard to see our happiness deferred again when such a little sum would give us to each other."

As she ceased, Nell looked for comfort into the countenance of her companion, never seeing through her tears how pale it was with sudden grief, how stern with repressed emotion. She only saw the friend whom Jamie loved, and that tie drew her toward him as to an elder brother to whom she turned for help, unconscious then of how great his own need was.

"I never knew of this before, Nell. You kept your secret well," he said, trying to seem unchanged.

The color deepened in Nell's cheek, but she answered simply, "I never spoke of it, for words could do no good. Jamie grieved silently about it, for he thought it a great sacrifice, though I looked on it as a sacred duty. He often wearied himself to show in many loving ways how freshly he remembered it. My grateful little Jamie." And Nell's eyes wandered to the green treetops tossing in the winds, whose shadows flickered pleasantly above the child.

"Let me think a little, Nell, before I counsel you. Keep up a good heart and rest assured that I will help you—if I can," said Walter, trying to speak hopefully.

"But you came to tell me something; at least I fancied I saw some good tidings in your face just now. Forgive my selfish grief, and see how gladly I will sympathize with any joy of yours."

"It is nothing, Nell. Another time will do as well," he answered, eager to be gone lest he should betray what must be kept most closely now.

"It never will be told, Nell. Never in this world," he sighed bitterly as he went back to his own room, which never in his darkest hours had seemed so dreary, for now the bright hope of his life was gone.

"I have it in my power to make them happy," he mused as he sat alone, "but I cannot do it, for in this separation lies my only hope. He may die or may grow weary, and then to whom will Nell turn for comfort but to me? I will work on, earn riches and a name, and if that hour should come, then in her desolation I will offer all to Nell and surely she will listen and accept.

"But yet it were a generous thing to make her happiness at once, forgetful of my own. How shall I bear to see her waiting patiently while youth and hope are fading slowly, and know that I might end her weary trial and join two faithful hearts? Oh, Jamie, I wish to heaven I were asleep with you, freed from the temptations that beset me. It is so easy to perceive the right—so hard to do it."

The sound of that familiar name, uttered despairingly aloud, fell with a sweet and solemn music upon Walter's ear. A flood of tender memories swept away the present and brought back the past—the thought of that short life so full of pain and yet of patience, of the sunny nature which no cloud could overshadow, and the simple trust which was its strength and guide.

He thought of that last night and saw now with clearer eyes the sacrifices and the trials silently borne for love of Nell.

The beautiful example of the child rebuked the passion of the man and through the magic of affection strengthened generous impulses and banished selfish hopes.

"I promised to be kind to Nell, and with God's help I will keep my vow. Teach me to bear my pain, to look for help where you found it, little Jamie." As he spoke, the young man gazed up at the shining cross, striving to see in it not merely an object of the dead boy's love, but a symbol of consolation, hope, and faith.

These words came to Walter's mind and fixed the resolution wavering there, and as his glance wandered from the gray tower to the churchyard full of summer stillness, he said within himself, "This is the hardest struggle of my life, but I will conquer and come out from the conflict master of myself at least. Like Jamie, I will try to wait until the sunshine comes again, even if it only shines upon me when dead, like him."

It was no light task to leave the airy castles built by love and hope and go back cheerfully to the solitude of a life whose only happiness for a time was in the memory of the past.

Thus, through the weeks that bore one lover home, the other struggled to subdue his passion, and he was as generous in his sorrow as he would have been in his joy.

It was no easy conquest, but he won that hardest of all victories—that of self—and found in the place of banished pride and bitterness a patient strength and the one desire to be indeed more generous than a brother to gentle Nell. He had truly "cleft his heart in twain and flung away the baser part."

A few days before the absent lover was to come, Walter went to Nell, and with a countenance whose pale serenity touched her deeply, he laid his gift before her, saying, "I owe this all to Jamie, and the best use I can make of it is to secure your happiness, as I promised him I'd try to do. Take it and God bless you, sister Nell."

"And you, Walter, what will your future be if I take this and go away to enjoy it, as you would have me?" Nell asked with an earnestness that awoke his wonder.

"I shall work, Nell, and in that find content and consolation for the loss of you and Jamie. Do not think of me. This money will do me far more good in your hands than my own. Believe me, it is best to be so; therefore, do not hesitate."

Nell took it; for she had learned the cause of Walter's restless wanderings and strange avoidance of her of late, and she judged wisely that the generous nature should be gratified and the hard-won victory rewarded by the full accomplishment of its unselfish end. Few words expressed her joyful thanks, but from that time Walter felt that he held as dear a place as Jamie in her grateful heart, and was content.

Summer flowers were blooming when Nell went from the old home a happy wife, leaving her faithful friend alone in the little room where Jamie lived and died.

Years came and went, and Walter's pen had won for him an honored name. Poverty and care were no longer his companions. Many homes were open to him, many hearts would gladly welcome him; but he still dwelled in the gloomy house a serious, solitary man, for his heart lay beneath the daisies of a child's grave.

But his life was rich in noble aims and charitable deeds, and thus, with his strong nature softened by the sharp discipline of sorrow and sweetened by the presence of a generous love, he was content to dwell with the memory of little Jamie in the shadow of the cross upon the tower.

AGATHA'S CONFESSION

I was poor and plain, with no accomplishments or charms of mind or person, and yet Philip loved me. Years of care and labor had banished all my girlish dreams. I never thought to be beloved, but tried to stifle my great yearning for affection. So when the knowledge came to me that I was dear to a human heart, it was like a magic spell changing the cold, solitary girl into a fond and hopeful woman. Life grew bright and beautiful. The sad past seemed to vanish, lost in the blissful present.

Philip loved me—and I was rich in my poverty. He found a charm in my plain face, and I envied no woman's beauty. I possessed the art of pleasing him and I desired no other accomplishment. He asked for "a little love," and I freely, gladly gave him the affection treasured up so long, waiting but a word to bid it gush forth strong and deep, bringing bloom and verdure to the lonely pathway of my life.

Philip was generous, ardent, and impulsive. He began by pitying and indeed by loving me, truly I hope, tenderly I know. And I was bound up heart and soul in this one passion coming to me like a radiant spring day in the midst of winter. I fed and cherished it until it became the ruling power of my heart, swaying me to good or ill.

I had one friend (or thought I had, may God forgive her the sin and misery she caused me) who possessed all that I lacked: youth, beauty, wealth, and those fresh charms that make a woman lovely in the eyes of men. I had not known her long, but loved and trusted her entirely, grateful that she turned from gayer friends to sympathize with me.

Philip admired her; and I was glad to see it, for, thinking his heart all my own, I neither feared nor envied Clara's beauty. So blinded, my happiness I enjoyed serenely with these two friends, whose truth I never dreamed of doubting till a sudden light flashed on me when most tranquil and secure.

A single look betrayed it all. I could not be deceived, for, knowing every change of Philip's face, I read it plainly as an open book. When I saw a tender glance like that which he first bestowed on me resting long and earnestly on Clara, I felt with a bitter pang that beauty might be more to him than love.

They could not see the sudden grief that fell on me as I watched them with eyes now keen as they were lately blind. They could not know how plainly I was reading in their faces the dawning consciousness that chased the color from my own, nor how clearly I detected the secret sympathy that gave such music to their voices as they sang.

They stood together, both beautiful and gay, in the flood of light that shone down from the shaded lamps. Dark and plain and sad, I sat apart in the twilight shadows, struggling silently to find some outlet from the maze of doubts and fears that filled my heart and brain.

I wanted to be generous and just, to forget self and think of Philip's happiness alone. But my great love rose up so importunate and strong, I could only listen to its pleading and cling fast to the old hope and faith, though both were broken reeds, I knew.

I watched and waited many days, trying to seem unchanged. But the veil had fallen from my eyes, and the blessed calm was gone that for a little while had brooded over me. Ah, what a little while it seemed! I saw the cloud coming nearer and nearer which should overshadow me and leave them in the sunshine I had lost.

At last, feeling that concealment was ungenerous and unwise, I went to Philip, saying calmly, though my heart was nearly broken by the sacrifice I tried to make: "Philip, if I have lost your affection, give me at least your confidence. If you love Clara, do not hide it from me, and I will break the tie that has become an irksome fetter, and henceforth try to find my happiness in making yours."

This touched him deeply, as I knew it would. He drew me fondly to him, saying half gaily and half sorrowfully while his frank eyes looked down into mine:

"I am but fascinated by her beauty, little friend. But tell her to be less lovely and less kind; it will be better for us both. Indeed I do not love her; so forget your fears, and believe me, I would give a hundred charming Claras for my one truehearted Agatha."

"But, Philip, a time may come when you may regret your generous pity for the poor, plain girl who would not be a burden, though she has no one else to love. Promise me that if such a time should come, you will freely, frankly tell me so. I could bear anything from you but falsehood or deceit."

"I promise, Agatha, so be your happy self again and prophesy no further evil, for it saddens me to see you look so grave and pale."

And so it rested for a while, and I saw with pride how earnestly my lover tried to keep steadfast in his faith to me, how studiously he shunned the fair face that always smiled on him, and how sorely his heart was tried by the divided passion that had found an entrance there.

Clara saw this too, and her vanity urged her to greater efforts to secure the love of one whose admiration had become so dear to her.

She had been my friend. But when I saw the evil nature hitherto concealed, which now prompted her to wrong and torture me by luring away the one heart I prized, she then became my enemy, and I watched keenly to defeat her cruel purpose. She was my guest, and I could not send her from the home whose peace she was destroying; so I waited patiently, hoping all would yet be well.

But at length I could no longer bear it. Philip was changed to me, and slowly I saw my happiness departing. Then my pride gave way, and I went humbly to my rival, beseeching her to give me back the one joy of my life, crying to her:

"You have beauty, youth, and many hearts to gladden you. I have nothing but Philip's love. Be generous and do not rob me of the only treasure I possess. You have the power to take him from me. Oh, be just and do not use it to my sorrow."

Clara listened with a scornful smile and chided me for a jealous child, saying coldly, "I want nothing of you. Why should I envy your one lover when I have the power to gain so many for myself? I do but try my charms on him, that they may not be wasted in this quiet place, and if he is weak enough to forget you for a smile, why, never heed it—he's not worth your tears."

"Oh? Clara, heartless as beautiful, how can you jest thus with my trouble? Be kind and go away before it is too late. Philip does not love you yet, but he will. I see it coming on him. Spare us this grief, and prove yourself the friend I thought you by leaving me, unclouded, the only happiness I possess."

I repented my hasty words as soon as uttered, for an evil light shone in Clara's eyes and an exulting smile flitted across her face. But she grew kinder, and promising to be and do all I desired, she left me with that strange smile on her lips.

As she went out, Philip came from the dark nook where he had sat unseen, and with a look of shame and half-remorseful sorrow, said to me, "Agatha, the time you once foretold is coming. I do not love you less, but that siren charms me as a serpent charms a bird, and robs me of the will and power to resist. I do not love her, but her image haunts me night and day and makes me miserable. I have kept my word to you, but I am impetuous and weak and may in some unguarded moment say to Clara what would wrong us both, pledged as we are. Help me, Agatha, to cast off this unhappy spell and make me worthy of your generous love again."

I read in his anxious face and eager words how earnest his desire was, and that gave me courage to say bravely, "Flee temptation, Philip. Leave the spot where we have been so happy before a rash word mars your future peace. Freed from the presence that enthralls you, this delusion will pass by, and we may yet be happier for the cloud that dimmed our sunshine for a little while."

Philip went, and peace came back to me, for he wrote cheeringly. The spell seemed broken, and I looked to welcome him again, tender and true as of old, when Clara should be gone.

A gradual change had fallen on her since Philip's departure. She was more gentle and confiding than before and seemed trying to banish from my mind all recollection of the past. But my distrust, once roused, never slept. I endeavored to be friendly; but I watched her steadily, for I felt that she would work me harm if any chance should offer; and my vague suspicions were not false.

Clara was not charitable, with all her wealth, and when she suddenly began to visit the poor cottages about the town and talked much of the suffering there which she should relieve, I was not blinded by it. I watched closer still to learn the hidden cause of this unusual benevolence, but waited long in vain.

She went and came with unflagging interest and seemed to find a marvelous content in doing it. As she passed smiling to and fro, many called her "the good angel of the poor" and blessed her "beautiful, bright face." This mystery perplexed me long, but I discovered it at last.

One miserable home she visited assiduously, and one day, despite her evident reluctance, I went with her. The mother of the family lay ill, and while Clara talked with her, I tossed the rosy baby to and fro before the little glass upon the wall. And as I did so, I saw plainly in the narrow mirror the woman give a letter to Clara, who concealed it with a warning glance toward me.

The child crowed and leaped unheeded after that, for my mind was filled with swift conjectures, whose truth or falsehood I resolved to know, urged by the sense of coming harm which haunted me continually.

That night, leaving me with a fond caress, Clara, complaining of fatigue, went early to her room. I followed several hours later. The night was chilly, and I was about to close my window when a light from Clara's nearby caught my eye. To steal noiselessly along the balcony and peer in through the vines and half-transparent curtains was a moment's work.

Her casement was open, and heedless of the night air, she sat near it, bending over her writing table with a flush on her cheek and the same exultant light in her eye that I so well remembered.

I had not watched her long when her maid's voice from her dressing room disturbed her. She rose with an impatient gesture and went to give her orders.

Quick as thought, I put aside the curtain, caught up the paper she had left, and read "Dearest Philip," my eyes at the same moment recognizing his handwriting on several of the half-open letters scattered on the table.

I laid the paper back and with a strange, stern calmness stood without, looking steadily at the fair, false friend who sat within, smiling at my blindness as she wrote tenderly to the man I loved as my own soul.

For a long hour I watched her, heedless of the cold wind sighing around me or the rain that fell unheeded on my uncovered head.

When Clara slept, I stole into her room, took the keys from her hiding place, opened her desk, and read every letter there. Then I went back to my sleepless bed to realize the great sorrow that had come to me.

From these letters (Philip's and copies of her own) I learned how she had first written to him on some slight pretext and so had slowly but surely led him on till, under the guise of friendship, she had won a rash avowal from him, thereby gratifying her pique and wounded vanity. I learned how she had told him I was happy in his absence, never speaking of him, never listening to her repeated entreaties for his recall, saying that I loved to show my power and was proud of the entire control I possessed over him. Skillfully, artfully she had worked upon his pride and temper, wronging me by every means she dared to use, overcoming his honorable scruples, silencing his self-reproaches, and mingling her falsehoods with such pity, sympathy, and timid, half-confessed affection that I could not wonder that Philip, ardent and impetuous as he was, should be deceived and taught to look on me as the hard, coldhearted girl my false friend painted me.

I had no power to tell my feelings in sweet words or even mute caresses, as she could. One glance from her beautiful eyes spoke volumes, while I could only *feel*, deeply and warmly, but in silence; ready to give my life for the one I loved, but powerless to tell that love in words. Thus, beneath my calm exterior my passion burned, a hidden fire to warm and brighten or to consume my life.

Philip's letters won my pity, but little of my contempt. He had not yielded without a struggle. I knew he did not really love her, for his last letter was full of remorse for his deceit toward me and regret that he had ever seen the fair face that had robbed him of his peace and self-respect.

I forgave and loved him faithfully as ever, for I thought him more sinned against than sinning. But such a hatred and contempt for Clara sprang up within me that I trembled lest it should lead me to some sudden act of retribution to be repented of hereafter.

I rose the next day with the firm resolve to save Philip and unmask my treacherous friend. Secretly, as they had wronged me, would I seek to right myself. The means I left to time and my own watchful mind.

"Susan tells me the fever is spreading among the poor of the village, so be careful how you and Clara visit them, for it is a dangerous and malignant disease," said my invalid old aunt, as I sat in her chamber a few days later.

There was nothing in the words to startle me. But I trembled and grew pale, for a black thought rose up in my mind and, like a demon, tempted me.

Clara would go to receive the answer to her letter at the sick woman's cottage. Doubtless the fever was already there; she might take it and then— Such a host of conflicting thoughts surged in my brain that for a while nothing was clear, but out of that confusion rose the wish that she were dead and Philip all my own again. I would not tell her of the danger she was in, but let her go and come till the blight fell on her, cutting short her life and treachery together. I had little fear for myself, for I was strong and healthful. But she, so delicate and frail, would scarcely struggle through a pestilence like that.

I sat and thought of these things till my temples throbbed and my heart beat quick with the guilty purpose stirring in it, for it seemed almost right and just to be revenged on her for the cruel wrong she had so deliberately done me.

Suddenly, as my eyes roved restlessly to and fro, they fell on Clara's figure passing down the green lane to the town. I knew her errand and watched her gliding away, looking lovelier than ever, with an expectant glow upon her cheek and a mocking laugh as she looked back at me and then went on, rejoicing in her conquest of my Philip.

That name, as I muttered it, seemed to wake my better self. Forgetting my hatred in my love, I put away the thoughts that made me so unworthy of it, and darting after Clara, told her of the danger she incurred and bade her go into the town no more. A look of sudden shame flashed across her face as I spoke, and with a shudder she turned back, thanking me warmly for my timely warning.

But it was given too late. She had been often to the cottage filled with the contagion, and a week from that night I watched beside her, listening to her incoherent ravings, thanking God that I had not yielded to the strong temptation and that if she died, it would not be through me.

For many days the fever raged, then left her wasted to a shadow and feeble as a child. I nursed her faithfully, trying to stifle my sinful regrets when told that she would live. Her white face haunted me and her feeble voice was a hateful sound. I could have forgiven her if any sign of penitence or sorrow had escaped her. But the utter falseness of her nature hardened my heart against her and left no room for any softer feeling than contempt.

Philip seldom wrote now, and knowing the cause, I as seldom answered his brief letters. I could not deceive him, and so waited till I could put an end to his struggle and my own.

I watched if any note or message from him came to Clara. But her maid was wary, and I discovered nothing till one night, as I lay apparently asleep in the deep cushioned chair in Clara's room, I saw her draw a paper from beneath her pillow, read it, kiss it, and then, concealing it, sink quietly to sleep, little dreaming whose eyes were on her.

I skillfully possessed myself of the letter, and found it, as I thought, from Philip, tenderer than any yet had been. I thrust it back into her bosom as if a serpent had stung me, and sitting in that silent room, brooded darkly over my unhappy fate till no sin or sacrifice seemed too great if it but won me back all I had lost.

As I sat thus gazing gloomily on Clara's sleeping face and wishing I had the power to blight its fatal beauty, a sudden gust of air from the half-opened window wafted the muslin drapery of her bed across the night lamp burning near. I should have risen and closed the window, but an evil spell seemed set upon me. I sat unmoved, watching with fascinated eyes the white curtains floating nearer and nearer to the dangerous lamp.

Clara lay in a deep sleep, the house was still, and solemnly across the moonlit meadows came the deep tones of the village clock tolling one. I heard the rustle of the rising breeze, saw the quickened sweep of the light drapery, but neither spoke nor stirred. A dreadful calm possessed me, and when a sudden blaze lit up the room, I only smiled—an awful smile—I saw it in the mirror and was afraid of my own countenance.

The flames shot up brighter and hotter as the woodwork caught, and Clara sprang up suddenly, stretching her arms through the smoke and crying wildly, "Philip, save me! Save me!"

Philip could not answer her, but he saved *me,* for the sound of his name now broke the evil spell that bound me, as it had done before. I tore Clara from the burning bed and fought the flames till they were conquered, finding a fierce delight in the excitement and the danger.

But when Clara lay asleep again, under the effects of a soothing potion, and the frightened servants were sent wondering to bed, then I felt as weak and helpless as a child.

Burdened with the weight of the crime so nearly committed and conscious of the power my unhappy love possessed to lead me into evil, I cried within myself, "This must end. I will lead this dreadful life no longer, for it is ruining me, body and soul. Philip must decide between us, and the struggle cease."

I looked at Clara, marked each grace of form and feature with a careful eye, and then scanned my own face in the mirror steadily, hoping to find some little charm, some single trace of power or intellect, to oppose against my rival's beauty. But there looked back at me a countenance so haggard, dark, and wild, I hardly knew it for my own. It had been calm and gentle once, but now it had grown stern and gloomy with the conflict at my heart. With a heavy sigh I turned away, feeling that it was no face to please a lover like my Philip.

I flung myself upon the floor and there wrestled with myself through that long night. Pride and hate were both subdued by my remorse. But my love would not be silenced, and it seemed hard, very hard, that the affection which had been the light and blessing of my life should now become its heaviest sorrow.

In the gray dawn I wrote to Philip, bidding him come home, simply telling him that I knew all and could forgive it if he would be true now to himself and end all doubt and misery at once. I sent the letter, told Clara what I had done, and besought her to make Philip's happiness if she truly loved him, for I had no claim upon him now.

She seemed surprised at my frankness, but not humbled at the discovery of her own treachery, called me "a romantic child," and said she would "see what could be done for Philip."

Her heartless words were daggers to me, but I bore it silently, longing day and night for Philip to arrive and have all over and past doubt.

Clara grew anxious and restless as the hour for his return drew near. She was still wan and feeble, but she rouged her white cheeks and made a careful toilette, that his eye should discover no loss of that beauty which had won him.

I never thought of my apparel nor my altered face; *I* had no lover to please now, no tender hopes and joys to flush my cheek and light my eye; *I* had nothing but an aching heart and a blank future lying drearily before me.

"He is coming, Clara! I know his step along the garden path. Are you asleep or faint?" I cried as, turning, I saw her lying in her deep chair with half-closed eyes and a look of pain upon her face.

"No, I am only weary with waiting. Bring him to me quickly, Agatha." She rose up in her old stately attitude, with flashing eyes and a proud smile on her lips.

"Philip," I said, detaining him as he came in, with an expression of mingled joy and shame flushing his handsome face. "Philip, let me say a few words first, for once with Clara, you will forget all else. I release you from the tie that has become a fetter. I want a free heart or none. Choose for yourself Beauty or Love. One word more, and I try to say it in a gentle spirit. Let me warn you that a false friend will not make a truehearted wife. Now, go and let it soon be over."

He faltered, looked down at me with a searching glance, but I stood resolute and calm, unable to express my sorrow as I had been to express my love, but feeling both the deeper for that very cause. He could not read my tortured heart, and thought me cold and unfeeling, for with a few hurried words of gratitude and regret, he bade me lead him in to Clara.

She did not rise as we approached, but sat in the crimson shadow of the curtains with a strange look in her eyes, which never moved as Philip took her hand.

"Agatha, what is this? She is cold as ice," he cried, looking at me with a startled face. I put away the curtains—and there, in the full glare of the summer sun, she sat with false bloom on her hollow cheek, a glassy stare in her half-open eyes, and not a breath to stir the lace upon her bosom. She was dead.

I had longed for this, even prayed that one of us might die, and had hoped to see her taken from my path. But now, when in one swift moment my wicked prayer was granted, I repented of it and almost wished her back again.

Philip seemed bewildered by the strange and sudden check his infatuation had received. The spell seemed broken, for when the first terror and surprise were over, he never spoke of her and seemed to wake from his short dream his old kind, tender self. I uttered no reproach, but by every silent means in my power showed how gladly I welcomed back the love, not lost but led astray.

The physician seemed but little surprised at Clara's sudden death, saying he had feared it, she being so frail and the disease hereditary. So when all restoratives had been tried in vain, we laid her, beautiful and still as a marble image, in her last narrow bed, and her friends came from their distant homes to carry her back to the only one now left her on the earth.

"Rest in peace, Clara. I forgive you now as I hope to be forgiven my own sins," I said softly to myself as, standing alone beside the coffin, I looked down upon the quiet face so powerless to harm me now. As I spoke, I bent to put away a lock of hair that had fallen on her cheek. In doing so, my hand touched her forehead, and a strange, quick thrill shot through me, for it was *damp*.

I put my hand to her heart. Her pulse and lips were still. I touched her brow again, but my hand had wiped the slight dew from it and it felt cold as ice.

I stood white and still as herself for a few moments while the old struggle raged in my breast fiercer than before.

Fear whispered that she was not dead—Pity pleaded for her lying helplessly before me—and Conscience sternly bade me do the right, forgetful of all else. But I would not listen, for Love cried out passionately:

"Philip is my own again. She shall not separate us anymore and rob me of the one blessing of my life."

I listened to the evil demon that possessed me, and hardening my woman's heart, I vowed a solemn vow that she should never win the prize she sought, *never*, if I killed her to prevent it.

And I muttered to myself, "Twice I have conquered my revengeful spirit, but to be more deeply wounded. Now I will yield to it, and if a word of mine could save her, I would not utter it."

I shut out from my sight the face I hated, and left her silently.

It was the last that I saw of her, and I never told the sudden doubt awakened in me. She was buried, and we fell back into our quiet, happy life again.

Philip was fonder than ever, trying by every gentle word and deed to atone for his past negligence. The future now lay clear and bright before me. My life would have been one of perfect joy, had not a sudden gloom fallen on it now and then like the shadow of a passing cloud, and a vague sense of guilt weighed on me, growing heavier day by day.

The horrible fancy that Clara was not dead haunted me like a ghost. I feared to tell it at first, lest she should come back to be the evil genius of my life. I kept the sinful vow I had made until it was too late to save her. But this secret fear became a specter to rise up before me in my happiest hours and mar my peace of mind. So, many miserable weeks rolled on.

We were to be married, and in the excitement of that time I hoped I might forget. But it was in vain. The fear was always lying heavy at my heart, and I could not drive it thence, resolve and reason as I might. It never left me, but was forever there, making my days wearisome and anxious, my nights hideous with evil dreams.

I would not believe it anything but a wild fancy, yet I felt how it was wearing upon me. I saw my cheek grow thin, my eyes lit with a feverish unrest, my spirits failing, and my life a daily struggle to cast off the gloom which marred my happiness—that happiness so long desired, so precious, but so darkened by the secret dread that, like a remorseful ghost, now haunted me.

My wedding day drew near, and I sought comfort in the hope that this great change might free me from my hidden trouble.

Once Philip's wife, I would so fill his life with joy and content, so bind him to me by every tie a woman's love can weave, and grow so near and dear to him that his affection should brighten every nook of my unhappy heart and banish from my memory the gloomy past.

I even hoped to see a time when I might freely, fearlessly confess my doubts and fears and all the wild, wicked thoughts that once filled my mind. He would forgive me, I knew well, and smile away my foolish fancies; then the burden would be lifted off and I at peace again.

I clung to this hope. Often in those miserable nights when that dead face looked at me from the darkness with a mute reproach in its dim eyes, scaring sleep from my pillow, I would be framing my confession into fitting words for Philip's ear—mingling self-accusations with whispered prayers for pardon and fond reminders that these trials and temptations were all caused by my great love for him.

Many a long, ghostly night I whiled away rehearsing this confession, for in it lay my hopes of future peace.

I did not fear the loss of Philip's heart, and when I could no longer bear my secret, I would tell him—but not yet, not yet.

The night before my marriage I lay down upon my bed with the old fear stronger than ever and fell into a deep sleep filled with troubled dreams, which held me fast till early sunlight falling on my eyes awoke me. It would have been better for me had I slept forever.

I sprang up with a sense of unutterable relief and for a while forgot myself in glad thoughts and preparations for the approaching ceremony.

The day was beautiful, and I was happy, for the phantom fears were gone. Our few friends came with smiles and all good wishes to celebrate our quiet nuptials. The hour arrived and all was ready, but Philip did not come.

We waited long—but still no bridegroom. Messengers were sent to find him, but returned saying he had gone out early that morning and had not yet returned.

Then my heart sank within me. My short-lived joy departed, and I sat racked with dark forebodings that almost drove me wild. But he did not come.

One by one the friends stole quietly away, and when the sun set, I was left alone with the good clergyman and my old aunt. They tried to reassure and comfort me, but their words passed by me like the wind.

I paced the room hour after hour, with eye, ear, and mind strained to the utmost to catch the first sound of the approaching steps. Still Philip did not come.

At length my aunt slept, the good man went away, and kind, curious neighbors ceased to trouble me. Then I was utterly alone, and the red firelight, which I had thought would have shone upon a happy wife, now glimmered faintly on a pale, anxious woman, with dead flowers on her bosom and bridal garments mocking her desolation as she sat alone, watching and waiting for the coming morrow.

Suddenly Philip's step sounded in the hall, and with a cry of joy that echoed through the house, I sprang to meet him. But there was that in his face which drove me back. Haggard and wild it looked, as with white lips and eyes dilated with some secret horror, he stood gazing at me till I was cold with ominous dread.

I could not bear the silence long and, going to him, would have put my arms about his neck with a glad welcome; but he shrank from my touch with averted head and hands outstretched to keep me from him.

"Philip, what is it? Do not kill me with such looks and dreadful silence. Tell me what has happened. I can bear anything but this," I cried, clinging to him with a desperate clasp.

A look of bitter pain swept across his face as his eyes met my own imploring ones. He held me fast a moment and then put me from him with a shudder.

I sat where he placed me, without power to move or speak, while Philip stood before me with a countenance hard and stern as rock, saying with an abrupt calmness far more terrible than the wildest agitation: "Agatha, last night I sat alone in this room long after you had left me. And as I sat here, a white figure with vacant eyes and pallid cheeks came gliding in, and standing there, it told a sad tale of deceit and wrong, of hidden sins and struggles, and confessed one crime which drove it like a restless ghost to betray its guilty secrets when most fatal to its peace."

"It was Clara, come back from her tomb to wrong and rob

me even now," I muttered, half unconscious that I spoke, the old fear was so strong upon me.

"No, Agatha, *it was you,* coming in your haunted sleep to tell the sinful secret that is fast wearing your life away. It was awful to see you standing there with no light in your open eyes, no color in your expressionless face, and hear the tender words meant to be spoken with repentant tears and fond caresses, uttered in low, unearthly tones by pale lips unconscious of their meaning, and then to see the self-accusing apparition glide away unmoved into the gloom, leaving such misery behind. Oh, Agatha, how I have been deceived in you."

"Forgive me! You must—you will—for it was you, Philip, who drove me to this pass. I loved you better than my own soul, and she came between us. I have been sorely tempted, but for your sake I resisted more than once. Did I not set you free when my whole heart was bound up in you? Did I not relinquish my life's happiness to render yours secure? Have I not proved how strong my love is by these sacrifices for your sake? Then do not reproach me now that I unconsciously betrayed the struggles I have secretly endured, nor chide me that I was rejoiced when Clara died; for *she is dead,* and nothing but my feverish fancy would have ever doubted it."

Philip's calmness vanished as I rapidly poured out these broken words. The horror-stricken look came back into his eyes, his tall figure trembled, and his voice sounded hoarsely through the silent room as he replied with lips that whitened as he spoke:

"She *is* dead, thank God! But she *was not* when they buried her. Aye, you may well fall on your knees and turn your guilty face to heaven, for you murdered her, Agatha. Filled with alarm by your last night's confession, and remembering the strange anxiety that has possessed you since her death, I went this morning to L——, where Clara lies. Alone I went into her tomb—but was brought out senseless, for she had been buried alive!

"There was no doubt of it, for she had turned in her coffin and, too weak to break it, had perished miserably. God forgive you, Agatha. I never can."

"Oh, be merciful, Philip. I had suffered so much from her, and I could not give you up. Be merciful, and I will atone for it by a whole life of sacrifice and penitence—but do not cast me off," I cried, overcoming in my despair the horror and remorse that froze my blood.

But he never heeded me, and his stern purpose never changed. He tore himself away, saying solemnly as he passed out into the night:

"God pardon us both. Our sins have wrought out their own punishment, and we must never meet again."

We never have.

LITTLE SUNBEAM

"What troubles you, my child? Are you cold and hungry? Tell me, what is it?" asked the kindhearted lady, stooping to raise the drooping figure of a ragged child who crouched in a doorway, weeping bitterly.

The little girl lifted a quick glance to the mild face bending over her and, reassured by the sympathy she read there, answered through her tears, "I can't find the place they sent me to, and I'm afraid to go back because they'll beat me. I'm so cold and tired, I can't bear it tonight."

"Beat you!" cried the lady, drawing near the forlorn little creature. "Who will? Your mother?"

"*My* mother!" echoed the child, with an irresistible sob. "I haven't any mother. They said bad children like me never had any, but indeed, ma'am, I ain't very naughty. Only it's hard being good without anyone to show me how."

"What is your name? And where do you live, my dear?" asked the lady, with moistened eyes and a compassionate smile that lit her serious face like sunshine.

"My name is Meg, and I live in —— Street with Mrs. Nelson, to do the work," answered the little girl.

"What work can such a child as you do?" The lady glanced incredulously at the slender figure and pale face of the child.

"I'm not very young, though I look so small. I'm nearly ten, and I can sweep and scrub and cook a little. I run errands and work all day and sometimes have the baby to take care of in the night when Mrs. Nelson is at parties and the servants go

242

away. Indeed I do, ma'am. Look and see if it isn't true." As she spoke, the child threw back her tattered shawl and showed her arms, still bruised and purple with the marks of blows, and her little hands, worn and hardened with unnatural labor.

"Poor thing, poor thing! I never knew of cruelty like this before. What can I do for you? Let me go with you and tell your mistress how it was. She will forgive you, I am sure, little Meg."

"She'll say she will, but when you are gone, I shall be beaten and starved as I was before. Oh, take me somewhere, ma'am, where people will be kind to me, and I will be *very* good." With a fresh burst of tears the child clung to the only hand that had touched her gently for many a day.

The lady paused a moment, glancing from the friendless child to the wintry sky—but her decision was soon made.

"Come with me tonight, and tomorrow we will see what can be done for you. You are not afraid to go with me, are you, Meg?"

"Afraid! Ah, no, ma'am. I'd go anywhere with you. It seems so nice to have folks kind to me," exclaimed the child as she gathered her ragged shawl about her and slipped her bare foot into the old shoe that poorly covered it. Then, holding fast the hand of her friend, she went confidingly to her new home.

But on the way sundry purchases were made. When little Meg found herself invested with warm shoes and stockings and thick shawl and hood, her heart overflowed with childish gratitude and she could only cling closer to her benefactress, sighing for very happiness and whispering in joyful wonder, "Dear me, dear me, how beautiful this is, and how very good you are to me."

Two brothers sat together in a twilit room. One was a gray-haired man of sixty, the other many years younger, both hale and handsome, but silent, serious, and stern. The firelight flickered on their faces, but met no answering gleam. The old clock ticked and the dog upon the hearth sighed in his uneasy sleep, but no other sounds broke the silence which had lasted since the waning light had faded from their books.

Years had passed since these two brothers had clasped hands or called each other by the old familiar names. The memory of their boyish love was darkened by a later and less holy passion, for between two hearts once tenderly united, anger, pride, and jealousy had raised a barrier which parted them more utterly than land and sea.

Both had loved one object, and neither had won the prize. But in the struggle they had lost what was far more valuable than a fickle woman's favor—their confidence and love for one another. Both were passionate and proud, and when the conflict was abruptly ended, all the bitterness of their mutual disappointment was wreaked upon each other till there stretched a gulf between them which nothing but a generous forgiveness could bridge over. But neither would utter that first word, so hard to say, so beautiful when humbly spoken.

Time went on, and the years that should have taught a truer wisdom only hardened their hearts and widened the breach between them.

They dwelt beneath one roof and met daily, and there grew up a cold and distant courtesy between them which few saw beneath, and to the world the brothers seemed unchanged. But to themselves the separation was still greater for the seeming friendship, and the happy past grew dearer as it faded dimly in the distance, leaving them nothing but a mournful present and a gloomy future.

The elder brother saw the younger solitary in the prime of life and, remembering how once he had filled the first place in that vacant heart, longed sometimes to knock at the closed portal and be welcomed in to the old friendship, which would warm and brighten his declining life. But the pride that had strengthened with his strength rose up to silence the tender feeling, which was thrust back to pine in secret.

The younger saw the gray hairs gather on the elder's head and age come slowly on, and felt how beautiful and right it would be if his strength supported, or his affections lightened, the burden that fell on the brother who was once the generous protector of his youth. But the jealous passion which had parted them still rankled in his heart and forbade the utterance of that word which would have made them friends.

So they lived on, outwardly cold, silent men busied with their life's cares and heedless of its affections. But inwardly each cherished a faint spark of the old love which, though burning dimly, never wavered nor went out.

The long silence which had brooded over the dark room was broken by the entrance of a lady. Her presence seemed to bring both cheerfulness and light; for the flames leaped upon the hearth, the dog awoke to give her a noisy greeting, and the brothers found a smile and word of welcome for her.

All the affection they withheld from one another was unconsciously bestowed on Cousin Rachel, an orphan like themselves and past the first bloom of life, who came to fill their home with the charm of a woman's gentle presence and who sought by every means she could devise to reconcile the brothers.

A stately woman was Cousin Rachel, with a beautiful, mild countenance whose early freshness had departed, leaving it serene and bright as a mellow autumn sky.

"What is that?" suddenly asked Mr. William, the elder brother, as they sat together later in the evening and the echo of a child's gay laugh came up from below.

"It is a pleasant sound in this still house. What is it, Cousin Rachel?" asked Mr. Frank, putting down his book to listen to the unwonted sound.

Cousin Rachel, glad of anything, however slight, which might relieve the monotony of the evening, told with unconscious pathos the tale of little Meg. The brothers, seeing her interest, promised to inquire into the child's position and better it if possible.

"Let me show you the poor thing, for in spite of cruelty and neglect she is a winsome child. Come hither, Meg. These are both friends, so do not be afraid," Miss Rachel said, beckoning to the girl as she paused timidly in the doorway.

Thanks to her new friend's care, Meg's tangled locks were parted smoothly on her forehead, all traces of dirt and tears removed from her cheerful face, and some slight alterations made, rendering her miserable dress more decent. As she stood looking with confiding eyes into the friendly faces around her, she was indeed a "winsome child."

Miss Rachel's plan succeeded; the evening glided cheerfully away, for Mr. Frank's heart warmed to the lonely little creature whose appearance told her simple story more eloquently than her childish words.

Mr. William sat silent, but listened from behind his paper with a sympathy he was too proud to show, while Cousin Rachel, with a woman's thoughtful charity, worked busily on a garment for the child, often pausing to watch the happy face that seemed too young and bright for tears.

Even the stately hound left his warm nook to make friends with Meg, who soon sat beside him on the rug with his great head upon her knee, chatting softly with him of the book of prints Mr. Frank had given her for her amusement.

The little figure, bathed in ruddy light, gave to that fireside a charm it had lacked before, and the childish voice made blither music than those walls had echoed to for years. The three beholders worked the change and felt its simple charm. The brothers' glances met with unconscious kindness as they fell on little Meg's bent head. Their voices took a milder tone as they spoke of the child, and over Cousin Rachel's face there shone a tender pity, making it more beautiful than youthful bloom.

The little sunbeam had stolen in, and its first rays were shining on them, though they could not see it yet.

A few days passed. Meg's wrongs had been made known, and she was freed from her hard servitude. Mr. Frank led her home to Miss Rachel and said as he gave the child into her arms:

"She is yours now, Cousin Rachel. My brother is willing, and I am very glad to have her here for your sake. Make her but half as good a woman as yourself, and she will never lack love or friends."

"Now I shall have a mother, and a father too, if you will let me call you so. May I, sir, if I am very good?" cried little Meg, looking wistfully from Cousin Rachel's close embrace.

"Call me anything you like, and be a faithful child to your new mother," Mr. Frank said kindly as he went hastily away. But all day long the image of the child on Rachel's breast floated before him, and the sweet names she had given them rang in his ear above the tumult of the world about him.

Thus Meg found parents and a home, whose light and joy she soon became, for with unconscious ease she won the love of all and bound three solitary hearts together by the magic of one generous affection.

The quiet house grew musical with childish song and laughter and echoed to the sound of dancing feet. Wherever Cousin Rachel moved, a little bright-haired figure tripped beside her, making the once irksome duties pleasant by its innocent companionship. Birds sang in the once silent rooms and flowers bloomed in sunny nooks, for the brothers remembered Meg and were repaid fourfold for every gift by the grateful love the child bestowed on them.

Coming wearily home at night from the care and turmoil of the day, they always saw an eager face watching for their return, always heard quick feet speed down to let them in, and always felt the clasp of welcoming arms whose light touch seemed to banish weariness and care and lead them to the blessed rest of home.

Night after night, through twilight gloom or wintry storm, the little face shone out like a cheery ray from their own hearthstone till the brothers learned to watch for it and love it silently. They never saw another, milder countenance, watching in the shadow patiently; they never knew how many acts of childish tenderness were prompted and encouraged by good Cousin Rachel, and never guessed how earnestly their household angels labored to reunite the broken bond and lure the brothers back.

Mr. William frowned when first he saw Meg making one in their domestic circle, but when he found the easy chair drawn to the warmest nook, his lamp lit and book laid ready, the slippers warm upon the hearth, and the fire brightened for his coming, he could not see the anxious face watching if he were pleased without kissing it and calling her his "thoughtful little Meg." He saw how gladly she forestalled his slightest wish and how carefully she checked her mirth lest it should trouble him. When he heard the patient sigh which sometimes broke the silence she forced herself to keep when longing to sing with her birds or join the hound, Black Douglas, in his uncouth play, the old man's heart was touched; and watching the delight his soul caresses gave, he felt happier for yielding to this gentle impulse of his proud nature.

To Mr. Frank, Meg was a child, clinging to him with all the warmth of her grateful heart and finding a generous return in the affection he bestowed on her.

The sweetest music in the world to him was the voice that called him "Father," even while it woke memories half melancholy and half glad; for he was not an old man yet and still felt the longing for a fireside of his own where the name that was so pleasant to his ear might be a household word on many lips.

This longing haunted him more often now than it had done for years, and when he saw the homelike group of little Meg beside Miss Rachel's knee and heard his cousin called by the blessed name which sanctifies the poorest woman, he often murmured sorrowfully to himself, "It might have been, it might have been."

But as the year rolled on and these two figures were before him day by day, regret ceased to sigh, "It might have been," and hope whispered timidly, "It may be yet."

For over Cousin Rachel there had come a change more beautiful than that which fell upon the brothers. The fresh young life so closely mingled with her own seemed to bring back her youth; the small hand always clasped in hers seemed leading her into a purer world of thought and feeling; and the bright head pillowed on her bosom seemed to stir the deep fountain of her woman's nature till it gushed forth, making the solitary pathway of her life fragrant with flowers that hid its roughness and made verdant its most dreary spot.

Fresh energy seemed given her, for a child looked to her

now for guidance; a great happiness possessed her, for she was beloved; and a sweeter beauty beamed in her tranquil face, for childish eyes looked there for sympathy and love.

The little sunbeam had shone warmly in on Cousin Rachel's lonely heart, ripening many a golden resolution and many a woman's affection, and the autumn of her life was fruitful with generous deeds and beautiful with noble aspirations.

"Why is my merry little Meg poring with such an anxious face over Cousin Rachel's sketchbook when she should be out at play?" As he spoke, Mr. Frank scattered a handful of flowers on the child's bent head and the pages of her book.

Meg started and looked up, smiling through the flowery rain. "I'm looking at these pictures, for I never saw them here before. Is it wrong? She did not forbid me when I had it last."

"No, child, why should she? Let me see the pictures that can keep you from your play this sunny morning." As he spoke, Mr. Frank glanced over her shoulder and saw the faces of his brother and himself.

"When did she do these? And how? We never knew of it," he said, lifting them with sudden interest, which increased as Meg replied:

"I've seen her working busily at something for a long time, and yesterday I found her crying softly at her work. See, this was it; the drops have spoiled your picture, Father. And when I asked what made her sad, she only held me close and bade me love her dearly, for she had great need of it. What did she mean?"

But Mr. Frank stood silent, looking at the tear-stained picture and pondering on the words more clear to him than little Meg.

"What are you doing here with all these flowers, my child?" As her low voice broke the silence, Cousin Rachel came in, stately and serene as ever. But a swift change passed across her face as Mr. Frank, with a questioning glance, turned the sketch he held, and Meg, half conscious she had done some wrong, eagerly explained that she had looked into the book to find the cause of her friend's grief that she might try to comfort it.

"I intended these as gifts, but have not finished Cousin William's yet, for he plays with Meg so much I cannot catch the likeness unobserved, as I once could when he sat reading silently. They will be ready soon." And Cousin Rachel hastily replaced the pictures and put by the book.

"How, then, did you catch mine so well? *I* always played and talked with Meg," asked Mr. Frank, a smile flitting across his face, which had grown bright and earnest as he watched his cousin.

"I know—I know how it was," cried Meg as Miss Rachel stooped silently to gather up the scattered flowers. "She knew it from the small one in the golden case that always hangs about her neck. I saw it in her hand when she was fainting once. But, dear Mama, what have I done? Why do you look so strangely? Indeed I meant no harm."

And Meg, startled by her sudden paleness, clung closer to Miss Rachel, who bent her face till it was hidden in the child's long hair.

"Oh, little Meg, you have done more harm than you ever can repair," said Miss Rachel with a voice still tender through all its reproachfulness.

"Cousin Rachel, there is one way to atone for Meg's innocent betrayal. May I tell it?" Mr. Frank drew nearer as he spoke. "I, too, have worn a picture, not *on* my heart but *in* it, where no curious eye could look—a picture that I once looked on as the likeness of a sister. But through this last year it has grown far dearer and more beautiful than ever sister's was, and I have learned to look upon it tenderly and reverently as the face of her I would call my wife. But remembering the bitter past, I feared to speak lest I should have deceived myself and but disturb your peace. But now that Meg has raised the veil that hid our hearts from one another, look upon the face I have cherished and know it for your own, dear Rachel."

Meg felt the hot tears falling on her hair, heard the quiet beating of the heart so near her own, and in the tightened clasp of the fond arms about her, knew that she was freely pardoned for the harm she had so innocently done.

"Cousin Rachel, you know me well, and if I *can* make your happiness, give me the clear right to do it. Look up and tell me if I may hope to see this good, true face beaming on me from a wife's place at my own fireside?"

Cousin Rachel's drooping head found a stronger, tenderer resting place as she said simply, with eyes that shone through quiet tears: "Dear friend, I have loved you all my life."

As they stood thus together, hand in hand, there came two soft arms around their necks and a golden head between their own, and thus the link that bound them was completed by the little sunbeam which had lit them to each other's love.

"No bright face at the window, no firelight on the hearth—where is our household fairy gone?" asked the brothers, coming home one autumn night and missing the glad welcome which made that hour so pleasant.

Little Meg was ill, and through long days and nights there was no rest nor joy in that sad house. Fear and sorrow looked out from anxious eyes, but found no vent in words. Hushed steps stole through the rooms where light feet once had danced, eager whispers breathed where the blithe carol of a childish voice had sounded, and the dark shadow of Death's wing lay over the once cherished home.

The brothers sat alone together, looking often at the empty chair, the drooping flowers, and the muffled cage, touching tenderly each little thing the child had loved, and murmuring sadly her pet names to poor Black Douglas, who went restlessly from room to room, seeking vainly for his gentle playmate.

They stole often to look in upon the meek face on the pillow or to listen to the patient murmurs breaking the stillness of the darkened room and then, with eyes that saw but dimly, went back to ponder on the love they bore the child and pray their little sunbeam might be spared to them.

There came at length that mysterious sleep which silently strengthens soul and body for a longer sojourn here or, gently severing the tie that binds them, deepens into that solemn slumber which has no wakening but in heaven. Through the long hours no sound but the child's faint breathing broke the stillness, but at midnight, when a change might come, there stole into the room two figures in whose worn and anxious faces there were no signs of the pride and sternness which once marred them.

Standing on either side of the quiet bed, the brothers looked down upon the little creature lying there with meekly folded hands, so white and still and so like death that each felt, in the sharp pang that sight caused them, how dear the child had grown and how desolate their home would seem without the cheerful presence that had brightened it so long.

The younger brother felt that *he* was not without comfort in the sorrow that might come; for Cousin Rachel's hand lay warm in his, and in her love he had a solace that would not fail him. But the elder was alone, and owned at last how strong had been the power of the frail child laying there, for silent as sunshine, she had shone upon his proud heart till it opened wide and took her in. Other children might sit upon his brother's knee and call him "Father," but none could ever be to *him* what little Meg had been. Silently a bitter tear flowed down his cheek, and he forgot all but one desire, to lay his gray head down beside the child and let her lead him through that other world as she had led him for a little while through this.

The younger brother saw the unwonted grief and read the thought that gave it birth, and in his own heart, pity, sympathy, and the generous wish for pardon rose up stronger than before. Something in the face beside him and the touch of the dear hand seemed to smooth the way and render easy what had seemed so hard before.

"Brother Will, let there be peace between us."

The old boyish name, uttered brokenly, with tearful eye and outstretched hand, found its way straight to the old man's softened heart. The little sunbeam had shone so long upon the barrier pride had built between them that it melted at the first frank word, and above the tranquil face upon the pillow, the two clasped hands, brothers in heart and name.

The heavy shadow faded and did not fall. Joy and not sorrow drew the united family still closer, and marriage bells soon rang out merrily where they had feared a funeral knell would sound.

Years passed. Children gathered about brother Frank and called Cousin Rachel "Mother," but Meg was still the cherished elder sister of the flock, looked up to and beloved by all. With no name but the one which grew a household symbol of all tenderness and patience, no fortune but the wealth of love lavished upon her gentle head, and no beauty but the sunshine of her cheerful heart, "our Meg" grew up to womanhood.

One tie most beautiful and strong bound her to the solitary brother, about whose hearth no wife or children sat. She was the old man's darling, hope, and pride, and he went cheerfully along the downward path of life leaning on that devoted daughter's arm and blessing the faithful sunbeam that shone on him to the last.

MARION EARLE; OR, ONLY AN ACTRESS!

"But, Mrs. Leicester, all are not weak, frivolous, and vain. I have known actresses as virtuous and cultivated as any lady whom you honor with your friendship. Faithful wives, good mothers, and truehearted women, who are an honor to their profession and would be an ornament of any class of society, were it not—pardon me—for prejudices like your own."

"Show me one such, Mr. Lennox, and I will conquer my prejudices—as far as I can. But it seems impossible that they can be all you describe, surrounded by such influences and leading such a life," and the lady glanced at the stage where a ballet was performing previous to the play.

"Ah, you see only the roses scattered in their way and fancy them butterflies," replied the gentleman. "There are more thorns than flowers, and their life is often a long and patient struggle with stern necessity. What is mere amusement to you is daily bread to them, and we little know, as they pass before us with smiling faces, what heavy hearts they may have. There is many a sadder tragedy played behind those scenes than any we see here before. You ask me to point you out an actress such as I have described; Marion Earle, whom you will see to-night, is such a one."

"You are a great admirer of Miss Earle's, and therefore, being an interested party, I fear I cannot depend on your opinion. With you gentlemen, beauty veils so many blemishes," said the lady with a reproving smile.

"Madam, I am proud to say that I am Miss Earle's friend,"

replied the gentleman gravely, "and my gray hairs should give some weight to my opinion. Marion's beauty veils only a good and tender heart, and if you will allow me to tell you a little of her history, I think you will look upon her with different eyes."

Mrs. Leicester bowed her acquiescence, and the eager old gentleman continued: "She was left an orphan, with a little sister dependent on her for support. They were friendless and poor, but (after vainly trying to support herself by the few occupations left to women) Marion had the courage to enter the profession for which her talents fitted her. She knew the dangers and the labor through which she must pass; but for the child's sake she ventured it, and that motive has kept her safe through all.

"By her own indomitable energy and patience, she has struggled up through poverty, injustice, and temptation till she has become a beloved, admired, and respected actress— aye, respected, Mrs. Leicester, for not a breath of slander ever touched her name.

"The little sister is being educated well, and Marion, by her own efforts, has secured a quiet home where she and May can be together all their lives. Surely such an aim is noble and such a woman must win respect, though she is only an actress!"

"O surely, you have made me quite impatient to behold this embodiment of all the virtues," answered Mrs. Leicester, smiling at her friend's enthusiasm. But she soon forgot both Mr. Lennox and his story in the interest of the scenes passing before her.

It was a comedy, and Marion, for the hour, put by her cares and was the gay and brilliant creature that she seemed.

Her beauty charmed the eye, her clear voice satisfied the ear, and the fire and feeling she threw into her part touched the heart and lent a womanly grace to every look and action.

Even Mrs. Leicester felt and owned her power, forgetting her pride and prejudice in the excitement of the hour, and heartily applauded what she had but just condemned.

Toward the close of the last act, after a splendidly played scene, Marion passed out with a jest upon her lips; a moment afterward a cry rang through the theater so sharp and bitter, it filled the listeners with wonder and dismay.

There was a stir among the audience, and the performers paused involuntarily for what should come. But nothing followed save a confused murmur behind the scenes.

The play went on, but it now received the divided attention of those who were absorbed before.

Contradictory rumors of the sudden cry were whispered about, and its mournful echo still seemed lingering in many ears.

When, after a long pause, Marion appeared, a quick murmur arose, for in her face there might be read a tale of suffering that brought tears of pity into womanly eyes and changed the comedy to a tragedy for those who saw that countenance, so lately beautiful and gay, now resolute and white, with a fixed look of agony and grief in its large eyes. It was a pitiful sight to see and a still more pitiful thing to hear the jests and joyous words that fell so mockingly from lips that quivered and grew white in the vain effort to recall their vanished smiles.

Apparently unconscious of the sympathizing faces looking into hers or the consoling whispers of her fellow players, Marion went on, mechanically performing every action of her part like one in a dream, except that now and then there flitted across her face an expression of intense and eager longing and her eyes seemed to look in vain for some means of escape. But the stern patience of a martyr seemed to bear her up, and she played on, a shadow in the scene whose brightness she had lately been.

Her task at length was done, all but a little song, which always won for her the plaudits of her delighted hearers.

With the same painful faithfulness she tried to sing it, but her voice faltered and failed. Her heart was too full, and she could only shake her head with a smile so sad and weary that it called forth the pity of her audience in the only way they could express it, by the heartiest applause they ever had bestowed upon her.

It touched her deeply, and feeling only the generous sympathy that made them friends, she forgot time and place and, stretching her hands to them, said imploringly, "Kind friends, pardon me—I cannot sing—for my little May is dead!"

The only sound that broke the silence was the rustle of flowers falling at her feet. Leaving her broken words and her great grief to plead for her, she bowed her thanks, and the curtain shut her and her sorrow from the world.

"My dear Grace, what are you weeping so bitterly for?" asked Mrs. Leicester as they prepared to go.

"I cannot help it, Aunt, I pity that poor girl so much. Who will comfort her, for she is an orphan and all alone now?" sobbed the warmhearted girl, too young to feel ashamed of her generous emotion.

"Don't be foolish, my love," whispered her aunt, wrapping her cloak about her. "Miss Earle has plenty of comforters; such people never feel these things very deeply. You see she made quite a good thing out of it; her tragic air was vastly effective, so never waste your pity, child—she is only an actress."

"There is a young person below who insists on seeing you. Shall I send her up?"

"Certainly not, I am engaged," and Mrs. Leicester sank back among the cushions of her lounge and resumed her novel.

The servant lingered, saying, "I am afraid she won't go, ma'am; this is the third time she has been this week begging to see you. Couldn't she come up and be done with it?"

"No impertinence, John; she wants work, probably. Tell her I have none, and let me hear no more of her."

John departed, but the door had hardly closed behind him when it was suddenly reopened; and the young woman entered, locked it behind her, possessed herself of the bell rope, and then, turning to the startled lady, said desperately, "Madam, you must hear me. Do not be alarmed. There was no way left but this. You would not see me; therefore, I have forced myself upon you. Only listen, and you will pardon me."

The girl's face was wan and wasted with recent suffering

and wore a look of mingled supplication, fear, and anguish, as of some timid creature hunted till it stood at bay.

"Who and what are you?" demanded Mrs. Leicester, recovering her self-possession.

"You ask me sternly, madam, and you shall have a stern answer," replied the girl steadily, while the hot blood burned in her thin cheek.

"I am a motherless girl, whom your son, promising to cherish and protect, robbed of the one treasure she possessed, and then left to the pity of a world which is merciless to the weak. I have watched and waited for him one long year, have borne pity, scorn, and pain most patiently, trusting he would come as he promised. But he never has, and when I learned that he had been across the sea, I forgave him and came here to his home to seek and ask him if he had forgotten me. Let me see him for one hour, one moment—he will set my heart at rest, and I will never trouble you again."

Mrs. Leicester fixed her cold eye on the face before her, saying haughtily, "If you desire money, say so boldly, but do not come to me with this old story, which I neither believe nor desire to hear."

"Heaven help us, madam. It *is* an old story, but Christian charity is never old. I only ask that from you, and justice from your son. It is all he can do now. Let him keep the word he plighted to me and give his little child a name!"

"Girl! How dare you come to me with a demand like this? You are an impostor, and your tale is false, utterly false!" cried Mrs. Leicester with an indignant frown. "My son is an honorable gentleman, and you—what are you that you have the audacity to demand justice for your own sin and folly?"

The girl's eye flashed, and she smiled bitterly as she replied, "I am used to looks and words like these, and for your son's sake I have borne them for a year. You speak of my sin; judge of his. I was an orphan, ignorant and young, trusting all who were kind to me—and he was very fond and tender for a while. God forgive me—how I loved him! Worldly fears disturbed our peace; he left me, promising to come again. He never has, and his falsehood has changed me from a happy child into a most miserable woman. O madam, which is the blacker sin, to love blindly or to betray a trusting heart? Which of us two, the lonely orphan or the 'honorable gentleman,' is the greater sinner?"

Mrs. Leicester rose with an angry flush upon her face, saying, "I will listen to this no longer. Were my son here, he would clear himself from your accusations at once; in his absence I will hear nothing, believe nothing against him. I know him too well. Go and never venture here again."

The girl turned away, but remembering that it was her last hope, she made one more appeal, crying humbly, "By the sacred name of "mother," which we both bear, do not cast me off! A little sympathy, a little pity, will save me now! O by the love you bear your son, have compassion upon mine and do not send us out, *two* helpless children, into the cruel world; for I am very young in all but sorrow, and there are so few to take me in. Be merciful and help me in my bitter strait!"

The hard face softened at the poor young creature's prayer, but worldly pride swept like a cloud across the ray of womanly compassion. Offering a well-filled purse, Mrs. Leicester pointed silently to the door.

The girl struck the money from her hand and swept past her with the mien of an insulted queen. Pausing on the threshold, she turned, saying:

"Madam, I did not sell my love, and gold cannot buy my peace. I shall remember this, and as you have dealt by my son, so will I deal by yours." Then, with a warning gesture, she was gone.

"Miss Earle, there is a poor girl below who wants to see you. I made bold to say she could, for you bid me always let the poor souls in."

"Poor and in trouble, doubtless. Yes, I will see her, Janet," and Marion left her flowers, murmuring softly:

> *"We do pray for mercy; and that same prayer*
> *Doth teach us all to render*
> *Deeds of mercy.*

"My child, what can I do for you?" she asked, turning toward the slight figure entering at her door.

The stranger looked eagerly into the face before her, as if fearing a repulse. But in that countenance so beautiful and benign she read no contempt. A tender pity shone in the lustrous eyes, and the music of the poet's words still lingered in the voice that called her "child."

The wild anxiety passed from her young face. Overcome by one kind word, the poor heart that had borne so much gave way at last, and with a burst of grateful tears she cried to Marion:

"I am fatherless and motherless. Oh, help me in my trouble and keep me from despair."

Lost in the tumult of her own emotion, the girl was but dimly conscious of the arm that gently enfolded her or the hand that uncovered her aching head and laid it to rest upon a friendly bosom.

But the low voice soon recalled her, saying tenderly, "Dear child, be comforted. Tell me your grief, and believe me that whatever it may be, you are no longer friendless and alone."

"Ah, madam," sighed the girl, "forgive my tears, but yours are the first kind words I have heard this many a day. I thought there was no charity in all the world for me, and when it came so bounteously, I could not bear it."

"It has been a cruel world to you, I fear. But tell me your trouble and take heart, for you are too young to despair," said Marion, looking down upon the face so youthful, but so darkened by remorse and care.

The girl shrank timidly away and answered brokenly, "You will despise and turn from me, as all have done, when I have told you more. But, oh, remember I was very young and very lonely, and it seemed so sweet to be beloved."

But Marion only drew her nearer, only lifted up the drooping head, and with a tenderer compassion shining in her eyes, said earnestly, "It is not for me to judge you or your error, but remembering my own weakness, to comfort and console, as I in my sorrow would have been consoled, and leave all judgment to a wise and pitying God, who knows our strength and our temptations. Look bravely up and tell me all."

And gazing steadfastly into the friendly face, the poor girl told her story. Through it all, the arm about her never fell away and the pitiful eyes looked down unchanged.

"What is this man's name?" asked Marion, with an indignant flush upon her cheek.

"That I shall never tell" was the resolute reply. "No one shall look coldly on him, and he never shall reproach me for bringing contempt upon him. He had a kind heart once, and it may lead him back to me at last. Till then I will trust and wait."

"True woman through it all," sighed Marion. "But tell me how I best can serve you. What are your present needs, your future hopes?"

"I ask only honest work to keep me and the child from suffering. I will do anything, however humble, anything for bread. My greatest fear has been that, cut off from human love, I should grow wild and wicked and be driven to despair or death."

"Never fear that again," said Marion. "I will see that you have a quiet home and simple work, a home where you can love your boy and lead a blameless life. But always remember that there is One who hears His children when they cry to Him, and when human pity fails, His great love takes them in."

"I will never doubt again, for in my extremest need He led me here. Ah, madam, if there were more hearts like yours, there would be fewer fates like mine. I heard of you from those you had succored, and hoping and fearing, I came here to be consoled as tenderly as if I were a sister. God in heaven bless you forever and forever."

But Marion seemed unconscious of the grateful kisses pressed upon her hand; the one word "sister" touched a chord in her warm heart and stirred a tender memory that drew her closer to the lonely girl.

She caressed the bright head resting on her shoulder as she had caressed another which could never lie there anymore, and with a sudden dimness in her beautiful, proud eyes, looked down upon it, saying softly, "I had a sister once, a little clinging child, who was the blessing of my life. We had no mother, and I loved her as a mother might. For ten happy years she was my comfort and my joy, and then, when I had gained the home for which I had toiled and struggled, this little sister died. Since then, for every child I feel a yearning tenderness and love them for her sake. In every young girl blooming into womanhood, I see my darling as she would have been had she been spared, and a great sympathy possesses me for all their innocent delights, their maiden hopes and fears. In every wronged and sorrowing woman, I behold some likeness of the child as she might have been had fate proved kind, and I feel a strong compassion and a longing wish to comfort and protect them out of love for her.

"So, looking into your wan face, I see my May's confiding eyes, and knowing that her feet might have faltered among the snares of this false world, as yours have done, I thank God she is safe. Remembering what might have been, I take you to the shelter of my love as I would have had some kind heart pity and protect my child."

They sat silent for a moment when Marion ceased. Then, with a blissful smile flitting across her face, she said:

"I am to be married soon, and then I shall have no cares but those of home. Come to me in a month and I will do yet more for you. If meanwhile you are unhappy or in trouble, write to me. I will not forget you even in my own great happiness. But tell me, child, what is your name?"

"My name?" echoed the girl. "I have disgraced the honest one my father bore, and *he* who should have given me one denied me his. I have no name but Agnes; call me that alone."

"You have another," Marion said, "that none can deny, none take away, a sweet and blessed name which will sanctify your life and take half its bitterness away when baby lips shall call you 'Mother.' Be true to that name, and though your child may never know an earthly father, remember he has a heavenly One who never will forsake you, though all the world may cast you off."

Agnes turned to go, but Marion bade her wait and, writing a few lines, offered them with a generous supply of money, saying as the girl drew back:

"Here is the name of the good woman with whom you will find a home, and here a little sum for future needs. I give it you in my lost darling's name, and I know that you will take it for her sake."

"It was offered once before, but not as now," murmured Agnes. "I will take it and pray with all my grateful heart that you may be a happy wife and mother with no shadow to disturb you all your tranquil life." Then, looking timidly up, she faltered—"May I kiss you, madam?"

The stately woman bent and gathered the outcast to her bosom, remembering nothing but that blessed charity which binds human hearts together and makes the whole world kin.

Had Robert Leicester been a poor man's son, he would have found in hard experience a teacher who would have made a strong and noble man of him, for he had generous impulses and a kindly nature. But born to wealth and early left fatherless, he grew up beneath the care of a proud, world-minded mother, whom he loved tenderly and whose will became his law.

Hoping to make an accomplished gentleman, she forgot that better thing—an honest man—and was content when he grew up handsome, gay, and courtly, with no ambition but to enjoy life and no knowledge of the duties wherein its true enjoyment might be found.

Easily led to good or ill, his was a character dangerous both to himself and others, for with winning manners and a generous heart, he loved and was beloved by all who knew him, even by those who saw the weakness and mourned the high powers misdirected, talents wasted, and the wrong early done a noble nature.

Meeting Marion abroad, whither she had gone after her

little sister's death, they had journeyed much together; and Robert, by his sympathy and kindness, had lightened her sorrow, won her confidence, and soon woke a warmer interest in the heart which longed to bless and to be blessed. From friends they glided into lovers; from lovers they were soon to pass into that closer union which makes the happiness or misery of two lives.

Marion saw her lover's faults, but felt she had the power to strengthen and direct, and was glad to feel she could do something for the friend who had made her solitary life so beautiful with hope and love.

And Robert looked up to Marion, loving yet fearing; for he felt he was unworthy of the generous confidence she bestowed upon him, and though bitterly lamenting it, had not the courage to become more worthy in his own eyes and in hers by sacrificing her love to the higher sense of duty that oppressed him.

Mrs. Leicester had no affection for Marion; of high birth herself, she felt that her son stooped to take her as his wife. But Marion had made a name for herself, and better men than he had thought it no dishonor to offer her their hand.

Marion was an actress, and the proud woman looked upon her profession with contempt. But Marion had buried down all doubts long ago. There was nobody in the land purer than she, nor prouder of the blameless life she led, and Mrs. Leicester, while she hated, must respect her.

Marion had fortune, too, partly gained by her own honest labor, partly bequeathed her by an admiring friend. The extravagance of Mrs. Leicester and her son had nearly squandered the property the elder Leicester left, so worldly caution triumphed over womanly dislike; and for her own sake the selfish mother left her son to the best and truest passion of his life.

Mrs. Leicester's spacious drawing rooms were filled with a throng of friends in honor of her son's wedding, for Marion would have no public spectacle and shrank even from the eyes that had often watched her play the part she felt so real and solemn now.

A sudden stillness reigned through the brilliant rooms, broken only by the voice which asked, "Robert Leicester, will thou take this woman to be thy wedded wife?"

Before the answering words could fall from the bridegroom's lips, a start and stir among the guests arrested them, and with an involuntary motion he turned—to see Agnes standing at his side with her child in her arms.

There was a fire in her eye before which his own fell, and her low voice rang like thunder in his startled ear: "*Will* you take that woman for your wife while I stand here with your child upon my breast? Where are the promises you made, the oath you swore? Will you deny them, with this innocent face to testify against you? Oh, Robert! Robert! I have hoped and waited all this weary year to find you here at last, false to yourself and me."

The young man, as she spoke, had cast one look of despair and dismay about him and then, covering up his face, had staggered to a seat and sunk into it, crushed by the weight of his remorse and shame.

Mrs. Leicester clutched Agnes by the arm and hissed a warning in her ear, endeavoring to lead her away. But the girl's spirit was roused, and shaking off her grasp, she drew her slight figure proudly up and, lifting the boy from her bosom, cried exultingly:

"I told you I would remember the hour when you cast me off! Have I not kept my word? I told you, as you dealt by my son so would I deal by yours. You left this child to shame and sorrow; he smiles in your face. Look at *your* son. On whose head lies the shame heaviest now? You would not believe me; ask him, whose word you cannot doubt, if what I say be not the living truth. Here before these witnesses I tell you, this is his child and in the eye of God I am his wife. Ask him if he can deny it."

White as her bridal veil, with a bewildered countenance and eyes dilated with a growing fear, Marion had stood motionless while Agnes poured out her excited words and pointed to the bowed figure that never spoke nor stirred.

"Robert, is this true?" The words came imploringly from

Marion's lips as she bent towards him with clasped hands, as if pleading him for life.

The young man writhed as if some conflict tore his heart, but lifted up his face and answered steadily, "Yes, Marion, all true."

She heard him with an incredulous gaze, but as he turned away with a bitter groan, a scarlet flush of scorn and indignation burned in her cheek, then paled and left it whiter than before. With one look at her lover she drew her veil across her face and prayed inwardly for help.

Agnes had caught a single sentence dropped carelessly from the lips of a lady for whom she had worked—"Young Leicester's wedding tonight."

It was enough for her. She had borne much, but she would see him once more, make one appeal, and then submit. She had not learned the bride's name, nor did she recognize her in her bridal robes until she heard her voice. Then, looking on the woman whose happiness she hoped to blast, she saw her benefactress.

Fierce and bitter were the passions surging in the poor girl's heart, but at the sight of that kind face, so blanched and sorrow-stricken, gratitude rose up and silenced the storm that raged within. She forgot herself, her wrongs, and only heard again the voice that comforted, only saw the friend who succored her; and dropping her boy upon the cushion where the happy bride would soon have knelt, she flung herself at Marion's feet, and clinging to her, she cried passionately:

"Oh, pardon me—I never knew that it was you who had come between me and my love. Forget what I have said, and I will go away, never to disturb your peace again. You can make him happier than I, a poor fond child, whose love has always been a sorrow to him. I forgive him all if he is but true to you. Heaven bless and keep you, dearest lady. See, I am going, never, nevermore, to be a shame or grief to any heart that has been kind to me."

Snatching up her child, she turned away, and Mrs. Leicester, eager to spare her son, stepped forward, saying with affected calmness: "Friends, forget this painful scene, and let the ceremony proceed."

"It shall proceed, madam," answered the voice few thought to hear, and Marion, plunging aside her veil, passed down the room, took Agnes by the hand, and led her back. As she took the child into her arms, she said, "Agnes, this is your place, not mine. For your sake and the boy's, obey me. Robert Leicester, this is the woman whom you promised to cherish and protect. Take her by the hand, and here publicly atone for the wrong you have done her, by giving her the sacred name of wife."

"He shall not—Robert, at your peril do you obey this mad request!" cried Mrs. Leicester, looking defiantly at Marion.

"Madam, he shall—I am the one to set him free or hold him to his bond. He owes me reparation for the double wrong he has done me and this poor girl, whose cause I make my own. Robert, I appeal to you, as you are a man and would win back some part of the regard I once bestowed on you. I command you to keep the word you plighted one year ago as you would have kept that which you vowed to me."

There was a flash in Marion's eye and a command in her tone that rang like a silver trumpet through the room and awed both haughty mother and wavering son to a complete submission.

Robert put aside his mother's hand and, with a resolute, pale face, silently took his place at Agnes's side. Marion spoke a few words to the aged minister, who bowed his white head and with a trembling voice pronounced the marriage ceremony.

Agnes never turned her gaze from Marion's countenance, and Marion, motionless and white as a marble image, stood with the child upon her arm, looking straight before her with eyes that saw only utter darkness.

As they rose up from their knees, Robert turned to Marion and said hoarsely, "Are you content?"

She only bowed her head, and without a word or look for his young wife, he rushed from the room. Then Mrs. Leicester was herself again, and sweeping disdainfully past Agnes's drooping form, she turned to Marion, saying haughtily:

"Miss Earle, my house has been made a stage long enough where you may play the queen. Oblige me by leaving it at once and taking with you your friend; for much as I admire the skill with which you have entrapped my son into this shameful marriage, believe me, neither he nor I will ever accept, or disgrace our home with, the presence of the wife you have thrust upon him."

Marion's eye lit, but she answered calmly, with a glance of pity and contempt that stung the proud woman more deeply than her words could have done.

"Madam, your son's wife will never ask the shelter of your roof unless he claims her, as I trust he one day will. Then you may feel some remorse for this most cruel deed. I have played out my part, not as a queen, I trust, but as a Christian woman; and I only ask of those who witness my last act to remember that when the lady and the mother cast forth that poor girl with scorn, the actress—at whom she sneered—taught by her own human errors, pitied the outcast and, remembering a divine example, comforted and took her in."

And with the little child upon her breast and the forsaken mother on her arm, Marion passed through the sympathizing throng, stately and calm, as if no bitter pain and desolation were lying heavily at her brave heart.

She did it well, for she was "only an actress."

Three years had passed since that unhappy bridal, and Robert Leicester had not claimed his wife. She still dwelt under Marion's roof, finding her only happiness in her boy and the love of that true friend.

Friends had warned and enemies had sneered, but Marion heeded neither and kept the forsaken mother and child safe in the shelter of her honorable home, answering both friends and foes by a few simple words, which silenced them forever: "Let him who is without sin cast the first stone."

And so they lived, two solitary women bound together by one sorrow and one love.

Mrs. Leicester, meeting with heavy losses, left the city soon after her son's strange marriage, and for three long years no tidings had been heard of them.

Agnes had written to her husband once, but receiving no reply, felt that she was deserted, and patiently waited, hoping for happier times to come.

Marion sat in the pleasant garden of her country home. The air was full of summer music, and Agnes's little son played in the sunshine at her feet. The wind idly fluttered the leaves of her neglected book, for her eyes were fixed upon the little face which daily grew more like the one she remembered well.

Time had passed lightly over Marion's head, bringing a riper beauty and a deeper experience. The first and last love of her life, abandoned as a hope, crushed as a passion, living only as a quiet grief and a pure remembrance, still kept its watch as guardian of her heart.

No bitter memories soured the gracious sweetness of her nature, no discontent darkened her brave spirit; she poured strength and happiness within herself and led a tranquil, cheerful life with Agnes and her son.

Marion's reverie was broken by old Janet, who came hurrying down the path, exclaiming, "Oh, miss, a poor gentleman has just fainted in the hall. He asked for you, and before I could answer, he fell like one dead. I've sent Joe for the doctor, but do come and see what can be done for him."

Bidding the child stay among the flowers, Marion hastened in, to recognize in the unconscious stranger her lover, Robert Leicester.

"Thank heaven, he has come at last, though it be only to die near us," she murmured to herself, holding fast the icy hand.

Then with quiet energy she gave all necessary directions for the sick man's comfort.

When Dr. Murrey arrived, he found his patient recovering from the deathlike swoon but already delirious with the fever burning in his veins, and Marion hovering over him, resolute and calm, though harassed by fears that filled her with the deepest anxiety.

"This is no place for you, my dear Miss Earle," said the doctor, turning from the sick man to the eager woman at his side. "This fever is contagious, and you must not expose yourself. I trust it is not too late. Send Mrs. Leicester and her boy away, and take all proper precautions yourself. We will have Nurse Clay to take charge of the poor gentleman."

"Nurse Clay is with her sick daughter, sir, and no other woman in the village would risk her life for an utter stranger. This gentleman is Mrs. Leicester's husband, and for her boy's sake she must not see him. But I have no fear, and I shall not leave him till the danger is past or he needs human help no longer."

As she spoke, there was a light in Marion's eye and a glow upon her cheek which told more eloquently than words the earnestness of her resolve and the joy her perilous compassion would afford her.

In vain the good doctor sought to intimidate and dissuade—she would not yield and soon won an unwilling consent from him to be allowed to stay.

The child was sent to its mother with a message from Marion, forbidding her to return from the friendly neighbor's where she chanced to be till all danger was over. Agnes, trusting all to Marion, obeyed her in this as in everything and lived upon the tidings that came hourly from her husband's room to allay her fears.

Marion set her house in order, released the timid servants from their posts, keeping only old Janet; and then in the darkened room sat down to her long watch beside the pillow of the suffering man, who never knew her, though he called upon her day and night, imploring her to pardon him and give him back his wife and his own dear little child.

A long night and a day had passed since the wild voice echoed through the lonely house, and Marion still sat beside the bed, bathing the burning head that found no ease upon its tender resting place or lifting a cooling draft to parched lips that could not thank her for her patient and untiring care.

The shaded lamp was lit, and its soft light fell full on Marion's anxious face. Tears such as she had seldom shed were falling fast, and broken words of love and sorrow mingled with her whispered prayers.

A slight sound startled her; looking up, she saw a gray-haired woman standing on the threshold. Wild-eyed and wan was the face that watched her from the gloom, travel-stained and poor were the garments that covered the tall figure bending towards her, and there was a world of stifled fear and anguish in the voice that cried to her:

"Where is my son?"

Marion, pointing silently to the head upon her bosom, beckoned the wanderer in and yielded up her place to the poor mother, who looked fearfully into the eyes that had no recognition in them and listened to the voice that could not welcome.

A sudden thought roused Marion as she stood aside watching that sad meeting, and drawing near, she said, "Dear madam, he was brought to me unconscious and has never known me since. Forgive me for seeking to banish you from your son, but it is not safe for you to stay—there is danger of contagion."

"Danger?" echoed Mrs. Leicester. "Then why are you here?"

"Because I could not leave him to a stranger's care. Because his mother was not here and his wife must live for her boy. I have neither child nor mother to lament my loss. I loved him once, and therefore I am here."

With a sudden impulse Mrs. Leicester stretched her hand to Marion and kissed the beautiful, mild face that smiled so cheerfully amid the danger and the gloom. Then, as if ashamed of the unwonted emotion, she said with a proud humility that showed how much the effort cost her:

"Miss Earle, I once turned you from my home. Can you pardon my discourtesy and for my son's sake shelter me a short time in your own?"

"Yes, madam, I can freely pardon all the past, for as I once foretold, your son has come to claim his wife. By his sad wanderings he has learned the remorse and penitence that led him here, and for Agnes's sake I can forgive a far greater wrong than you have ever done me."

And Marion proved the truth of her words, for no daughter could more anxiously forestall a mother's needs than she. Abating nothing of her own quiet dignity, she paid a respectful deference to her guest's wishes, which soon won its way to the proud woman's heart, grown softer through the sharp discipline of poverty and pain.

The three years which passed so quietly in Marion's home had been years of suffering to mother and son. Too proud to ask help from friends, they went among strangers to conceal their poverty. They were unused to labor, and life had been a sore struggle to them both and had taught them stern lessons, for which both were made humbler and wiser.

For his mother Robert labored patiently at any work he could obtain. For her son Mrs. Leicester put away her pride and plied her needle as diligently as the poor seamstress she had so often pitied.

They might have been happy in spite of their fallen fortunes but for the bitter thoughts that haunted the son, who in his hour of trouble learned compassion for the grief of others.

The loss of Marion's love he could have borne, but Marion's esteem he longed to win again, and would have come to claim his wife had he not been deterred by his mother's entreaties.

She never gave him the letter Agnes generously sent, and suppressed the few her son insisted upon writing, thus convincing him that Agnes and Marion would not forgive and had cast him off forever.

Mrs. Leicester, in her humbled state, could not bring herself to ask pardon or relief from those she had wronged; and so they struggled on till Robert, worn out with unaccustomed labor and the grief that preyed upon him, yielded to the uncontrollable desire that possessed him, and in his mother's absence wandered away to find Marion, caring only to be forgiven and set free from the burden of remorse that oppressed him.

All this Marion had learned from his unconscious lips and Mrs. Leicester's inadvertent words. She never spoke of it to her guest, nor made inquiries into her past life; the worn and aged face told the sad history, and the altered manner showed that misfortune had softened the high spirit that was once so pitiless and stern.

Day and night the two women kept their watch in the sickroom, learning to know each other better, and drawn closer by the one anxiety that possessed them both.

"If your son wakes conscious from his deathlike sleep, he is safe—if not, be prepared, dear madam, for the worst. I shall not leave you, so take heart, for I predict a favorable change," and with a cheerful smile old Dr. Murrey stole into the anteroom to guard the sleeper's rest.

Twilight faded into evening, evening deadened into night, and still the watchers, like pale images of patience, sat beside the quiet bed.

Marion, with folded hands and eyes that never left the white face on the pillow, prayed for the wavering life as if it had been her own. Mrs. Leicester, from the deep shadows of the parted curtains, watched her long and keenly, reading the unconscious countenance like an open book and musing bitterly within herself of the wrong she had done her.

"I thought her ambitious, loving my boy only for the high place to which he could lift her, but now I know she loved him for himself and for the right gave him up. I see lines in her tranquil face that only a great sorrow could have left, a sorrow she has conquered but never can forget. I hated and despised her, and she has repaid me thus. God forgive me for the wrong I did her noble nature, and spare my son that we may both atone for the injustice we have done her."

And Mrs. Leicester kept her word.

Night waned slowly and the gray dawn came stealing in. A single ruddy gleam shot across the sky and shone into the room. Marion pointed to the ray as to a blessed omen, and as if awakened by the light, the sleeper's eyes unclosed and looked into her own.

"Marion here, then all is well," he murmured feebly with a faint smile of recognition, and then sank again into a healthful slumber.

Marion covered up her face, remembering nothing but her great gratitude until she felt Mrs. Leicester's arms about her and the mother's tears upon her cheek. No words were uttered; but heart spake to heart, and the silence was eloquent with the forgiveness so generously bestowed, so humbly received.

Robert Leicester, a pale shadow of his former self, sat in the sunny garden waiting for the wife he once cast so cruelly from him. As she had longed and watched for him, he now longed and watched for her, forgetting even the quiet figure at his side who looked wistfully upon him with eyes dimmed by long vigils for his sake.

A child's voice broke the summer stillness; and at the sound Marion arose and, with a solemn beauty shadowing her quiet face, laid her hands on Robert's bent head, saying earnestly, "God bless you in your happiness, dear friend, and send you a fair future to atone for your sad past. Be a true husband to my sister Agnes, a wise father to your little child, and sometimes think of Marion."

"How can I forget you, the good angel of my life?" cried Robert fervently. "Where are you going, Marion? You were with me by my bedside in my darkest hour—why leave me in the brightest I have ever known?" he asked, as she turned away with the solemn light still shining in her wistful eyes.

She only answered, "It is better so," and stole away.

But from a distant nook she watched him still, forgetting the dizzy pain that dimmed her sight and the fierce flame that burned and throbbed in every vein—watched till she saw his mother place Agnes in the shelter of her husband's love, till she saw the gray head bent tenderly above the little golden one and the divided family united once again. Then, with a blessing on them all, she went silently away to lie down upon the bed from which she never rose again.

Her fortune was left to Agnes's son and her summer home to Mrs. Leicester, with the hope that she might "love it for the giver's sake." Then, having bestowed all she possessed to give—her life, her love, and earthly wealth—as she had lived she died, "quiet, amid grass and flowers and charitable deeds," and this home was Marion's monument—a noble one, though she was *but an actress.*

MARK FIELD'S MISTAKE

Love took up the harp of Life,
Smote on all its chords with might,
Smote the chord of Self, that, trembling,
Passed in music out of sight.

—Tennyson

"Where is Milly, Mrs. Low?"

"In the orchard since morning, reading your book, sir."

Mr. Field's grave face relaxed into a smile as he paced slowly through the green old orchard, saying to himself, "The child has more taste than I gave her credit for if she has given a whole day to the romance. I wonder if Miss Douglas will ever do as much," and his eyes turned wistfully to the city spires shining in the distance.

Mildred sat in the tall grass, whence morning shadows had long since fled. The melting sun now shone athwart the sward, touching her brown hair with gold and flickering on her earnest face, as with eyes and lips apart she sat brooding over the book upon her knee.

Silently Mark Field stood in the shadow of a neighboring tree, watching the changes flitting across the girl's attentive face. Swiftly her glance went to and fro, and she turned the pages eagerly, as if impatient of any pause or hindrance. Intense interest flushed her cheek, lit her eye, and kept her lithe form bent and motionless, unconscious of fatigue.

A sudden blithe laugh echoed through the orchard, but

Milly did not pause nor lift her head, though smiles rippled over her bright face and low peals of laughter broke from her lips. The young man smiled too, more flattered than he cared to own by Milly's interest in the children of his brain.

Lost in a pleasant reverie, he stood gazing through the green vistas till a quiet sob recalled him to his watch. Tears now were falling upon the book, but with impatient hands Milly brushed them off and read on, though half blinded by fast-coming drops.

"If all my readers shared Milly's enthusiasm, my success were easily predicted," thought Mark Field, and asked himself reproachfully, "Why can I not be contented with the smiles and tears of innocent hearts like Milly's? Why long for worldly commendations far less sincere, for worldly interest far less inspiriting and rewards whose worth seems lessened by possession?"

"Well, Milly, how is it?" Mark asked. Emerging from the shadow, he looked down into her rapt face as she closed the book and, leaning her head upon her hand, gazed dreamily into the western sky, as if continuing the romance there.

"It is good, *very* good, and I am so glad, so proud for your sake, Mark!" cried Milly, with her innocent heart's delight shining in her upturned face. "But one thing troubles me. Your heroine was too strong a character to end in that weak way. I was disappointed, for she might have been so noble."

A good deal surprised at the "child's" frank criticism, Mark asked, "What would you have done, Milly? It was a good bit of tragedy and cannot be very unnatural, for the tears are not yet dry upon your cheeks."

"If I cried, it was because I grieved that her life should end so poorly. *I* would have had her live to show how strong a woman may be and to shame the weak despair that leads so many to fly like cowards out of life when the battle first begins. A woman with such gifts should have conquered her own grief and 'made death proud to take her' by a life of brave devotion. Humbler women have done so."

"I should have made her a 'martyr' and given her a 'mission,' should I, Milly?" asked Mark with a scornful smile.

"Yes," answered the girl steadily. "Better a 'martyr' for duty's sake than a passionate creature throwing life away when its sweetness seemed gone. We all have a 'mission.' Yours is a very noble one; be true to it. Mine is not yet clear to me, but I am sure to find some work in the world to do and shall stand ready to accept whatever comes. You may laugh at me, Mark, but your Eleanor, with all her intellect, grace, and beauty, was not as true a woman as cheerful little Dolly, with her brave patience and unselfish love."

Mark Field looked down upon the girlish figure in the grass, saying with a touch of wonder in his voice: "Why, Milly, where did you get your ideas of love and life? Not from my book, I can testify."

"My eighteen years and my father's teaching have given me all I know of either," answered Milly. "It is not much, but I believe it is a knowledge which will help me to become what I desire to be: a useful, happy-hearted woman."

"Not a great one, Milly?"

"No, not what you call 'great,' for I possess no such gift to bestow upon the world, and so I am content to be learned in the simple lore of womanly affections, sympathies, and duties. There is so much to be done; I am only anxious to do my part and am not afraid I shall be forgotten if I do it well."

A look half sorrowful, half fond passed over the young man's face as he replied, pacing with restless step before her: "You are not ambitious, Milly. I am, and I'll tell you why. For years I have been fighting my way up from obscurity, conscious of a power that must find vent. But I was young, poor, unknown, and the world set its stern face against me. I have worked for daily bread and barely earned it. I have borne want and grief and disappointment, and in spite of all, I have conquered. The stern face begins to smile, and the pen that brought me bread now brings me the honor I have hungered for. I will not have suffered thus in vain. For every year of weary work and hope deferred, I will have my reward, and the world that would not help me when most I needed it shall yet heap favors on me and be proud to do it. These are dreams now, but they shall yet become realities. My poor room shall be changed to a pleasant home, my solitary life become full of power. My humble name shall be on many lips, and my ambition shall at last be gratified."

"You are changed already, Mark," said Milly sorrowfully as she watched the restless figure crushing the daisies under its impatient feet. "You have lost your cheerfulness. You are more worn and anxious than when you labored helplessly, and in the eager fire of your eyes I can see the spirit that has taken possession of you. Ah, the happy past will never come again!"

A sudden silence fell upon them both. In the stillness both looked into their own hearts and each felt the truth of Milly's words. She soon spoke again, asking cheerfully:

"How will you work your miracle? It will take years of patient labor, and you may find your granted wish no blessing, Mark."

The young man did not look into the questioner's uplifted face, but answered with a sense of shame he would not own: "I shall marry a rich wife, Milly—a woman beautiful enough to gratify my taste, gifted enough to share my aspirations, and skillful enough to rule my house and make it a fit home for the friends I shall gather around me."

"Shall you be happy then, Mark?" As she spoke, the girl's wistful eyes looked steadily into his own and seemed to read the quick denial his heart gave, but not his lips.

"Yes, Milly, as happy as men expect to be in this troublesome world. Do you fancy I shall be disappointed and find a bitter drop in my full cup?"

A look of sharp anguish stirred the sweet composure of the young face that had never turned from his gaze before, and there was a mournful cadence in the music of the voice that answered him so fervently: "May you never feel again the pangs of disappointment, Mark. May you be very prosperous in your noble work and very happy in your home."

There was a struggle in Mark Field's breast, a struggle often felt before, but never so keenly as in that brief moment. A generous passion rose up from the secret place where he had hidden it, and stood beautiful and sweet before him, pleading to be heard. But a stronger power silenced it, and the short conflict ended there, leaving a wound behind that never healed. A grateful memory came smiling from the past and spoke in his altered voice as he asked half tenderly, half gaily:

"When I am a great man, Milly, what shall I bestow on you, the true friend who stood by me in my hardest struggle? I have not forgotten how, when I came here sick, despondent, and unhappy, you made your home a pleasant one for me, and through two years of labor and success you have cheered my way and made it easier by your innocent companionship. What shall I do for you? What *is* your ambition, Milly?"

"To be very brave and just, very faithful to my work, and very patient all my life."

Something in the girl's meek face checked the false gaiety that rose to Mark Field's lips, for in all his ambitious dreams such hopes had no place. The strong contrast of Milly's earnest desire with his worldly longings smote him painfully, and her innocent nature spoke to his more eloquently than her words, uttering a rebuke for generous purposes neglected, wasted gifts, and life devoted to selfish aims.

A vague feeling of remorse oppressed and kept him silent till Milly rose and, offering the book, said in her old cheerful voice: "I thank you for a very happy day, such as I shall not spend again till you lend me another to enjoy."

"Keep it, Milly, for our friendship's sake," he replied, and writing her name in it, he gave it back, adding earnestly, "My next shall be better, for I will put a creature in it as simple and as good as one I have lately learned to know and—" Pausing abruptly, he asked as they reached the porch: "Have you any commands for town? I shall ride in tonight."

"Bring me pleasant news of your success and more notices of the book, but only favorable ones, for no one must find fault with it but I, because no one can admire it so much or feel so proud of it as I who have watched its progress all this happy year."

He promised, and rode thoughtfully away, but looking back from the riverside, saw Milly still standing on the porch with sunshine flickering on her bent head. He could not see how fast her hot tears dropped upon his gift, nor feel how dark a shadow had fallen on her happy life.

Helen Douglas was no longer young, but beauty, culture, and position made her the center of attraction to a large and brilliant circle. Alone in the world, of strong character and independent will, she had no ties to bind her, no fear of opinion to control her, and ruled her little kingdom royally, admired by all, feared by many, and beloved by few.

Mark Field admired her, was proud of her friendship, and fancied that he loved her, though in his secret soul he knew her sole attraction was the power she possessed to bestow on him all his ambitious heart desired.

She saw his growing interest and encouraged it, for, wearying of pleasures that had once been sweet, she began to long for a calmer life and a home less solitary than her own when friends and flatterers were gone. There was little love in her desire; she wished for no stronger arm to lean upon, no firmer will to guide her, no deeper heart to love. Her imperious nature must rule, and the husband she might choose must remain a subject to her, though king of all the world beside.

Mark possessed genius, reputation, youth, and a high name in the future if the gracious promise of the present was fulfilled. His frank admiration pleased her by its sincerity; his fine face satisfied her eye; his growing fame gratified her pride and filled her with a true desire for his success.

Never had her fine eyes shone more graciously upon him and never had her manner been so full of interest as when she greeted him that night. A quick smile lit up her face, and the music of her voice gave added sweetness to the flattering congratulations she bestowed on the young author and his work.

"See," she said, taking a richly bound volume from the table at her side, "I have had your beautiful creation clothed right royally in gold and purple, as it should be, and have given it the place of honor in my treasury. Will you add one favor more and let me see my name in it, written by your hand?"

A stately figure bent to lay the book before him, a fair hand offered him the pen, and the young man with a glow of gratified pride could but bow and acquiesce. But as he wrote, his thoughts passed swiftly from that brilliant scene to the green solitude of the old orchard, and the fair woman smiling down on him changed to a brown-eyed girl couched among the tall grass. The graceful flatteries sounding in his ear seemed empty words while remembering the eager voice that cried so joyfully, "It is good, Mark, very good." He wrote silently and rose up from his task with an altered mien.

Miss Douglas glanced at the newly written words as she returned her thanks, and a sudden change passed over her expressive face. But with a look of calm surprise she held the book before him, saying playfully:

"A slight mistake in the name, Mr. Field—mine is Helen Douglas, and I shall be proud to number you among my 'true friends,' if I may."

"Milly Low, from her true friend, Mark Field" were the words which met the young man's eye. Crimson with shame and anger, he tore out the offending page and carefully repaired his error—that slight error that led to a far greater one, which he bitterly rued all the days of his life.

Miss Douglas skillfully changed the current of his thoughts, and when her duties as hostess called her away, she saw his eye followed her and that he still kept the seat beside her own, lost in deep thought.

Hitherto she had been content to feel her power and live in the pleasant dreams she had conjured up. But the sight of the unknown name written with such unconscious care aroused her fears, and she resolved to make her dreams realities at once, if she possessed the power.

When Mark joined her again, there was a softness in the eye that seldom fell before another's, a winning tone in the voice that spoke so frequently to him, and a wistful look upon the handsome face, half proud, half tender, that filled his heart and brain with a bewilderment of hopes and regrets and fears never felt before. He lingered till the last and, before he left, had asked and won a beautiful hand that gave him money when it should have given love.

Through the soft spring moonlight he rode home, and sat down by the fire shimmering on his hearth, still lost in thought, still troubled by the vague sense of remorse that would not be appeased.

He tried to think of Helen, but imagination turned traitor. From the red embers he conjured up a picture that haunted him through all that night—a quiet country home, full of sweet sights and sounds; a twilight orchard path where a slight figure walked beside him, listening to his desires and disappointments, encouraging with quick sympathy or comforting with womanly cheer. Through the summer gloom he seemed to see soft eyes looking up to him with confidence and love in their brown depths, while from the small hand folded in his own there seemed to come a touch that warmed and strengthened his whole nature.

The same figure seemed to float through all the changes of his waking dream—sometimes beside him as he wrote, waking fresh memories and high thoughts by its welcome presence; sometimes near him at his fireside, pillowing his weary head upon its gentle bosom and "smoothing off the day's annoy," cheering grief or soothing pain. In the shadows of the summer light or the ruddy circle of the firelight, the figure was always the same—always a household spirit walking by him steadfastly, with faith and innocence and love still shining on him from its cheerful eyes.

This winning vision beckoned, but he would not stretch his arms to greet it. The wistful face grew dim and faded, never to be again recalled by prayer or invocation.

The red embers turned to ashes, the light wavered and went out, and dawn was stealing through the curtains, gray and chill, before Mark Field rose from his long vigil a poorer and a harder man for that night's defeat, conqueror though he believed himself; for he had sacrificed the purest passion of his life and lost a blessing never to be won again. Seeking to gain laurels, he forgot that the little flower called heartsease blossoms oftenest at our feet.

Of all the sad words of tongue or pen,
The saddest are these, "It might have been."
—Whittier

Ten years had come and gone, and Mark Field's name was a "household word" on many lips. His ambitious dream *had* become a living truth, and his long struggle ceased forever.

But there had come a change in him and the books he wrote. The same powerful hand wielded the pen, but the spirit that inspired it was an altered one. The tender pathos with which he once touched human sin and sorrow was now gone, and in its place, sarcastic pity or reproach. The genial humor which once painted the lighter foibles and pathos of the world so kindly that a tear came with the smile was replaced by a keen, cold wit that often wounded when it sparkled brightest. The household figures that won friends by their simple joys and sorrows were changed to worldly shadows taken from the darker, sadder side of life. Thoughtful women and innocent girls laid down his books wondering if the world were in truth as full of misery and falsehood as he painted it. Young men full of generous aspirations felt their faith in honesty and honor shaken as they read, and even while they relished the keen satire and the brilliant wit, were conscious of a sentiment of pity for the bitterness of spirit which marred what might have been both powerful and sweet.

Mark Field felt the change which had befallen him, and lamented it. But the regrets which poisoned his own peace darkened all the world to him, and as he saw he wrote. The genius which should have made poetry of Life's prose and by its power served humanity had been perverted by ambition and embittered by remorse till half its strength and sweetness was destroyed.

Milly's fervent wish was yet unfulfilled. He felt a sharper pang of disappointment than he had ever known before, for when he raised the full cup to his lips, the "bitter drop" was there and all its sparkling water could not quench his thirst. He had been "prosperous" in worldly things, but had grown poor in wealth of heart and soul. He was not "happy in his home," for its true charm was wanting. A stately woman's presence graced it, and he was thought a happy man. But "wife" was not a blessed word to him, full of tenderness and trust, and the tie that bound him was not the sacred bond of love, unseen but ever felt; it was a golden chain that seemed more irksome for its glitter. The fair woman looked upon and admired him afar off as others did, but never laid her proud head on his bosom, never came and took her place within his heart.

All he had asked was granted, but a regretful and longing spirit still possessed him. An inward voice he feared to listen to seemed crying mournfully, "Oh, Milly, faithful Milly, come and comfort me."

A sudden pestilence fell on the city, and it became a scene of suffering and terror. It spared neither rich nor poor, but among the latter its ravages were fearful. Many a poor soul to whom helpless creatures looked for hope and comfort died for lack of care, while wealth had power to purchase skill and save some lives that were better ended.

The pestilence was at its height when through the city there crept rumors of a brave-hearted woman who came daily from without, bringing a blessed air of country peace and freshness with her presence, and who went fearlessly among the poorest and most neglected sufferers, saving many and leading many calmly out of life.

The simple story came like a ray of sunshine to many terror-stricken hearts. To the forsaken poor it gave again their faith in Christian charity, while to the rich it was a rebuke which in that hour of suffering and fear touched their consciences.

Sums of money from unknown benefactors were given for her mission, and a little band of self-devoted women followed the example set so silently and went through the troubled city, true "Sisters of Mercy" to the helpless and the poor.

That humble figure passing to and fro upon its errand of perilous compassion was greeted with a reverence the most sincere. Many a full hand pressed her own, many a high head bent low before her, and men listened to her words, simple, wise, and few, as they had seldom listened to the most eloquent in calmer times. Always serene and cheerful, she came and went through scenes of grief and dread and was so strong and tender that many prayed to her as to a guardian saint. In their simple ignorance they believed a wondrous power lay in the touch of her skillful hand and the echo of her soothing voice, and no sound woke more or called forth warmer blessings than the humble name of Mildred Low.

"There is the nurse, sir. She offered to come when others refused!" As the servant spoke, Mark Field looked up from his bed of pain to see Milly standing at his side.

The mild face, worn with those labors of love, looked back at him with a benign compassion shining in its tranquil eyes as the voice so long unheard asked cheerily, "What can I do for you, dear friend?"

"Oh, Milly, help me make life worth living for, or let death take me from your hands." And in his hour of suffering the strong man clung to that frail creature as his only hope, with no fear of repulse, no doubt of sincerity and love.

A blissful sense of happiness filled Milly's heart as she felt the touch of those feeble hands and saw the eagerness which lit the feverish face uplifted to her own. "He feels the need of me at last," she thought, and lent her whole soul to the work she came to do.

There was a soothing calm in look and word that fell like balm on Mark Field's troubled spirit, a light in her eye that banished despair, a gentleness of hand that made its least touch comforting; and when he spoke of this, there came a smile upon her countenance more beautiful than any he had ever seen upon her girlish lips.

"Ah, Milly, *you* are unchanged," he said, scanning her face wistfully. "The years that have gone by have not robbed you of your peace nor soured the gracious sweetness of your nature. You have no sharp regrets to haunt you, no sins to embitter life. Thank God for that, Milly, and pity me from your kind heart."

"I do, Mark, but I am not content with pity. Let me serve

you, as I did so long ago. Let me heal and comfort you, for that is my 'mission' now." And as she spoke, a brief smile flittered over Milly's face and vividly recalled the past to Mark's remembrance.

"A blessed mission it has become, Milly, one that will do you more honor than that which *I* chose, and keep your memory green when I am forgotten. I smiled at your ambition once; how poor my own looks now. Yours was the nobler one; I felt it then, but see it clearly in our lives this day. I followed a vain shadow and lost my peace of heart; you chose duty and have found happiness. You *are* happy, Milly?" he asked earnestly.

"Yes, Mark, but only after years of prayerful endeavor. I too have had errors to lament and regrets sharper, perhaps, than yours. My life is far from what it should be, and must fail in many things. But it is growing sweeter to me every year, richer in duties, braver in sacrifices, and fuller of those records of humble labor which I would see before the book is closed forever."

"Oh, Milly, how shall I read the pages of the book I have been writing these ten years? It may be nearly done. What judgment will be given when it shall be read?"

Softly the voice beside him answered his despairing cry: "The mercy of God endureth forever."

Silence fell upon the room and remained unbroken till Mark, turning wearily upon his pillow, said, "Tell me more of yourself, Milly. I have known so little of you all these years. It soothes and satisfies me but to listen to the echo of your voice and makes the truth that you are sitting here beside me seem more real."

"There is little that can interest you in the history of these years, Mark," and a shade of patient sorrow swept like a passing cloud across the cheerful face bending so watchfully above him. "My mother's place is empty, but I am not a lonely woman, as I feared I should be, for the old house is full of little children, fatherless and motherless like myself. They make it very dear to me, for its once empty rooms are bright with winsome faces and musical with loving voices that call me

'Mother.' In their simple cares and sorrows I forget my own, and by their innocent companionship I keep my spirit blithe and young. I have my twilight hours, Mark, when things look cold and dim, but soon there comes some earnest work to shame me into action, some stirring purpose that gives energy and sweetness to my life. These dark hours come seldomer as years go by, and the sunshine lingers longer till at last I feel that I can truly say, 'Thank God, I am happy now.'"

Mark Field covered up his face and wept as he had not done since he sobbed upon his mother's breast as a tender-hearted boy.

Milly prospered in her ministering of love, and Mark was spared to rise up from his bed of suffering a wiser, humbler man, for, lying in the shadow of death, he had learned how beautiful and brave a thing life might become.

The fell fever had followed them to the country home to which they had fled, and would not be appeased until the mother and three little ones had fallen victim to its power. Through all the fear and anguish of that heavy time, Milly was the stay and comfort of the stricken household. One by one the little heads drooped and grew still upon her bosom. One by one she laid them down to that long sleep that needs no lullaby, weeping motherly tears above them and uttering words of consolation to the hearts left desolate.

Her brave sincerity led husband and wife to know each other better, and in these last hours of agony and death, they saw and pardoned the great wrongs they had done each other. Mark felt the solace of this mutual confession and forgiveness in after years, and Helen died happily in the love that came so late, and clinging fast to faithful Milly till the light of that mild countenance passed from her sight forever.

"Milly, I must go away," said Mark. "This place is so full of memories and regrets that I must leave it till time has laid the ghosts that haunt it now. One thing only holds me back—my motherless child."

"Not motherless, Mark, while I am here, not homeless while I have a home." And Milly folded the little creature closer to that bosom which seemed so fit a refuge for its help-less innocence.

"God bless you, Milly! Be to her what you have been to her father, and in her affection may you find some return for the great debt he already owes you."

So they parted—she to the great duties of her home, he to cross seas and lands in search of balm for self-inflicted wounds. Years passed before the wanderer turned homeward. Time had been kind to him and had healed his heaviest griefs, and fresh hopes were blossoming on their graves.

"Yes, I will go home and rest," he said within himself. "It is not yet too late, and these years have not been quite wasted. I am wiser for this sad experience, humbler for this sharp disci-pline of pain. I will begin anew. Milly shall teach me how to live and lead me up to better things. Oh, to recall the time when I *knew* she loved me—to unsay that one false word, to undo that one rash deed! Heaven forgive me and grant the one good gift I rejected when it came to me."

Autumn sunshine danced upon the floor, but nothing else stirred in the old familiar room as Mark Field paused upon the threshold. All the happy hours spent there seemed crowding back to stir his heart and lure him in, the pictured faces on the walls seemed smiling on him, and the sunny silence grew mu-sical with the echoes of remembered voices speaking as they spoke of old.

His eye, wandering from one well-known object to an-other, fell on a book that lay apart as if it were a cherished thing. It was his own first, best book, given to Milly years ago. He held it long and turned its pages lingeringly. It was worn with frequent reading and stained with many tears, but was more beautiful and precious in his sight than that other gold and purple volume whose leaves were never cut—for Milly's hands had often touched it, Milly's tears had fallen when she read, and he felt sure that Milly still remembered him and kept his first gift for the giver's sake.

A sound of childish voices roused him from his reverie and led him through the well-known path into the orchard, where all the air was full of the faint fragrance of ripening fruit and little figures flitted to and fro, their glad voices making blither music than the summer birds.

"Are you looking for Mother, sir? She is behind the trees with Nell," said a little damsel, pausing in her play to glance half shyly, half confidingly into the stranger's face and then dart away before he could reply.

In the old place, on a rustic seat, sat Milly with a child upon her knee. Time had touched her gentle head so lightly that it bore no trace of years; there was the same serene face, still the same clear glance and cheery voice. Nothing seemed gone but the shadow of unrest and secret sorrow which once came and went across the quiet countenance, and all the grace of a noble womanhood now crowned her with a charm mere beauty could not give.

Apple blossoms had whitened all the boughs and shed their tinted petals on the girl's brown locks when Mark Field last beheld her there. Now a ruddy harvest bowed the branches above the woman's head, a fitting symbol of the life fast ripening to its gracious prime. The unseen watcher felt and owned the truth of Nature's silent lesson and, remembering whose hand had rudely shaken that fair tree, thanked heaven that its blossoms had not all been scattered.

Milly was singing a little song that Mark knew well, and as she sang, her eye dwelt musingly upon the young face looking fondly into hers.

The figure moving in her thoughts came suddenly before her, and the voice which first taught her the simple melody spoke to her: "Milly, am I welcome home?"

He read the answer in her cordial greeting and soon sat beside her, full of content and happiness till quick-coming hopes and fears disturbed the quiet current of his thoughts.

"Do you remember when we last sat here, Milly?" he asked at length, folding her hand closer in his own.

"Yes, Mark, fifteen years ago. A long, long, long time it sounds, and yet it seems but yesterday."

His eyes were on her face as she replied, scanning it with eager scrutiny to read some sudden glow, some brief emotion that might give him hope. But the steadfast eyes never dropped nor turned away, and the friendly smile remained unchanged till he spoke again, fervently and fast:

"Milly, if I could recall that day and answer again the question you then asked, how different it would be—I shouldn't covet the poor things I once desired, for my sole ambition now is to possess the gift I should have asked for then had I not been blind to its great worth. Now, when it is the one thing I desire, it may be too late to claim it. I want a home—a quiet place where I may forget the past and know a happy future. I want a friend to purify and strengthen me, a woman wise and tender who will lead me out of my gloomy self into a fresh, fair world again, one who can forgive much and sweeten pity with her love. The home I long for is here, and the woman I would call my wife means your shape, Milly. Can these things ever be?"

"No, Mark, never."

He looked into her face incredulously. There was a world of pain and pity in her answering glance, but neither doubt nor love, and her voice, so firm yet gentle, sounded like the knell of his cherished hopes.

He dropped the hand he had held so closely, and bent his head upon the bosom of his little Nell, accepting silently the punishment he felt was merited.

Milly's womanly heart smote her for the pain she must inflict, but her frank nature would not let compassion silence truth. With a light caressing touch upon the bent head so thickly sown with gray, she answered his appeal in tones that often faltered, often failed, but never lost their brave sincerity:

"Mark, fifteen years ago I had a friend whom I loved with all the fervor of a maiden heart, and was beloved in return—I believed so then, I *know* it now. And yet he chose another wife, not for love's sake but ambition's. I never reproached him, for no vow bound us, no word had ever passed between us. But we had looked into each other's eyes and read the secret of a mutual love—a love fresh and ardent as youth, innocence, and hope could make it—and this knowledge should have been as binding as betrothal ring or plighted word. To me it was and ever will be, but it was a bitter moment when I learned how far apart our paths must be and how false my friend could be to himself and me.

"Mark, it was a moment full of sharper anguish than I can ever know again, for I could not speak and must submit. I did, and silently buried my lost love deep out of sight, there to be a consuming pain for many years. God only knows how fierce the struggle was; for I was passionate and young, and life seemed barren when the affection that might have been a blessing proved a burden. But let that dark hour rest among past things. The flame purified me while it tortured, and at last patience rose from passion's grave, an angel beautiful and strong to solace and support my wavering feet. No tears for me, Mark. I am glad to have felt the sweetness and bitterness of love and am the richer and more human for the blessedness and pain of this great passion.

"I have spoken frankly, that I may not seem unkind. The man I loved lives only in my memory now, and these long years of strife and conquest have made my heart a sacred place where that first and last love lives forever. No hope, no fear, can stir its calm. Then leave me this one hidden joy and the peace I have so hardly earned."

Mark Field put the child down from his knee and rose, saying with humility sorrowful to see in one so proud: "It is just, Milly, but very hard. As you submitted long ago, so will I now, as silently if I must, as patiently if I can. But my sustaining hope is gone, and without that there seems little worth living for. Yes, it is too late to be what I might have been."

"It is never too late," cried Milly. "There is noble work in the world to do, and who so fit to do it nobly as those who have been taught by suffering and time? Oh, Mark, what I, a woman, have lived through, surely you, with a man's power and courage, may yet conquer. You shall not despair, but work—and in the griefs of others find a solace for your own. You have wealth; make it a blessing, not a curse. You have power; use it for high ends. You have eloquence; plead it for those whose wrongs keep them dumb. Sing no dirges over the past, but dedicate heart, tongue, and pen to some grand work, and make life a brave battle full of victories."

Milly stood before him transformed by the energy of the purpose at her heart. Her eye lit and her countenance glowed with the fervor of her words, while her voice sounded like stirring music to his ear.

"Ah, Milly, if I had again the power I have lost, I might do what you ask, but I am forty-five—too old to begin anew—and the autumn of my life never can be gladdened by a harvest such as yours," and he smiled drearily, glancing from the little figures singing in the sunshine to the withered leaves beneath his feet.

But Milly pointed to the fields of yellow grain that waved along the hillside, saying softly, "The reapers have not come yet, Mark, and these golden days were given to ripen and perfect the generous promise of the year. There is yet time. Then go out to your work, and from among the tares garner up the wheat sown in your springtime and neglected until now. Go, and when weary, come and grow young again among little children in the old home always yours."

He stood erect and stretched his hands to child and woman, saying bravely, "Milly, I will—but my sheaf will be poor and scanty, my offering a few dead books, while yours is a rich store of living charities. Lead your father, little Nell, for he has wandered very far. Teach me, Milly, and become the sweet, strong angel of my life."

"Yes, Mark, your friend forever."

Thus, led by his little daughter's hand and leaning steadfastly on faithful Milly, Mark Field began the world anew.

MARK FIELD'S SUCCESS

Still waits kind Nature to impart
Her choicest gifts to such as gain
An entrance to her loving heart
Through the sharp discipline of pain.
—Whittier

"A Merry Christmas, Father!" cried little Nell's blithe voice as Mark Field came in from the winter night to the warm glow of Christmas fires, the music of happy voices, and the peace of Milly's presence. She sat among her little flock, telling them the sweet old story of the divine Child whose birth night was being celebrated far and wide over the earth His advent had so blessed. Like flowers turning toward the sun, the thoughtful little faces were uplifted to her own, drinking in like dew the words that fell so simply and reverently from her lips.

Mark Field sat down among his children and listened like a child to the wondrous story of the Judean peasant, feeling rebuke that he had never so truly seen the power and the beauty of that life before.

The story done, the children soon flitted away to their Christmas games, and Mark and Milly sat together in the ruddy circle the firelight cast about them.

"Milly, I want something to do," Mark began, rousing himself from the sweet and bitter memories awakened by the familiar spot, the quiet hour, and the beloved presence at his side. "The new year must find me busied about some better

293

work than weaving romances. I am tired of my phantoms; their fictitious joys and sorrows weary me. Show me some human grief that I can assuage, some real wrongs that I can relieve. Give me some earnest work, that I may feel my life is better worth the living. Teach me, Milly, for I have been a selfish soul and am very ignorant of any sufferings but my own."

Milly's clear eyes beamed upon him with a glance of frank approval as she answered, "Mark, I have hoped for this, feeling sure that a time would come when human woes and wants would touch your sympathies and rouse your interest in the great duties of this life. There is a work which you can share with the just, compassionate, and brave of this and every other Christian land—a work in which you can labor with both tongue and pen, winning for yourself God's blessing and a place among the true heroes of the world."

"What is it, Milly? Where shall I find it?" cried Mark, eager to follow where the beloved voice should call him.

"There is a symbol of the work, Mark, and a brave little laborer to lead you on," and Milly pointed to a group in a distant nook of the long, old-fashioned room. A colored child, deformed and feeble, sat in her little chair apart from the merriment about her, but not alone nor sorrowful, for Nell, with her childish countenance beautified with love and pity, stood beside her, selecting from her store of gifts the dainties for poor lame Bess.

Mark Field looked at the little picture till it grew dim before his eyes as he remembered the story of the crippled child. Poor Bess, rendered helpless and loathsome by disease, had been a friendless creature till, when all other doors were closed to her, Milly's opened wide and she took her home with that love which takes all to its warm shelter, with that faith which recognizes the divine in the saddest human wreck, and that patience which conquers all things. Milly saw in the forlorn outcast a *child,* and remembering by whose blessing little children were forever sanctified, she took it to her bosom and was to it as a mother.

Mark recalled this womanly deed of hers, the last of many

charities, and felt that he need not fear to follow the guide who walked so meekly through the byways of the world, a sweet Samaritan to any who had need of help.

Milly watched him silently, and when he turned to her again, she said, still pointing to the childish group: "Mark, I would have you 'go and do likewise.' Give as freely of your gifts to many as Nelly gives of her little store to one. See in poor Bess a symbol of her race—that race so wronged, neglected, and forsaken. Make their cause your cause, and in serving them you will serve God."

"Milly, if I put my hands to this work, I sacrifice much that is dear to me," Mark replied. "I shall lose many friends and much wealth; the former I grieve to lose for my own sake, the latter for Nell's. Helen's wealth came from the South, and at my death will be Nell's. It is her all, for I have been very idle these last years and shall have but little for the child. Therefore, if I give myself to this work as an honest man, I must put away the fortune unrighteously accumulated and must rob Nell to free the poor souls who by law are mine. God knows I pity them and deplore the miserable fact, but what can I do? Were I alone concerned, I should not waver long, but I think of Nell, and hesitate. Need I—ought I to do this, Milly?"

"Yes, Mark, you *ought,* and if I know your heart aright, you *will,*" replied the voice that seldom spoke in vain. "Do not let your love blind your conscience, nor selfish fears weaken your integrity. A brave life devoted to humanity will be a nobler heritage to Nell than a hundred fortunes stained with blood and tears. Do the right fearlessly, and God will provide for Nell."

"Ah, Milly, I am selfish, vain, and weak," sighed Mark. "I cannot give up my ease, my high place so hardly won, my friends, and all the nameless solaces and pleasures these afford me, for the self-sacrificing life you offer. I honor those who have done so; I desire sincerely to do well, but falter here before the first hard step. Give me some of your courage, Milly, some of your self-denying spirit and integrity."

Before Milly could reply, Nell came and laid her bright head on her father's shoulders, caressing his anxious face and asking what disturbed him on that happy night. He drew her on his knee, and looking into the innocent countenance that knew no guile, he asked, half playfully, half seriously:

"Nell, if I should tell you that by giving up all these pretty toys treasured so carefully in this little apron, you could make Bess strong and well again, would you do it? Nay, more," he added, seeing a quick assent in the child's eyes, "would you give away your flowers, let loose your birds, and part with all the things you value? Could you bear to have your little friends turn from you, to hear them say harsh, unkind words of you and know you had lost their love? Could you do all this for poor black Bess?"

Nell listened with the smile fading from her lips as Mark went on, growing so grave and earnest as he spoke that she believed his appeal must be true and paused a moment in deep thought as he ceased. Then she said slowly:

"If Milly said it was best, I'd try, Father."

"What, all these precious things, Nell? Bess is not your sister. Why should you rob yourself for her?"

Nell turned toward the distant recess where the little cripple sat, and gazed long at the misshapen figure, dark skin, and uncouth features. It was not a fair sight, but a sad one; and as she looked, the child's eyes grew deep and thoughtful, her lips trembled, and her little bosom heaved. Silently she laid her treasures one by one in her father's hand, and then, looking bravely up into his face, as if her sacrifice were made, she said earnestly:

"Bess is a *child,* Father, and I call her my sister, for she has lost her own. She is not pretty like these toys, but she loves me and will last when these are gone. Yes, I'll give my precious things to make her well if God will let her be, for He loves her, Father, and doesn't mind her poor little body because He knows her soul is white."

The father bent and kissed the eager face, saying tenderly, "Keep your treasures, darling. Bess shall be helped without this loss to you. You have rebuked your father, Nell, and taught him to put away *his* toys to serve a race of sadder sufferers than Bess. You are my little Gospel, Nell—a fair, sweet book full of simple wisdom and consolation. I shall read it often, for I need its teaching very much."

"I am but a little book, Father. You will soon read me to the end," cried the child as she laid her soft cheek upon his own.

"Heaven forbid, my darling!" and Mark held her closer, as if his arms were a shield from every ill. "Milly must fill these white leaves with precious records of deeds and virtues like her own, that I may solace my old age with such rare reading and leave the volume yet unfinished when my poor history ends."

Silence fell upon the three, unbroken but by the murmur of gay voices from above and the sound of dancing feet. Milly broke in, saying with a glance into the thoughtful face bent down upon Nell's golden hair:

"Mark, a brave poet said, 'To long and weave a woof of high, heroic deeds is enough for a feeble soul, but nobler is the stouthearted striving that makes the dream a reality.' Dear friend, cease longing and put heart and soul into your work. Welcome poverty, injustice, and neglect for the truth's sake, and believe me, though your fortune passes away, you will find yourself rich in peace of heart; though old friends desert you, the good and true will take you by the hand; and for every worldly loss you will find a blessed gain in the growing strength and power of your own soul. Oh, Mark, your ambition proved an empty thing. Look higher for your happiness, and remember the divine voice has said, 'If any man would come after me, let him *deny himself*, take up his cross, and follow.'"

"Milly, I will try" was all Mark said, but in the firm grasp of his hand and the clear glance of his eye she read an answer that filled her with hope and cheer.

"Good night, my darling. I shall miss this sunny face in my solitary home, but it is better here, and I'm content. Good night, Bess. A merry Christmas and a happy future to you and your kindred. God bless you, Milly. Help me on with your brave words and patient care, and I will prove a grateful pupil to you all my life."

Mark went out into the winter night. But the bleak winds could not chill, the darkness could not bewilder, nor the solitude make afraid; for the snowy pathway seemed to shimmer with a fire's warm glow, and he seemed to bear a generous purpose on his heart while, in the guise of little Nell, a good angel walked beside him, smiling on him with a glance as beautiful and bright as that he left behind in Milly's eyes.

New Year's Eve was coming on, and in the early gloaming Mark Field went toward his lonely home. He lingered on his way, and when at length he stood before it, he looked up at the darkened windows, thinking of the faces that years ago were wont to smile a welcome on him as he came. As this thought jarred the tender chord of love and memory, his eyes fell on his study window: A radiant light streamed out through the frosty panes, and a little shadow seemed to dance upon the wall.

The steps that had fallen so bravely trod lightly as a boy's as Mark entered at his door and hastened to the room where gloom had vanished when the little shadow came.

"Milly sent me as a New Year's gift, dear Father. She said you were alone and needed me to be your sunbeam. Are you glad to have me come?" cried Nell as she sprang into his arms.

"Glad, Nell? A whole summer of sunshine could not make such happiness as your small self. I *was* alone, gloomy, and sad, but now there will be joy in the sight of your winsome face, cheer in the sound of your blithe voice, and comfort in your innocent companionship, my Nell." And Mark sat down upon the hearth a happy man.

Milly, with a true woman's instinct, had read the struggle in Mark's mind and judged wisely in sending the child to plead unconsciously for the right, to rouse his better nature, and to keep his spirit from the gloom that often darkened it. Thenceforth Nell dwelt with her father, taking root like a little flower in his heart, softening his nature with the touch of its clinging tendrils, and covering the ruins of a bitter past with the tender verdure of its love.

*　　*　　*

The year rolled around and brought another Christmas Eve to Milly's home. The children were keeping their simple revel as gaily as before, but "the mother" did not join in their play as she was wont to do. With an anxious shadow on her quiet face, she paced to and fro, looking often out into the night, watching and waiting for the guest who always came to sit beside her Christmas fire.

In sending Nell away, Milly had resigned her dearest treasure, and many a secret pang it cost her, for without the child's sweet presence she seemed to lose the solace of her laborious life. Nell was a childish shadow of the Mark she had so truly loved, an image of her happy youth with all its bloom and freshness still untouched by grief or time. But silently as the early affection was relinquished, the later love was given up and made a blessing to herself in seeking to bless Mark.

Milly had lost another happiness in parting with the child. Mark found his home so cheerful that he seldom came to the old place now, not that he loved Milly less, but Nell more. He did not know how welcome his presence had become, how refreshing to Milly, when the duties of her day were faithfully performed, to sit and listen to the conversation so rich in the varied charms which travel, thought, and culture gave it, and to feel the charm of that true friendship and the knowledge of her power to strengthen and to cheer.

He came but seldom, and Milly watched the changes coming over him with womanly solicitude. He had never spoken of the work she had offered him, but she heard of him as one seeking for light and willing to be taught, and in her faithful heart prayed fervently that the promise of his manhood might not fail as that of his youth had done.

A step on the threshold woke her from her reverie, and looking up, she saw Mark standing before her with a face so like little Nell's in its humility and timid joy that her heart went out to greet him, though her lips only said, "Welcome, Mark. Come to your old place and tell me what glad tidings I read in these wistful eyes, dear friend."

Mark stretched his hands to her, saying, "Milly, they are clean, but very empty now."

"No, Mark, not empty while my little store remains," and Milly held them fast in both her own, baptizing them in quiet tears.

"The first hard step is taken, and I see my way before me now," Mark continued as they sat together on the hearth. "I am a poorer and a richer man, and your words, Milly, did not fall upon a careless ear; they took root and in God's good time, I trust, will blossom and bear fruit. This has been a year of trial. Pity, contempt, distrust, and injustice have been my portion; angry remonstrances, harsh names, and the falling off of friends, my daily trials; hard, very hard to bear, but I shall learn to receive these wounds meekly and find a balm in the approval of my conscience and my own true friend. The leaven your example has infused into my nature is slowly working, Milly. I already feel a power unknown before. My fears grow less, my courage greater, and I cannot hesitate, for like old Behmen, though 'without his contempt within, there is a fiery striving' that will not let me pause."

"Ah, Mark, what I desire you have the power to perform," said Milly with a sigh, looking into the earnest countenance of her friend and marking the youthful ardor that had replaced its melancholy gloom.

Mark smiled as he replied with the humility which seemed to have come to him with his new aspirations: "Nay, Milly, *you* are the sower of good seed, *I* but the gardener, who, with the help of heaven's sun and dew, may gather a little knot of herbs and flowers from my neglected garden to make my autumn fair."

A shade of sorrow swept suddenly across his cheerful face as he spoke. With an altered voice he said, "Milly, my little Nell needs you. Will you come to her? She is weak and wasted, but I never knew how much she needed care till a friend's womanly eye saw the change and showed it to me. I am not a fit guardian for such a tender charge. My blindness proves it, and this year's absence from your motherly care has robbed my little blossom of the fostering sunshine which has been her life."

"Let her come back to me, Mark. I will cherish and heal my

darling as no other woman can," cried Milly, with a host of foreboding fears starting into life and banishing the sweet composure of her face.

"She will not come, Milly," answered Mark. "I spoke of home and you, but though her little heart was full of love and longing, she still clung to me, urging, 'It is better I should stay with you; tell Milly so with my dear love.'"

A sudden rain of tender tears dimmed Milly's eyes, for she remembered now her farewell words to Nell—"Cling to him and love him, darling, for he needs you very much"—and Nell had been faithful to her short, sweet ministry of love.

"I will come to her, Mark. There are many now who can fill my place here, and none to whom I will yield my place by Nell. Tell her I remember and will come," Milly said, as Mark rose like one with a burden newly laid upon him. He paused in his farewell, saying fearfully:

"Milly, if the shadow that seems gathering should wrap my darling from my sight, how shall I bear it?"

"God will give you strength, Mark. He never sends more sorrow than a human heart can bear" was Milly's low reply.

He looked down upon the gentle face that looked back at him with faith and meek submission shining through its tears, murmuring regretfully, "I have no blessed faith to comfort and uphold me, and in my sorrow know not where to turn. Oh, Milly, teach me this truth, and be very near me when the dark hour comes."

"Yes, Mark, your griefs and joys are all my own."

Nell lay on her little bed, a patient shadow daily growing dearer as she drifted down the solemn river, farther and farther from the reach of those whose love grew powerless to stay the rapid waves that bore their treasure so serenely to the sea.

Mark hoped against hope and struggled manfully to accept the great grief as he should, but the father's heart bled sorely and clung despairingly to the one happy love of his whole life. Day and night he hovered near the pillow where faithful Milly sat, learning of her a little patience and a little faith. She was his refuge when his despair grew strong, and for his sake Milly strove to conquer and conceal the motherly anguish that tore her heart with so sharp a pang.

The quiet room became a sacred place to Mark, and when he entered there, all selfish hopes, all poor ambitions and vain desires, seemed to stand rebuked by the innocent presence that sanctified the spot. Looking daily on the fragile wreck before him, Mark felt the blessing of a sinless soul, for no bitter memories had power to mar Nell's peace, no doubts to disturb, no fears to dismay; and seeing this, the coming change lost half its gloom. Life was but a poor gift to desire for her who was so fit to lay it by, and Death, no longer a stern phantom, seemed like a beautiful, benignant angel standing unseen in the silence of the air and blessing them.

So many weeks went by while

> *Lying patient in the shadow*
> *Till the blessed light should come,*
> *A serene and tranquil presence*
> *Sanctified that troubled home,*
> *Earthly hopes and cares and sorrows,*
> *Broke like ripples on the strand*
> *Of the deep and solemn river*
> *Where those little feet must stand.*

In the soft spring twilight Mark sat by his little daughter's bed, gazing on the wan face that slept on Milly's bosom. So fair and spiritlike it looked that he was smitten with a sudden sense of loss and a yearning grief that would not be appeased.

"Milly, surely God might spare me this one from the little flock he has taken from me," Mark cried bitterly. "She is too young to die when her life might be so beautiful and precious to us both. I think, Milly, of the good her gentle spirit might accomplish if she were spared us now."

"I feel it, Mark, and my love clings to her as passionately as your own; but it is not for us to judge, only to suffer and be still. But do not think her short life wasted, her sweet ministry ended when she passes from our sight. Some lives, Mark, are long conflicts; some, vain desires or evil wanderings; but there are some which, though short, are like sweet hymns, devout and simple, but more beautiful than any song the human heart has ever sung. Such a life is Nell's, and its beloved melody will cheer your spirit when it faints and strengthen it like some brave psalm. Do not lament, but listen, dearest friend, till the bitterness of grief be charmed away and nothing but its blessedness remains."

As Milly spoke, the child stirred on her bosom and awoke.

"When will it be morning, Father? I am tired of the night," said the feeble voice as Nell's large eyes wandered to and fro with strange wistfulness.

Mark lit the shaded lamp and drew it nearer, saying cheerfully, "It will soon be morning. See, I have made it bright for you and wish I could bring on the dawn so easily for your sake, darling. My child, what is it? Can you not see me, Nell?" he asked suddenly, as he saw the small hands grasping blindly for his own.

"No, Father, I cannot see your face, but I know you are near. Though it's very dark, I shall not be afraid." And the patient child smiled faintly as she laid her head upon its tender resting place again.

Mark and Milly looked into each other's eyes for one brief moment. Then Milly put her hand in his, and clinging fast to that support, the human father sought for strength to yield his daughter to the heavenly One who was leading her away.

Watching silently, they saw Nell fold her wasted hands and heard her murmur faintly to herself.

"What is it, Nell? What shall Milly do for you?" Mark asked, bending low to catch the broken words.

"I forgot to say my little prayer, and it seems going from me when I try to speak. Say it for me, Father, and then good night."

Mark took the small hands in his own and tried to repeat "Our Father," but his lips refused to say, "Thy will be done," and Milly's low voice finished what his faltering tongue had left unspoken.

The childish voice that should have echoed the "Amen" was

silent—for on the wings of that divinest prayer the little spirit had ascended from the long twilight of this life to an eternal morning.

"No more weariness nor pain for you, my Nell. Good night, my darling, sleep in peace and wake to a mother's love in heaven," Milly murmured as she laid the smiling image of the child to its last slumber, weeping softly as she touched the bright hair and smoothed the wasted limbs that would never need her tender care again.

Mark sat staring tearlessly, with that look of stony grief so awful in a human countenance, that speechless anguish more eloquent than words, more pitiful to see than the bitterest tears that ever fell.

Milly went to him and drew the desolate father to the shelter of those arms where all his little ones had lain, saying with a voice that fell like music on the solemn stillness of the room: "Dear heart, be comforted. The little reed you leaned upon is broken now, but this grief, like a veiled angel, shall lead you through tears and anguish to a strength that cannot fail—a love that cannot die. Believe that, Mark, and let Nell's innocent faith teach you to trust and wait, saying, as she said, 'I cannot see you, Father, but I know that you are near, and in the darkness I am not afraid.'"

Mark Field laid his gray head down beside the little golden one and, from the depths of his afflicted heart, prayed his child's prayer. He groped in the darkness for the consolation no human voice could give. The Infinite Father's arm enfolded him and he was comforted.

> *Henceforth vowed to life's broad duty,*
> *Man's great business uppermost, not woman's beauty.*
> —E. B. Browning

Years came and went, and the world was better for the presence of Mark Field—an earnest, upright man humbly doing any work that served humanity, steadfastly adhering to the better part he had chosen, careless of honors, fearless of opinions, generously trustful of others, humbly doubtful of himself alone.

The two great sorrows of his life had been his best and sternest teachers. The loss of his little child led him to believe and, believing, to desire with his heart and soul that peace which blesses and is blessed. The love of a noble woman purified his nature and became a North Star that led him up from doubt and gloom to a higher freedom and a truer life.

The world never knew the secret of his wise benevolence, his severe self-renunciation, for when tired and troubled by outward and inward cares, he went like Numa to his Egeria. In the vernal solitude of the old orchard, or beside the friendly fire, Milly soothed his restless spirit, counseled, warned, and cheered, awakening his sympathies anew, rousing his intellect, appealing through his heart to his head and honor, and, with her clearer perceptions of the simply true, showing him the moral right and warning him of the fair-seeming wrong.

Like all true men, he was not ashamed to learn of a woman, not ashamed to own whose counsel guided him, whose friendship made him what he was: a tender yet brave-hearted man.

Thus Milly walked beside him as a good angel in a woman's form, but another spirit kept its watch and wore deep in his secret soul. Little Nell was with her father still, leading him to heaven as Milly led him on earth. The little shadow that had danced upon the wall was still visible to his fond eyes, making the long twilight hours sweet seasons of communion with the spirit of the little creature who had ceased to be a shadow as she flitted from him into perfect day, leaving only a wraithlike symbol of her presence to console him by his solitary household fire.

This love and sorrow, which had come to him so like a spring day in the midst of winter, with its brief sunshine, thawed the ice that years of selfish gloom had brought about his heart, and with its warm rain called forth those flowers that blossom lowly in the grass but make the air a fragrant benediction with the hidden virtues they possess. When his way seemed darkest and his life most desolate, when temptation came or weariness in well-doing, he went silently away into a lonely room and, laying his head upon that empty pillow, prayed again his darling's prayer and then went out to take his burden bravely up, better for the softening touch of a pure sorrow, stronger for communion with the Giver of all strength.

"Mark, we have often helped and counseled one another since our friendship first began. Help and counsel me now in a weightier matter than any we have ever spoken of before," said John Howe, a new-made but much honored friend of Mark's, as they sat together in the summer moonlight.

"Tell me freely, and my best wisdom shall be given to your cause, John," answered Mark, watching with a touch of wonder the sudden color in his friend's dark cheek and the unwonted hesitation of his manner.

"Mark, I love Milly," he said slowly, as if it cost him much to tell the sacred secret of an honest heart. "Yes, I am bold enough to love that noble creature so rich in many virtues, but I dare not tell her this, for much as I should suffer if she should deny me, she would feel it more. To her generous nature it is hard to refuse the poorest favor to a friend. You know her well, Mark; you have seen us together and heard her speak of me. Then tell me sincerely, do you think she loves me, or may learn to love?" John's deep voice grew tremulous with strong emotion as he spoke.

The peaceful moonlight turned to blackest night before Mark's eyes as his friend's words fell upon his ear. The patient hope of many years seemed suddenly destroyed, and the reward for which he had so hardly labored seemed snatched away forever. For vague as his hope was of earning Milly's love, it was still a hope, cherished faithfully, though how deeply he never knew till a friend's hand lifted the veil and showed him the real object of his life.

Swiftly the sharp pang came and went. He thought of Milly's solitary lot, of his own past wrong to her, of John Howe's integrity of heart and life, and said within himself,

"He is worthier than I, and if I can atone to Milly by this silent pain, surely I am man enough to do it and rejoice if they are happy."

As he thought thus, half unconsciously he drew a little chair more near than his own and softly laid his hand where a bright head always used to meet its touch. It was empty now, but the magic of a tender memory filled it with a living presence. With his hand still lying there, Mark looked into his friend's wistful face, saying bravely:

"I would I had the power to set your doubts at rest, John, but Milly's heart is a veiled temple where no human eye can look. I know she honors you and highly values your esteem. More than this I cannot read, but believe me, of all who might aspire to fill that sacred place, you are the worthiest, John."

"God bless you for that, Mark. Your approval gives me hope and courage. I will earnestly seek to win the blessing of Milly's love, and if I do, Mark, believe me, it shall prove no barrier to the friendship which has been so much to me," cried John Howe fervently—little dreaming how hard a test that friendship was now called to undergo.

He sat late into the night talking of Milly and his love till Mark felt in his despair as if he could raise his strong right arm and silence him forever. He went at last, and Mark watched him as he crossed the lawn with buoyant steps and head erect, his whole figure full of youth and hope and high resolve—and as he looked, his own young days came back, not blushingly as they might have done, but like remorseful ghosts to haunt and torture him.

All night he sat in the silent room or paced the green aisles of his blooming garden, learning now the bitter lesson he had taught Milly long ago and repenting as he never had repented before the first great error of his life.

The dark hour went by at last, and silencing the eager hopes that still possessed him, he put away his own desires and listened only to the low voice of his better self.

"Life looks desolate and fate seems unkind. My heart is full of bitterness and pain, and where can I look for human sympathy and consolation now? Oh, come to me, my little Nell, and solace me for my great loss," he cried, stretching his arms into the empty air with a sense of desolation never felt before, for now no Milly could console him, no strong-hearted friend uphold.

Mark called for help and it came, not visibly; but from the depths of his own spirit there arose a strength born of sincere desire, while to the father's yearning cry there came an answer in a subtle sense of nearness to the child and the blessed knowledge that no power could rob him of that love.

He folded his arms upon his breast as if he gathered a living Nell in their close embrace and felt that he was not desolate. So comforted, he wandered through the green solitude, feeling nature's simple magic till the calm brightness of the summer night filled his troubled spirit with a patient courage to suffer and be strong.

Mark's place in Milly's home was filled with another now, for John Howe went often to sun himself in the cheerful warmth of Milly's presence. They had many mutual interests, and he used them as innocent pretexts to meet the woman whom he loved. But as yet by no look or word did he betray that love, waiting patiently for some sign of deepening affection from unconscious Milly.

She never varied in her friendly regard, but longed for Mark and grieved in secret that her home had lost its power to draw him thither. She never knew the stern self-denial that, like an iron hand, plucked him back when every desire of his heart lured him to her side.

One fair midsummer day she sat among the vines in the old porch, plying her swift needle as she mused on many things. Straining her thoughtful eyes afar off through the green vista of an orchard path, she saw the object of her reverie—Mark—standing where he stood so many years ago and looking down upon the daisied bank where the girl Milly had sat and read. Ah, both were altered now. The young man's ardent face was deeply lined with care, and his eager eyes had lost their fire. The young girl's brown locks were touched with gray, and on her blooming countenance the soft shadow of an earnest womanhood now lay. But as the fruit is fairer than the blossom, so the man and woman in the autumn of their changeful lives were nobler than the youth and maid before the sunshine and the rain of God's wise providence had ripened and perfected them.

Screened by the vines, Milly looked, unseen, and waited eagerly for his coming, but he only cast a wistful glance at the old home and then turned away, stealing through the trees, as if he would escape unseen.

A sharp pain shot through Milly's heart as she saw him go, and with a sudden impulse she sprang to the doorway, crying, "Mark! Mark, come back to me!"

He heard, wavered a moment, and then came back with a young man's speed and eagerness.

"Forgive me, Milly, if I seemed unkind, but I knew if I came, the old spell would be upon me and I should wish me gone," he said in answer to her mute reproach.

An unwonted color gleamed in Milly's cheek, a soft beam lit her eye, and a slight tremor sounded in her voice as she replied, "Never doubt your welcome, Mark, nor fear to come. *I* do not weary of my friends."

"Nor I, Milly. But my days are full of duties, and my nights of thought. There will soon come a time, I trust, when I may be a frequent guest, a frequent sharer in your happiness." As he spoke, Mark sat down on the rustic seat beside her, murmuring with a sigh of satisfaction, "Milly, it is very pleasant to be here."

She did not answer, but sat looking down upon her busy hands with an expression of entire content on her mild face. Mark saw it—saw the fresh bloom of her cheek, the luster of her eye—and with another and far-heavier sigh, said within himself:

"It is the presence of a happy love that beautifies her thus. John has not waited in vain if his companionship has wrought this change. I *will* be glad for her sake, and he shall keep his old place in my heart through all."

Milly broke the silence, saying with a kind glance, "What

troubles you, old friend? You are grave and sad. Can I serve you, Mark?"

"Yes, Milly, you can give me something that I covet. Shall I ask you for it?" answered Mark, with a sudden desire to realize a purpose often pondered, but never spoken of till now.

Milly looked into his face with a quick, keen glance, and the knot of heartsease on her bosom rose and fell with her quickened breath. But she answered steadily, "Ask freely, Mark. I like to grant you favors; you have bestowed so many upon me."

"Have I, Milly? I am glad to know it and will ask my boon fearlessly, sure that you will grant it for our long friendship's sake," Mark replied, still looking half sadly, half fondly at the countenance so near and dear to him. He paused a moment and then continued: "I am very lonely, Milly. I want a companion to fill the empty place in my home and heart. You can give me what I need, but I fear you will hesitate to trust me again when I proved so blind before. I am wiser now and will prove a better guardian of my trust. Will you give me something you have cherished long if I will promise to be very wise and watchful, Milly?"

"If I can, Mark," Milly answered, still with downcast eyes and swiftly moving fingers.

"I will show you the gift I covet, and for Nell's sake I think you will not deny it." As he spoke, Mark rose and passed into the house.

Milly's work fell on her knee, and with eyes dilating with wonder and something akin to fear, she sat with fading color listening for his return.

He came at length, bearing in his arms—poor Bess. A long sigh of relief parted Milly's lips, but she did not speak. Mark resumed his place, saying earnestly:

"Milly, I want the little friend my Nell loved so well. I need a child's voice in my silent house, a child's face to look into my own, a child's affection to keep my spirit young. Give me Bess. I will deal gently with her and make her life all I desired to make my Nell's."

"Take her, Mark. I freely give her to your care, for my

home is full of children and yours is desolate. Will you go, Bess, and be a little daughter to this friend?"

"Yes, anywhere with dear Nell's father" was the quick reply, for in the caressing touch of the hand upon her head and the benign face smiling down into her own, Bess read the tenderness and truth of her new friend, and clung about his neck, where childish arms had not rested since death took the last and dearest of his flock.

"She will go with me today, so bring me her small possessions, Milly. We will be on our way before the sun gets low, for my little daughter is not strong," Mark said cheerfully, still holding the gentle creature on his knee, still hoping to satisfy the hunger of his heart with pity, since love was denied to him.

Milly silently obeyed, but when the child wept softly on her breast at parting, she held her close, feeling as if the last link that held her to Mark would be broken when Nell's little friend was gone.

"Come often, Mark. I too am lonely, even amid my flock," Milly said as he proposed to go.

"Lonely with John's blithe company!" Mark replied with a brief smile. "Nay, Milly, you flatter me, but I will come soon and bring you tidings of the child to prove that I am grateful for the gift. Farewell, dear Milly. Come, my little Bess."

Thus, cradled tenderly in Mark's strong arms and pillowed on his generous heart, the child of that rejected race was borne away to become a spirit of consolation in his solitary home. But Milly clasped her hands before her face, saying brokenly, "Oh, Mark, you cannot read my heart."

John Howe went often to his friend to tell his hopes and fears, for there had come a change in Milly which seemed the sign he waited for.

A quiet melancholy had fallen upon her, and though she tried to be her cheerful self again, it was in vain. Some secret longing seemed to haunt her, and a patient hope sat in her eyes, making their brown depths luminous through unshed tears.

Mark wished his friend "Godspeed," manfully striving to be

just and kind and true in word and deed, though each hour of John's society was a brief martyrdom. For Mark's love had grown with his growth, and now the ardent but unstable passion of his youth had become the strong, deep desire of his manhood that grew dearer as all hope died out, but cherished still for its own sake as he learned its worth and felt its power in his life.

So through silent suffering, Mark learned the austere charm of self-denial, and feeling that henceforth he must labor for love of God, not love of Milly, he prayed that the divine affection might sanctify the human and in its sacred fire consume all pride, ambition, and self-love.

He felt that he might conquer, but when a mission across the sea was offered him, he accepted it, saying to himself, "It is braver to flee temptation than to seek it. I will go away for a little time, and when Milly is my friend's happy wife, I will come back and take my old place in their midst. They shall never feel a shadow of the cloud which might have made our friendship dark."

As he sat in his study the night before his departure, John Howe came in, saying with a vain endeavor to speak cheerily: "It is all over, Mark. Take your friend back and comfort him."

Mark read his meaning in the altered face, so full of sudden gloom, and told his sympathy in a silent pressure of the hand.

"Yes, Mark, she has no heart to give me, and I have but grieved her in offering mine. May you never know how hard a thing it is to bear, old friend," and John turned away to hide the drops wrung from his strong nature by the bitterest disappointment his hard life had known.

"I do know, John, and Milly taught *me* the same hard lesson, gently and generously, as I feel sure she has taught you," Mark answered, speaking reverently, as one speaks of sacred things.

"You, Mark!" cried his friend. "You never told me this."

"Why should I, John, till I could tell it as a bond of sympathy to bind us yet more tenderly together? I loved Milly in my youth. I love her still, with no hope of return now, no thought of asking for the good gift I once flung away."

"Oh, Mark, teach me your patience and let my love make me what you are!"

"It needs no teaching, John, and with you it need not be a sorrow long, for you are young, with life before you. There are noble women who will be proud to take a wife's place in this true heart of yours. Time will be kind to you, and even if you never find a friend, Milly's friendship remains. Yes, John, we are both better, happier men for loving, though in vain, a woman like our own Milly. Let us be worthy of this love, that it may sweeten, not embitter, the lives it has so blessed."

The friends looked into each other's faces with eyes full of noble fire and felt their hearts made one by the same great pain and passion. Silently they clasped hands and parted.

Mark went by to say farewell to Milly, for his word was pledged and he must go. He hoped nothing for himself, for what so good a man as John Howe had failed to gain he dared not think of winning, unconscious in his humility that Mark Field was the better, stronger man.

Milly knew of his approaching departure, and whatever sorrow it had caused her, no trace of it remained. She met Mark with a smiling face and walked with him through the orchard paths, talking cheerfully of his long absence and the good work he went to do.

Pausing in their walk, at length they both stood silent, looking down the green slopes to the quiet river gliding murmuringly by. Mark seemed lost in thought, but Milly stood a little apart, gazing, with her whole soul in her eyes, upon the friend whom she never might behold again.

Mark, turning suddenly, saw the steadfast gaze fixed on him, and smiled, saying, "What do you see in the old man, Milly, to call those tears into your happy eyes?"

Milly did not turn her glance away, but her face grew colorless with deep emotion as she replied, "I see a good man, Mark. Young in heart, though time has touched his head with snow. Upright in life, though his integrity was won by many sacrifices and much pain. A humble man, unconscious of the virtues which have blossomed from the soil, watered by honest tears, enriched by generous deeds. A man whose name is loved and honored by the good and wise and uttered by the poor with prayer and blessing. I see all this, Mark, and remembering the past, thank God that your life has been no failure, but a brave success."

Mark had bowed his head and listened, like one in a blissful dream, to the beloved voice whose fervent commendations were the reward for his long labors, the crown to his hard-won victories. As she ceased, he looked up, saying with proud humility:

"I am a *rich* man also, Milly, for I have a generous friend who made me what I am and now gives me the rare praise which all belongs to her. I am your work, dearest Milly. See me as I am."

"I do, Mark, and I see the man I love."

The words fell from Milly's lips with brave sincerity, in answer to the unspoken love which shone forth clear and strong in Mark's whole countenance.

A blessed future broke like a summer dawn through the gray patience that had filled his heart with its somber twilight for so long. Life suddenly seemed full of bloom, and the deep river seemed to chant a marriage hymn as it rolled musically by.

Mark bent to look into the face turned from him in a glow of maiden shame, saying softly, "Milly, shall I go alone?"

The countenance so dear to him was lifted frankly to his own, with love in the tender eyes, truth on the honest lips, and all the fervor of a woman's full heart trembling in the voice as Milly laid her hand in his.

"No, Mark, never alone, for I will walk beside you through the light and shadow of this world till God shall bid us 'Come up higher.'"

THE MONK'S ISLAND

A LEGEND OF THE RHINE

"Mother, we are ready now for the promised story of the old carved chest. Throw on another log, Alaric. Cousin Constance, cease your spinning, and Minna, come sit with me in the chimney nook where we so often sat together years ago."

The blithe voice won obedience to its commands, for it seldom asked a boon in vain. The brother trimmed the fire and sent into the room a ruddy light, which glowed upon the dusty rafters, flickered on the steel-bound chest, and deepened the blush on pretty Minna's cheek as she took the proffered seat beside the young man who had been her playmate and was now her lover. Mild-eyed Constance smiled at his boyish eagerness as she pushed her wheel away. Widow Lenhart, seeing the circle of expectant faces, readily complied, saying as she glanced at the old chest, which stood apart, as if occupying the place of honor in her simple room:

"Years ago, when as boys you asked the history of that quaint relic of the past, I told you that when you were men, you should know it. Your father was five and twenty years when his father told it on his dying bed. You, Alaric, are five and twenty this night, and in obedience to my husband's wish, I tell the tale, hoping it will serve you as it served him and keep you true and steadfast to your duty, as it kept the brave old grandfather whom you never knew."

Alaric, leaning on the high back of his mother's chair, turned his thoughtful eyes from Minna's face to meet his mother's glance, so full of tender wistfulness and anxiety that

315

it called a sudden flush into his cheek and won his close attention to her words.

"Your grandfather was a merchant in the silk and spices of
the East, and his ships went to and fro year after year, bringing rare and costly wares to our good city of Strasbourg. He
was a young man at the time I tell of, betrothed to Gertrude
Brenner, the daughter of the rich armorer whose place our
Minna's father now fills. Bernhard was to be married after one
more voyage and sailed full of blithe hopes, promising a
speedy return.

"He was a comely man, tall, keen-eyed, and strong, as all
our race have been. And it is little wonder that the damsels of
the East looked with favor on the handsome, fair-haired
stranger of whom they caught stolen glimpses when he came
to traffic with their fathers. I know not how this may have
been, but it is true that one young creature loved him with all
the fervor of her passionate nature and watched for his coming with unfailing patience, though many months went by between his visits and her existence was unknown to him.

"She was the only and beloved child of the old merchant
with whom Bernhard oftenest stayed. She had no mother to
warn or to control her, and when she confessed the passion
which possessed her, the father consented that she should wed
Bernhard, Christian though he was, little doubting that the
sight of such beauty would soon win the young man to forget
his country and his God.

"Bernhard saw the fair Zaidee, heard the story of her patient love, her many virtues, and her great wealth, but refused
them all, telling them that a betrothed bride waited for him in
his native land and that as a Christian man, he could wed but
one. In vain the lustrous eyes shone on him and the fair face
smiled; in vain the father, for his child's sake, offered every
bribe to tempt the young man's avarice and pride. Bernhard
was firm and left them sorrowfully, for he was human and the
hopeless anguish of the fond girl touched his heart and awoke
a tenderer pity than he knew.

"The ship sailed and was far away when, as he paced the
deck one summer night, the vision of Zaidee seemed to stand

before him. He spoke to it as to some fair wraith, bidding it depart. But a sweet voice answered, and falling at his feet, the loving maiden with passionate words and tears implored his pardon and, appealing to his compassion, offered to serve him like a slave if she might but be near the object of her love.

"Wildly she wept and tenderly she clung, her beauty and devotion pleading more eloquently than her broken words. Remembering all she had left for him, the young man's growing pity pardoned that which seemed unmaidenly and wrong.

"In that hour a great temptation beset Bernhard's soul. He looked to his love for Gertrude as a shield and found with terror that the calm affection he had cherished was not love. Her image never haunted him as that of the Eastern girl had done, smiling on him in his dreams and mingling with his waking thoughts—an object ever beautiful and dear. The touch of Gertrude's hand, the sight of Gertrude's placid face, had never sent a thrill to heart and brain like that which then kindled such a subtle flame. Her voice never seemed like tenderest music to his ear, her glance like sunshine filling his life with sudden warmth and bloom. In one brief moment Bernhard's heart awoke from its long sleep and showed him the weakness and the strength of his own nature. A great passion and a bitter duty stood before him—his love for Zaidee and his pledge to Gertrude. A swift vision passed before him of his betrothed making ready for the bridal far away beside the Rhine, and it seemed a dark, distasteful picture when he looked upon the one before him—the boundless sea, the wooing winds, the soft gloom of the summer night, and at his feet the creature whom he loved, praying for a little pity and a little hope.

"For one hour he dreamed a dream of bliss. The beautiful imploring face lay on his breast tearless and serene while with eager words, half sorrowful, half gay, the tender voice poured forth its little tale of hope, despair, and flight. Bernhard listened, looked, and loved, knowing the hard duty that lay before him, yet yielding for a time to the enchantment that surrounded him.

"He sailed upon a charmed sea and longed to sail forever. A wondrous beauty filled the night, mysterious murmurs sounded from the waves, strong fragrance came upon the winds, and the mellow moonlight shining on the countenance uplifted to his own seemed more radiant than any sunshine he had ever known.

"The hour passed, and with an effort which rent his heart, he told poor Zaidee that their bright dream was over and that his home never could be hers, and implored her to help him do the bitter duty that now lay before them both. Bewildered by the altered manner, which seemed almost stern in its steadfast calmness, Zaidee bent to his will and like a little brokenhearted child obeyed his slightest wish. There was a single passenger on board, a venerable man returning from some pilgrimage, and placing the poor girl in the safe shelter of his years, Bernhard went away to struggle like a man to conquer the ardent love which seemed to have fallen like a spell upon his tranquil heart. Stung by self-reproach, he shut out all hope, silenced all self-pity, and prayed to be delivered from temptation.

"In the silence of the night the ship was put about, and while Zaidee slept with weariness and grief, the freshening breezes bore her toward the home she had deserted for a fruitless love.

"From her own words Bernhard had learned that she had been brought on board in a chest among the other merchandise her father had sent. It was yonder box of scented wood, quaintly carved and bound with steel. A treasure chest, Zaidee called it, but when it was examined, nothing could be found but the few jewels she had brought to offer the happy bride, whom in her childlike ignorance she hoped to serve.

"In a sad maze of sweet and bitter thoughts Bernhard passed that night, but morning found him resolute and calm, though strangely altered from the blithe young man who kissed away his Gertrude's parting tears. All day he paced the deck or labored with aimless energy at some needless task, pausing often in his fitful work or restless walk to listen to the music of a voice that came up from below, singing plaintively, as if to ease an aching heart or win a passing thought from one who needed no such tender lure.

"The rude sailors marveled at the unknown singer, but respect for their young master kept them silent till the sudden apparition of a woman's form explained the mystery of the mermaid's song. Bernhard stood alone looking with gloomy eyes into the sea, heedless of the sunset glories mirrored there and only longing to be down in its cool depths, lost in that dreamless sleep which human griefs and joys can never mar. A light touch fell upon his folded arms, and Zaidee's mournful eyes looked up into his own as if to read some hope of mercy there.

"With a look that held her silent, Bernhard pointed to a faint line lying on the far horizon, saying briefly, lest his heart should fail: 'I have been true to my word, for yonder is your home. Better never see my Gertrude more than meet her with another love beside me. Zaidee, spare the tears and prayers that drive me wild, and like a loving child, return to the old father whom you have left so desolate.'

"A single despairing cry fell from Zaidee's lips as she saw the distant shore that told her fate, and with one glance of mute reproach she fell like a broken flower at his feet. Down into the little cabin Bernhard bore the pale shape, believing he had murdered her, and calling the old pilgrim, he poured the tale into his ear, beseeching him to keep poor Zaidee from his sight until he gave her back into her father's arms. Then, waiting only to see returning breath part the lips he pressed for the last time, he rushed away, white and wild, as if fleeing for his life.

"Day was dawning when Bernhard was summoned below, where the old man with pallid face tremblingly confessed that, wearied with his long vigil, he had slept and, waking, had found Zaidee gone. The jewels and a raven tress lay on the pillow, but though it was wet with tears, the fair head was not there. A shred from her garments fluttering in the clasp of the narrow window told her fate and assured them that she was at peace.

"Bernhard flung poor Zaidee's gifts into the sea and turned homeward with all speed, commanding silence from all on board. The truth was known, however, and his men, full of rough sympathy, obeyed for love of him. He reached home so changed that his betrothed scarce knew him. But she soon learned the cause, for, watching by the sickbed where for weeks he lay, she gathered from his wandering words the story of his brief and tragic love. Unknown she heard, and unknown she pardoned the seeming wrong, believing it well atoned for and hoping still to heal and make the wounded heart her own.

"When he rose up from his bed of pain, Bernhard found another Gertrude than the one he left—not a pensive girl but a woman strong and tender, with a world of silent love in her meek eyes and a nameless charm in every look and tone, which soothed his troubled spirit and appeased his keen remorse. They were married, and Bernhard never crossed the sea again, but led a quiet burgher's life, respected and beloved by high and low. No word of that sad passion ever passed his lips till on his deathbed he told it to his son and learned then for the first time how wisely and how well his good wife had loved him and how faithfully she kept his secret five and twenty years without one jealous doubt, one womanly reproach. Your father received the story with the chest, bequeathing both to his eldest son, and on this your birth night I bestow the gift on you, my Alaric, trusting that like the two good men gone before, you will flee temptation and walk upright in the path of duty, even though it be across the dearest hopes of your young life."

Alaric, standing in the shadow of his mother's ancient chair, believed his changeful countenance unseen. But Constance, watching, sadly read the secret of his earnest sympathy in Bernhard's love, for in the eyes that seldom turned from Minna's blooming face she saw a passion hopeless as poor Zaidee's. In the shade of patient pain that fell upon his countenance she saw as keen a grief as Bernhard ever knew. When, the story being done, he bent his head upon his hands, she felt that he was echoing his mother's prayer, though her eyes grew too dim with sudden tears to trace the tender secret further.

Soon Minna rose to go, and Conrad sprang for cloak and lantern, jealous of the right of guarding her through the wintry streets.

"Good night, Alaric. May you see many a blithe birthday and find a fair wife to fill your goodly chest with linen of her own spinning. Can I wish you a better gift than that, grave master scholar?" said the pretty damsel as she dropped a curtsy to the hero of the hour.

"Yes, wish me a patient spirit and a docile will, sweet neighbor. They are rarer and better gifts than a busy housewife's love and labor," answered Alaric, with a vain endeavor to answer her gay words gaily. Then, holding her hands fast in his own and looking steadfastly into her smiling eyes, he added, "Tell your father that the matter we last spoke of can never be as he desires, and tell him I will set his mind at rest tomorrow. Remember, Minna, and so good night."

"Nay, you shall have a little kiss to lighten the weight of your many years, and with it this pouch for your books, embroidered by my own busy fingers. 'Tis a poor gift, but full of kindly wishes, Alaric."

The young man took the offering and bent as if to touch the laughing lips, but whispered softly as he pressed her hand: "Heaven bless you, dearest Minna, but give the kiss to Conrad for my sake."

With a shy glance and a vivid blush Minna shook her head and went merrily away with Conrad, who had listened with frowns and gestures of most loverlike impatience.

Constance stole from the room, and when Alaric returned to the fireside, he found his mother there alone. Both were silent for a time, the widow's eyes upon the dancing flames, the son's upon the ancient chest, which henceforth seemed a symbol of himself—a household shape wherein were locked mournful memories of unprosperous love and unfulfilled desires.

"Mother," he said at length, turning to look into the mild face always so full of sympathy and cheer, "Mother, I shall accept Uncle Wilhelm's offer and become a monk at Unterlinden. I have wavered too long and wasted time that should have been far better spent. I will delay no longer, but depart at once."

"Why must you leave me, Alaric? Are you not happy here?" asked the widow with a wistful sigh.

"Mother, I must flee temptation. Let me go," answered the young man almost sternly, as he paced the room with restless feet.

"My good son, I will, though with you goes the sunshine of my house. It is a quiet, charitable life, so like your own that it will scarce be the change you hope. But heaven will bless your honorable purpose and send the peace you seek."

The tender sympathy that shone in the mother's eye and trembled in her voice fell like balm upon the son's sore heart and touched it deeply. With a sudden impulse he threw aside the calmness he had assumed, saying in faltering tones:

"Mother, forget that I am a man, and let me come to you for comfort as I used to when a little child. I cannot go to Conrad, and where should I turn if not to you? Oh, Mother, pity and console me, for I am very miserable."

The young man knelt upon the little footstool where the boy had often sat, and now, as then, was gathered to the shelter of his mother's arms, comforted by the simple magic of her caressing touch, the tears that fell for him, and the music of the voice that whispered soothingly, "I know your grief, my son, with all its bitterness and pain, and can only love you with a prouder love for the brave patience with which you have suffered silently. None know your secret but myself, for a mother's eye is quick to see and a mother's heart to divine the sorrow that afflicts her child. Conrad and Minna are blind to any passion but their own, and this has made them careless of your pain. It is too late to change the maiden's choice, too late to ask the sacrifice of Conrad, and nothing now remains for you but to bear your sorrow manfully and let your mother comfort you, my son."

The first pang of despair being past, Alaric raised his head and, still leaning on his mother's knee, replied with self-accusing bitterness, "Mother, I have been tried and found wanting in integrity and truth. Minna's father believes that she comes hither not for love of Cousin Constance, but for me, and he has spoken to me in the friendliest manner, bidding me press my suit and promising her hand. That was my temptation, for I knew Minna would obey his will and that his sanction would do much to win her. I was weak enough to hold my peace, for my heart leaped high at the thought that she might yet be mine. Conrad has not yet spoken. They are not yet betrothed, and it is not yet too late, for Master Eckart will favor my desire. Nay, this very day he chided me for my slothful wooing and threatened to tell Minna that I was her promised husband. And even then I dared not speak, but bade him leave me to my own devices a few days longer and left him, more wretched than before. I could not mar my brother's happiness, and I was not brave enough to sacrifice my own to make his sure forever. Oh, Mother, I am very weak."

"No, Alaric, you are strong. For, looking in the fair face of the woman whom you loved, you silently renounced all hope, and through the lips that might have called you 'husband' sent the message that has sealed your fate. Bernhard did no braver thing, and if the story of his trial strengthened you for yours, it was not told in vain. Dear child, I know the generous, upright nature that will not shrink from a hard duty, for in these honest eyes, the clearer for their tears, I read a noble purpose. And I am prouder of my son than if he laid a laurel crown upon my knee."

With a vain effort to meet his mother's smile with one as cheerful and serene, Alaric replied, "Yes, Mother, I am my better self again. The love I bear my brother is no longer poisoned with a jealous fear. The perfect confidence between us is restored, and the peace of my own soul shall be unmarred by any selfish aim or low desire. I will plead Conrad's cause to Master Eckart, and to the voice that makes their two hearts one I will, with heaven's help, sincerely say 'Amen.'"

And Alaric Lenhart rose up from his mother's knee twice a man for having been in heart a little child again.

A quick step sounded at the door, and Conrad sprang into the room, crying with a triumphant voice and beaming eyes: "Give me joy, Mother! Give me joy, Alaric, for Minna is mine! I won only a single word from her, but my happiness is sure if Master Eckart will be content with the younger and the poorer son for his daughter's husband. He dropped a hint of his desire in the matter not many days ago, but I told him Alaric was to be a monk and had no eyes for pretty damsels. He looked wondrous wise and answered me that many a quiet man won hearts where we gay wooers failed."

"*You* shall not fail, dear lad, if words of mine can help your cause, for I love you and little Minna far too well to see your happy dream destroyed," replied Alaric, grasping his brother's hand with an energy that cheered the young lover's heart as no words could have done.

The widow looked fondly on her two handsome sons, but her glance lingered longest on the elder's face, for the peace of a conquered spirit made sudden sunshine there.

But Constance sat alone weeping softly, though her heart sang to the music of the spinning wheel: "Gertrude learned the secret of the heart she loved, and waited long until she won it. I, too, may hope and fill the old carved chest for Alaric with the webs I weave amid my tears."

Five and twenty years went by. The widow had rejoined her husband, and the housemother's chair was filled by Minna, a comely matron now, with a band of sons and daughters growing up around her. Conrad, a thriving burgher, was as hale and cheery in his manhood as he had been in his youth, and was a blithe companion to his high-hearted sons, a tender father to his blooming daughters, and a devoted husband to the woman he had loved as maid and wife through the changeful scenes of these many years.

Alaric became one of the brotherhood at Unterlinden. But the gloom of a monastic life never cast a shadow on his cheerful spirit, and never in the contemplation of the divine attributes did he forget pity for human frailties or sympathy for human griefs. In his native city he was honored for the learning he possessed and the piety that made his presence seem like a benediction, and his life like a sermon, to the high and low.

In his brother's home he was the most welcome guest that crossed the threshold. By him childish sorrows were consoled, motherly fears relieved, and fatherly anxieties dispelled, for "Uncle Alaric" was the friend, confessor, and counselor of all.

He took a vow of poverty, and his portion of their father's wealth was given to his brother, and Alaric kept nothing but his books, saying as Conrad shrank from the rich bridal gift: "Dear lad, what need I of gold or silver, house or land? My 'spouse' needs no fireside, and my 'children,' these beloved books, no food nor raiment. Then why refuse me the happiness of seeing you and yours lifted high above all want, all need of irksome labor, and the cares that grind and fret? Minna shall fill my mother's empty place and keep the dear old home unchanged. And think you not I shall be trebly paid when, years hence, I see the lovely rooms lit up with little faces looking at me with your friendly eyes and find your children playing where we played? Say no more, but take the gift and let me keep my old familiar nook beside my mother's chair."

And Alaric was right. No want or care disturbed the tranquil home, and he was still the elder brother of the house. They never guessed the secret of his early love, and the mother marveled much at his affection for the little Minna when her winsome sons were by. She never knew that to his eyes the little maid was a softened image of the Minna he had loved, and he took her to his heart as some atonement for the loss that left it desolate.

The child's voice was always the first to welcome him, her arms to give the tenderest embrace. Her place was always on his knee when he told saintly legends by the winter fire, and her small feet always tripped beside him to the city gate when he reluctantly departed.

Thus Alaric lived, serene and full of cheer. But far away from human sight the grave of a buried passion lay, watered by many tears, hallowed by many prayers—the secret spell that kept him humble, just, and true. For the sepulcher of that lost love became a shrine, fragrant with the pure desires and musical with the cheerful hopes that made perpetual summer in his heart.

But Constance, doubly orphaned when the widow died, and doubly friendless when Conrad married and Alaric became a monk, went out from that altered home to hide her desolate despair among the gentle nuns at Engelheim, whispering as she told her beads: "He dedicates his life to heaven and charitable deeds, hoping to heal his wounds. God give me grace to follow in his steps and stay my stricken heart with a divine affection, since it can never know an earthly one."

Two gaunt specters, War and Famine, passed across the land, bringing terror and dismay to Strasbourg. Enemies were without the walls, suffering and strife within; for in that hour of general want and fear, knight and burgher, artisan and priest, forgot all human rank and struggled each man for himself. The streets were scenes of contention, robbery, and wrong, for the thought of hungering wives and children made men deaf to all pity, heedless of law; and what gold could not buy, force obtained.

Conrad's eldest son, young Otto, joined the army, and the father, as a good citizen, labored night and day to restore peace and order to the distracted town. Alaric left his monastery to partake of all the dangers that surrounded those he loved and shield their weakness with his strength.

When he was returning from a long vigil by a dying bed one gloomy night, his steps were arrested by a feeble cry. The hour was late, the streets deserted, but he paused and listened to the voice that called on God. The dim lights flickering athwart the overhanging gables cast deep shadows down into the street, but groping to the spot whence the low cry came, he found a wounded man seemingly near death.

"Heaven help you, friend. How came you in this plight? And how can I best serve your need?" he asked with quick sympathy, seeking to stanch the blood that welled up from the wounded side.

With a sudden effort of departing strength, the prostrate man clasped his arms about the other's neck, crying brokenly, "Oh, Alaric, my brother, shrive me, for my hour has come!"

A keener pang than he had ever known before smote Alaric's heart as he laid that beloved head upon his breast and thanked God that he had come in time to succor and perhaps to save.

"Nay, move me not. I am too nearly spent for that, brother," sighed the wounded man as Alaric strove to raise him, speaking of his wife and home. "I shall never see them more, so let me lie here on your faithful breast and breathe my life away in one last prayer for them. Tell my Minna that an unknown hand smote me down as I was hastening home with fresh supplies, and taking from me the food more precious than the gold I offered, left me here to die. I have lain long in agony. But now my pain grows less, and in the mortal faintness that oppresses me, I feel the swift approach of death. Alaric, my wife, my children, I bequeath to you. Oh, befriend them in this bitter hour for love of me."

"Brother, I will," and Alaric sealed his vow upon the dying man's cold lips.

Priestly voices, sweet and solemn, sounded from the dim cathedral near, and as the melody soared upward with triumphant swell, Conrad's spirit passed, leaving a stately ruin on his brother's breast.

Alaric kept his promise nobly, for through the heavy year that passed, he was a father to the fatherless and a tender comforter to the widow's heart.

Time had scarcely lightened the burden of one great grief when another fell. War ceased, but Otto did not come. His comrades returned, but brought no word of him, though none had seen him fall. One believed he had been taken prisoner, but nothing certain could be known.

Minna's heart pined for her firstborn with a yearning grief that would not be appeased. Day and night she sorrowed for her boy, finding no consolation in the presence of the children yet remaining to her. Their affection brought no balm to her wounds, and Alaric's devotion no peace to her troubled spirit. She had mourned for Conrad with sincerest sorrow, but she knew he was at rest, and time, the comforter, had eased her pain. But Otto's fate was unknown, and the doubts and fears that tortured her sowed her brown hair with gray, robbed her countenance of light and bloom, and seemed wearing her very life away.

"Minna, I cannot see you grieving thus without endeavoring by some new means to ease your sorrow. The country is at peace again, and if your son yet lives, he shall be found," said Alaric, as they sat apart from the young people's evening merriment and he saw the tears that dropped so fast upon her busy hands and heard the sighs that mingled with the whirling of her wheel.

"How, Alaric, how?" she cried. "Have we not sent far and wide and questioned each returning neighbor of my boy? I cannot seek him, and who else would watch and wander as I would for my child?"

"He who promised his dying brother to be a father to his children, Minna. Rest in peace; for with a patience as watchful and untiring as your own will I seek Otto through the world and, if God wills, restore him to his home again."

"You, Alaric, so worn with cares for us and so unused to the tumult of the troublous world! No, no, I cannot let you go! It were a selfish deed to send you on this weary quest when you are suffering for rest." As she spoke, there shone in the mother's eye so strange a hope, so keen a joy, that they belied her words and confirmed the purpose Alaric had formed.

"No, Minna, let me go my way, and rest assured the love I bear you all will make me strong and wise. I shall be happier journeying to and fro than watching the light of your eyes grow dim with silent tears and the content of your life over-shadowed by this grief. Minna, lay your burden on my shoulders, and let me bear it as I would bear every sorrow heaven sends you. Dear heart, be comforted and think no more of me, for mine will be the blithest spirit in all Strasbourg when I see you smile to me from Otto's arms."

With a rain of tender tears the widow blessed his faithful love, and Alaric cheerfully took up the burden which had proved too much for her.

East and west the patient pilgrim wandered, but in vain. Month after month went by till two weary years were gone. Yet Otto was not found, and Alaric would not shorten his long exile while the faintest hope remained. Minna began to look upon her son as one surely dead, and bade the wanderer return. But among the grateful words that recalled him Alaric always found some lines of "hope and heartbreak" that spurred him on to redoubled efforts for the mother's sake.

Wintry winds were sweeping down the quiet street and

raindrops pattered on the window pane. But within, the fire-light shimmered pleasantly on little Minna's face and lit the illuminated missal on her knee as in soft, reverent tones she read the evening prayer. The widow, with bent head and folded hands, sat in the ancient chair where a meeker widow once had sat, and a fair son knelt upon the little footstool where another and a nobler son had gone for comfort from a mother's lips.

As Minna ceased, a deep voice cried "Amen!" and Uncle Alaric's hand fell softly as a blessing on her head. Poverty marked his threadbare garments, and cares had fallen like snowflakes on his head till the brown locks were white. But those years of anxiety and hope deferred had not broken the cheerful spirit, though the once upright form was bent, nor altered the benign face so worn with the weariness the lips would not confess. Benignant and serene, it smiled upon them as if their granted prayer arose in that beloved guise.

Minna sprang into his arms, blond Ulric seized his staff, and blooming Hildegard drew forth the father's chair with loving eagerness. But the mother only stretched her hands to him with eager eyes, as if imploring her lost son.

Alaric took those trembling hands in both his own, answering her mute appeal with a look more eloquent than speech, for with a cry that thrilled the silence of the room, the widow fell upon his breast and blessed him through her tears.

Soon, seated in his fireside nook, with his little maid upon his knee and a circle of April faces gathered close about him, Alaric told the glad tidings that he brought.

Following a slight clue from place to place till it led him into the far North, he had found Otto at length, and nothing but a heavy ransom now kept the captive from his home.

Conrad's wealth had been greatly lessened by the war and subsequent misfortunes, leaving the widow but a small store for future needs. Ulric labored with the armorers, old Master Eckart's sons, and added but little to the household purse. So late into the night they sat devising means to raise the ransom that should give Otto to their arms again.

"See, Uncle, here are all our trinkets, even the costly chain

Herman gave to Hildegard. We give them freely for Otto's sake and only grieve that we have no more," cried little Minna, emptying her casket eagerly while brighter jewels from her joyful eyes fell on her precious hoard.

"Dear child, I never grieved before that I was poor. But I, too, have an offering to make, a small one, but my all." Alaric's eye turned wistfully upon his treasured books, stored there for safety while he was away.

"Your books, Alaric! Nay, that is too great a sacrifice. I had far rather sell the webs stored here for Hildegard's bridal than see you bereft of your beloved friends," the widow replied, lifting the ponderous lid of the old chest and showing piles of linen snowy with the dews that bleached and fragrant with the herbs that strewed them.

But Alaric answered, smiling, "Which shall be sacrificed, your children or my own, dear soul? But listen, your words have shown me another source of help. Your brother Heinrich desired years ago to buy that ancient chest for its rich ornaments of burnished steel and offered me a goodly price, which, though I laughed at then, I will most gratefully receive in our present need."

"Oh, Uncle Alaric, the house will never seem like home if that be gone!" cried Minna, joining the group that gathered around the chest.

"Will it seem less like home than it does now, with Otto gone?" asked Alaric, looking down into the young face he loved so well. "Nay, my little maid, why weep? I love it well, for next my mother's countenance, it is the first thing my childish eyes learned to know. But rather than increase the loan which we must ask of friends, I would sell far dearer things if others felt their worth like me. Ulric, bring hither some tool that I may remove this center ornament to show the armorers tomorrow. It will recall the chest to mind and perhaps save our old friend a fruitless journey if Heinrich repents his former offer."

With a careful hand Alaric bent to detach the curiously wrought ornament, but in so doing, touched unconsciously some hidden spring, for the cover lid sprang apart and there lay poor Zaidee's treasure, glittering in the light.

"Otto should canonize that Turkish girl and pray to 'St. Zaidee' as his patron saint, for she has saved him in his greatest need," laughed Ulric, lifting out the shining pile when their first joy and wonder had subsided.

"No, my boy, St. Alaric is the guardian of our house—first to help and counsel, strengthen and console. Look to him, Ulric, for though walking in the byways of the world, he carries heaven in his heart." As she spoke, a smile shone on the widow's face that was more beautiful to Alaric's sight than all the early bloom she had lost.

"Farewell! Farewell! God speed and bring you safely back to us!" cried tender voices as Alaric set forth anew on his long pilgrimage to bring the lost one home.

Pausing, he looked back to feast his eyes upon the happy faces clustering on the threshold of the door.

The widow leaned upon her boy's arm with the old light in her eye, the old smile on her lips, so blithe of heart and full of hope that he seemed to see again the Minna of his youth. Hildegard waved her handkerchief and Ulric tossed his cap, but the little maid wept silently and, holding back the golden curls that fluttered in the wind, gazed with her whole heart in her eyes, as if she looked her last.

Thus, with smiles and tears, blessings and fond farewells, they watched the departing figure, till the last glimpse of the beloved face was lost and the sound of the slow footfalls died away.

Otto came home, and "the widow's heart sang for joy." In the rapture of that first hour, even little Minna forgot to ask for Alaric. But Cousin Constance, the pale nun who had left her cell to welcome the wanderer home, never forgot that name, and when the first tumult of delight had passed, her mild voice was heard asking anxiously:

"Otto, why are you come alone?"

A sudden gloom swept over the young man's face, so worn and haggard with captivity and pain, and a deep silence fell upon them, broken only by little Minna's fearful whisper: "God forgive us that we could forget! Otto, he is not dead?"

As if nerving himself for some dreaded task, the young

man drew still closer to his mother's side. With her hand in his, as if to gather strength from its fond touch, he looked into the apprehensive faces paling around him and replied:

"Uncle Alaric is not dead, though to my poor human sight it seems as if it would be better if he were. Listen, and give me help and counsel for the love we bear the prop and blessing of our house. On our homeward way, as we rode blithely over a desert moor, we passed a miserable hut, whence came a cry that made my heart stand still, it was so full of suffering and despair. Uncle Alaric drew bridle and sprang to answer that imploring voice. I followed, but paused upon the threshold of the door, fearing to enter there, for on a wretched pallet lay the specter of a man wasted by disease, who stretched his arms to us and with parched lips prayed for water. Mother, it was a leper—forsaken alike by God and man and sent into the wilderness to die. I plucked my uncle back, bidding him fly with me from the place, but he looked into my face with eyes of mild reproof, saying as he raised the poor soul to his knee and held his flask to the eager lips: 'Blessed are the merciful, for they shall obtain mercy.'

"Mother, what could I do? I pleaded with Uncle Alaric to come away for love of us, but he only pointed to the grateful face upon the pillow and replied, 'Dear Otto, go your way home, and when your mother asks for me, tell her I stayed to comfort a poor youth whose mother had forsaken him. Tell her to have no fears for me and bestow no reproach upon you. My duty for a time is here, for if I succored you for love of her, surely I should succor this deserted creature for the love of God.'

"Then, leading me away, he blessed and bade me go, desiring sundry comforts to be sent him from the nearest town. I obeyed, for I could give no aid; and my heart yearned so tenderly for home, I could not risk the life so hardly purchased by his care. But at the neighboring town I waited for him. Days passed and cheerful messages came from the lonely hut upon the moor, but Uncle Alaric bade me shun him and go on, leaving him to follow as he might. I would not, and when at length the leper died, blessing the Samaritan who had smoothed the road to death, Uncle laid the friendless creature tenderly to his last sleep and went serenely on his way again.

"I saw him but once, for he feared his perilous companion might cost him dear and he would endanger none by his companionship. I reproached him for his rash deed and implored him to come home with me, but he was firm, saying cheerfully:

"'My son, when I took upon me the vows of a monk, I, as a follower of Christ, devoted soul and body to the service of God, and whenever any human creature calls for help, however cursed by sin, disease, or woe, there my duty lies. No doubt nor dread should stay my hand, no selfish indolence lure me away, no human love render me forgetful of the meek obedience vowed to God. If this affliction comes, it can be borne, for with the sorrow heaven will send the patience, too. Go home, dear boy, and I will follow. Send Dr. Tauler to me at the summer cottage on the riverside, and time will set our fears at rest.' Thus we traveled home, and there I left him, so serene and cheerful still that I cannot think this curse will fall upon him. But if it does, Mother, what can be done?"

As he ceased, Otto bowed his head upon his hands and wept like a boy. But Constance glided like a shadow from the room.

In those superstitious times that mysterious malady was looked upon with unmingled abhorrence and dread; and when the heavy tidings came that Alaric was a leper, through all the grief that fell upon the hearts that loved him, that unconquerable fear rose up, withholding many a sympathizing soul from throwing wide their doors to take the outcast in.

At the city council friendly voices spoke of him and sought to devise some cheerful place of abode where, though isolated from kindred and human companionship, he might feel as though some link of sympathy still bound him to his race.

A man so well beloved for unnumbered deeds of charity and the beauty of his humble life could not pass from their midst and not leave a host of grateful memories behind him, and with sincere grief the worthy burghers mourned the misfortune which deprived them of so true a friend.

Some selfish souls among them, forgetful of all but their fears, urged Alaric's banishment with angry zeal, and hot words passed. The strife of tongues was at its height when the unwonted spectacle of a woman's figure in their midst brought sudden silence on them all.

A nun's somber garment shrouded it, but when the close hood fell, the meek face of Sister Constance shone upon them like the countenance of an angel, beautiful and calm. Many a father there had seen that figure in his home in times of suffering and death, for the nuns of Engelheim were Sisters of Mercy and had borne a noble part in the scenes of agony and terror which had filled the city in the time of war and famine. Now they listened willingly to the voice which had lulled their suffering little ones or comforted their sorrows for the dead, as it cried imploringly to them:

"Oh, men of Strasbourg, for the honor of our city, deal most tenderly with that afflicted man. By the love you bear your wives and children, do not banish him from all communion with the household whose good angel he has been. By the reverence you bear to the memory of his brave brother, whose blood cries from your streets, do not doom him to a long exile in a foreign land! Hear and grant my boon, and the sincerest prayer lips ever uttered shall go up to heaven from the sisterhood of Engelheim!"

"Speak, Sister Constance, without fear, for there are few favors we would not gratefully bestow upon the holy women of your house!" replied the venerable Master Eckart, to whom Alaric was as a son.

Constance gathered courage from the friendly faces around her and the purpose of her faithful heart, for with pleading eyes she said, "Yonder in the river lies the lonely island where the hermit Berthold dwelt. The hermitage stands empty now. But the little garden blooms, and the old man's orchard is a fruitful place. Let Alaric's home be there, for the city lights shine cheerfully across the water and the evening bells will sound like friendly voices to his ear. Messages of love can reach him there and household gifts make his lone island seem a home. I will make the hermitage a welcome spot and see that Alaric knows no want that affection can supply. This is my desire. Oh, grant it for the sake of all that noble man has done for you!"

With one accord they granted Constance's prayer, and through her fearless love Alaric found a home.

The day of his long exile came, and many gathered on the riverbank to catch a farewell glimpse of their departing friend. The threshold of his door was heaped with garlands and the path which he must tread bestrewn with flowers, for tender hearts were with him and thus mutely asked forgiveness for their desertion.

The boat, laden with gifts, lay at shore. Of all the creatures Alaric had served, the two humblest were the only ones whose love was greater than their fear—a pardoned criminal and a poor Magdalen—and were now leaning on their oars awaiting his approach. The man stood with head erect, as if this deed canceled many sins, and the girl with downcast eyes, weeping softly as she thought of him whose pity had raised her up when she was most deserted and forlorn.

The widow with her children pressed nearest, watching with eager eyes, while all along the pathway stood groups of poor souls whom Alaric had befriended—old men and maids, mothers with their little ones, the monks of Unterlinden, and many an honest burgher with softhearted wives and daughters on their arms, all waiting to cast their farewell blessing at his feet.

Slowly down the flowery path a shrouded figure came at length, walking with feeble steps and bent head. As he passed, out from the crowd a woman stepped and like a shadow followed him, unseen by Alaric's eye, but eager to support his wavering feet and to remove the mournful sense of desolation that surrounded him. Tears fell and broken voices greeted him. But still with bowed head the old man passed them by till, on the margin of the stream, he reached the household group that waited there.

"Alaric, farewell! We are not divided in heart, though we can never see you more. Oh, remember this and bless us as you go!" cried the beloved voices as he came, and little Minna, breaking from her brother's hold, sprang to his side and clung about his neck in such a wild abandonment of grief that all his hard-won calmness ended in a flood of tears.

For one brief moment he held fast the dearest treasure of his life, then gently unloosed the clinging hands and laid her, pale and still, in Otto's arms, saying fervently, "God keep you all, dear hearts, and reunite us on the shore of that diviner land where separations are unknown."

The shrouded figure paused an instant and, having stretched its arms as if in benediction on the mournful throng, then passed into the boat.

As the divided waves came rippling to the shore, a single clear voice suddenly arose chanting a brave old psalm. Solemn and sweet it echoed on the summer air, till voice after voice caught up the strain and sent it pealing far across the river that now rolled forever between Alaric and his home.

A few years came and went, but Alaric was not forgotten. Weekly a laden boat crossed the Rhine and took back richer gifts than it bestowed. For, though dwelling there shut out from all mankind, he found a spell to link him still in spirit to his race. In the green solitude his love and longing found a voice that touched and delighted every heart, for across the river he sent hymns devout and holy, songs sweet as the old knightly lays of love, and ballads full of tenderness and grace.

In him the people found a minstrel who wove into simple melodies the joys and sorrows of their humble lives and made them cheerful by the magic power of song.

Monks loved the pious faith that sounded through the solemn chants. Lovers found a wonderful charm in the soft strains that told their hopes and fears with such tender truths, and little children sang the birdlike songs that seemed to flow from a heart as childish as their own.

Thus, with true wisdom, Alaric met affliction with a smile and made his solitude a cheerful song.

Constance, from the lonely cottage on the riverside, looked night and morning for the spire of smoke that floated upward from the hermitage, and strained her eager eyes to catch a glimpse of the dark figure moving through the trees or pausing on the shore. A pale, gray-haired woman she was now, but the early passion burned unchanged in her constant heart and held her there, a solitary soul, when many pleasant homes were offered for her choice.

Hildegard had left her mother's house to become the mistress of young Herman's. Ulric was a bridegroom and Otto a proud father. Little Minna, though a winsome creature, was a maiden still devoted to the mother and to Uncle Alaric, who still stood first in her affection. But Constance left convent and kin to dwell alone beside the river that flowed between her and the heart she loved.

"No smoke among the trees, no figure on the shore for two long days! Alaric is in need of me, and now, when no other hand can minister to him, I may at least be welcome to his sight." And with an eager step, as if she went to some blithe festival, Constance hastened to the boatman who weekly plied across the stream.

"Good Rudolph, bring your son with you when you come for your load tonight. I purpose to send a chest of comforts to Brother Alaric, who is somewhat ill in health. It is a chest he values much; therefore, deal with it carefully, and leave it in the shadow of the lindens, where it may be sheltered from the dew till he shall find it on the morrow. Fail not to come. For your faithfulness to that good man, accept this gold of me and share it with poor Agatha, for Alaric still remembers her."

The evening red shone on the city spires and dyed the waves that rippled on the island shore. The linden boughs swayed in the freshening wind, and the departing boatman's song had died away when the lid of the ancient chest was lifted and a female figure glided from within.

No phantom Zaidee, beautiful and young, but a faded woman with a world of silent anguish in her eyes.

Lightly she trod the path that Alaric's feet had worn, and stood with quickly beating heart upon the threshold of the half-closed door.

A little bird flew to her hand, as if it missed some accustomed voice or caress. But its soft note of welcome filled her heart with foreboding fears, and when she entered silently, the timid creature's joy was explained. Pale and still lay Alaric upon his bed, the soft light shining on his silver hair and folded hands, but nothing else stirred in the room.

"Alaric, I am come! Oh, speak to me and tell me I am not too late. God pardon me that I delayed one hour and left him here to die alone!" cried Constance, kneeling by the narrow bed.

The sweet sound of a human creature's voice seemed to reach Alaric's ear even through the sleep that softened the approach of death. A faint smile swept across his lips, but left them voiceless as before.

The far-off vesper bells were chiming softly and the sound of whispering waters filled the air. The little bird lit on the pillow, mingling its blithe song with the mellow music of the bells. But Constance saw nothing but the serene face on her breast, heard nothing but the fluttering breath, felt nothing but the utter powerlessness of love to stay the life ebbing so fast away.

Sleep departed, and its diviner brother Death stood waiting when Alaric looked up into the face that bent above him. A blissful smile sat on his lips, hope beamed with sudden radiance in his eyes, and a celestial joy shone on his countenance. With a wild yearning for one look, one word, to feed the hunger of her patient heart, Constance bowed yet nearer to receive the last words trembling on his lips. But from its hidden grave the spirit of that early love arose, transfiguring the pale nun to the semblance of the fair idol of his youth.

"Minnie!" he cried, and serenely followed the mild Presence beckoning him away.

LOVE AND SELF-LOVE

"Friendless when you are gone? But, Jean, you surely do not mean that Effie has no claim on any human creature beyond the universal one of common charity?" I said, as she ceased and lay panting on her pillows, with her sunken eyes fixed eagerly upon my own.

"Aye, sir, I do, for her grandfather has never by word or deed acknowledged her, or paid the least heed to the letter her poor mother sent him from her dying bed seven years ago. He is a lone old man, and this child is the last of his name; yet he will not see her, and cares little whether she be dead or living. It's a bitter shame, sir, and the memory of it will rise up before him when he comes to lie where I am lying now."

"And you have kept the girl safe in the shelter of your honest home all these years? Heaven will remember that, and in the great record of good deeds will set the name of Adam Lyndsay far below that of poor Jean Burns," I said, pressing the thin hand that had succored the orphan in her need.

But Jean took no honor to herself for that charity, and answered simply to my words of commendation: "Sir, her mother was my foster child, and when she left that stern old man for love of Walter Home, I went too, for love of her. Ah, dear heart, she had sore need of me in the weary wanderings which ended only when she lay down by her dead husband's side and left her bairn to me. Then I came here to cherish her among kind souls where I was born; and here she has grown up, an innocent young thing, safe from the wicked world, the comfort of my life and the one thing I grieve at leaving when the time that is drawing very near shall come."

"Would not an appeal to Mr. Lyndsay reach him now, think you? Might not Effie go to him herself? Surely the sight of such a winsome creature would touch his heart, however hard."

But Jean rose up in her bed, crying almost fiercely, "No, sir! No! My child shall never go to beg a shelter in that hard man's house. I know too well the cold looks, the cruel words, that would sting her high spirit and try her heart, as they did her mother's. No, sir—rather than that, she shall go with Lady Gower."

"Lady Gower? What has she to do with Effie, Jean?" I asked with increasing interest.

"She will take Effie as her maid, sir. A hard life for my child! But what can I do?" And Jean's keen glance seemed trying to read mine.

"A waiting maid? Heaven forbid!" I ejaculated, as a vision of that haughty lady and her three wild sons swept through my mind.

I rose, paced the room in silence for a little time, then took a sudden resolution and, turning to the bed, exclaimed, "Jean, I will adopt Effie. I am old enough to be her father, and she shall never feel the want of one if you will give her to my care."

To my surprise, Jean's eager face wore a look of disappointment as she listened and with a sigh replied, "That's a kind thought, sir, and a generous one, but it cannot be as you wish. You may be twice her age, but still too young for that. How could Effie look into that face of yours, so bonny, sir, for all it is so grave, and seeing never a wrinkle on the forehead nor a white hair among the black, how could she call you 'Father'? No, it will not do, though so kindly meant. Your friends would laugh at you, sir, and idle tongues might speak ill of my bairn."

"Then what can I do, Jean?" I asked regretfully.

"Make her your wife, sir."

I turned sharply and stared at the woman as her abrupt

reply reached my ear. Though trembling for the consequences of her boldly spoken wish, Jean did not shrink from my astonished gaze; and when I saw the wistfulness of that wan face, the smile died on my lips, checked by the tender courage which had prompted the utterance of her dying hope.

"My good Jean, you forget that Effie is a child and I a moody, solitary man with no gifts to win a wife or make home happy."

"Effie is sixteen, sir—a fair, good lassie for her years. And you—ah, sir, *you* may call yourself unfit for wife and home, but the poorest, saddest creature in this place knows that the man whose hand is always open, whose heart is always pitiful, is not the one to live alone, but to win and to deserve a happy home and a true wife. Oh, sir, forgive me if I have been too bold. But my time is short, and I love my child so well, I cannot leave the desire of my heart unspoken, for it is my last."

As the words fell brokenly from her lips and tears streamed down her pallid cheek, a great pity took possession of me; the old longing to find some solace for my solitary life returned again, and peace seemed to smile on me from little Effie's eyes.

"Jean," I said, "give me till tomorrow to consider this new thought. I fear it cannot be, but I have learned to love the child too well to see her thrust out from the shelter of your home to walk through this evil world alone. I will consider your proposal and endeavor to devise some future for the child which shall set your heart at rest. But before you urge this further, let me tell you that I am not what you think me. I am a cold, selfish man, often gloomy, often stern—a most unfit guardian for a tender creature like this little girl. The deeds of mine which you call kind are not true charities. It frets me to see pain, and I desire my ease above all earthly things. You are grateful for the little I have done for you, and deceive yourself regarding my true worth. But of one thing you may rest assured—I am an honest man, who holds his name too high to stain it with a false word or a dishonorable deed."

"I do believe you, sir," Jean answered eagerly. "And if I left the child to you, I could die this night in peace. Indeed, sir, I never should have dared to speak of this but for the belief that you loved the girl. What else could I think, when you came so often and were so kind to us?"

"I cannot blame you, Jean; it was my usual forgetfulness of others which so misled you. I was tired of the world and came hither to find peace in solitude. Effie cheered me with her winsome ways, and I learned to look on her as the blithe spirit whose artless wiles won me to forget a bitter past and a regretful present." I paused and then added with a smile, "But in our wise schemes we have overlooked one point: Effie does not love me and may decline the future you desire me to offer her."

A vivid hope lit those dim eyes as Jean met my smile with one far brighter and joyfully replied, "She *does* love you, sir, for you have given her the greatest happiness she has ever known. Last night she sat looking silently into the fire there with a strange gloom on her bonny face; and when I asked what she was dreaming of, she turned to me with a look of pain and fear, as if dismayed at some great loss, but she only said, 'He is going, Jean! What shall I do?'"

"Poor child! She will miss her friend and teacher when I'm gone, and I shall miss the only human creature that has seemed to care for me for years," I sighed—adding as I paused upon the threshold of the door: "Say nothing of this to Effie till I come tomorrow, Jean."

I went away and, far out on the lonely moor, sat down to think. Like a weird magician, Memory led me back into the past, calling up the hopes and passions buried there. My childhood—fatherless and motherless, but not unhappy, for no wish was ungratified, no idle whim denied. My boyhood—with no shadows over it but those my own wayward will called up. My manhood—when the great joy of my life arose, my love for Agnes, a midsummer dream of bloom and bliss, so short-lived and so sweet! I felt again the pang that wrung my heart when she coldly gave me back the pledge I thought so sacred and so sure and the music of her marriage bells tolled the knell of my lost love. I seemed to hear them still wafting across the purple moor through the silence of those fifteen years.

My life looked gray and joyless as the wide waste lying hushed around me, unblessed with the verdure of a single hope, a single love; and as I looked down the coming years, my way seemed very solitary, very dark.

Suddenly a lark soared upward from the heath, cleaving the silence with its jubilant song. The sleeping echoes woke, the dun moor seemed to smile, and the blithe music fell like dew upon my gloomy spirit, wakening a new desire.

"What this bird is to the moor might little Effie be to me," I thought within myself, longing to possess the cheerful spirit which had power to gladden me.

"Yes," I mused, "the old home will seem more solitary now than ever. If I cannot win the lark's song without a golden fetter, I will give it one, and while it sings for love of me, it shall not know a want or fear."

Heaven help me! I forgot the poor return I made my lark for the sweet liberty it lost.

All that night I pondered the altered future Jean had laid before me, and the longer I looked, the fairer it seemed to grow. Wealth I cared nothing for; the world's opinion I defied; ambition had departed, and passion I believed lay dead. Then why should I deny myself the consolation which seemed offered to me? I would accept it, and as I resolved, the dawn looked in at me, fresh and fair as little Effie's face.

I met Jean with a smile, and as she read its significance aright, there shone a sudden peace upon her countenance, more touching than her grateful words.

Effie came singing from the burnside, as unconscious of the change which awaited her as the flowers gathered in her plaid and crowning her bright hair.

I drew her to my side and in the simplest words asked her if she would go with me when Jean's long guardianship was ended. Joy, sorrow, and surprise stirred the sweet composure of her face and quickened the tranquil beating of her heart. But as I ceased, joy conquered grief and wonder, for she clapped her hands like a glad child, exclaiming:

"Go with you, sir? Oh, if you knew how I long to see the home you have so often pictured to me, you would never doubt my willingness to go."

"But, Effie, you do not understand. Are you willing to go with me as my wife?" I said—with a secret sense of something like remorse as I uttered that word which once meant so much to me and now seemed such an empty title to bestow on her.

The flowers dropped from the loosened plaid as Effie looked with a startled glance into my face. The color left her cheeks and the smile died on her lips, but a timid joy lit her eye as she softly echoed my last words:

"Your wife? It sounds very solemn, though so sweet. Ah, sir, I am not wise or good enough for that!"

A child's humility breathed in her speech, but something of a woman's fervor shone in her uplifted countenance and sounded in the sudden tremor of her voice.

"Effie, I want you as you are," I said, "no wiser, dear—no better. I want your innocent affection to appease the hunger of an empty heart, your blithe companionship to cheer my solitary home. Be still a child to me, and let me give you the protection of my name."

Effie turned to her old friend and, laying her young face on the pillow close beside the worn one grown so dear to her, asked in a tone half pleading, half regretful: "Dear Jean, shall I go so far away from you and the home you gave me when I had no other?"

"My bairn, I shall not be here, and it will never seem like home with old Jean gone. It is the last wish I shall ever know, to see you safe with this good gentleman who loves my child. Go, dear heart, and be happy. Heaven bless and keep you both!"

Jean held her fast a moment and then with a whispered prayer put her gently away. Effie came to me, saying with a look more eloquent than her meek words:

"Sir, I will be your wife and love you very truly all my life."

I drew the little creature to my breast and felt a tender pride in knowing she was mine. Something in the shy caress those soft arms gave touched my cold nature with a generous warmth, and the innocence of that confiding heart was an appeal to all that made my manhood worth possessing.

Swiftly those few weeks passed, and when old Jean was laid to her last sleep, little Effie wept her grief away upon her husband's bosom and soon learned to smile in her new English home. Its gloom departed when she came, and for a while it was a very happy place. My bitter moods seemed banished by the magic of the gentle presence that made sunshine there, and I was conscious of a fresh grace added to the life so wearisome before.

I should have been a father to the child, watchful, wise, and tender; but old Jean was right—I was too young to feel a father's calm affection or to know a father's patient care. I should have been her teacher, striving to cultivate the nature given to my care and fit it for the trials heaven sends to all. I should have been a friend, if nothing more, and given her those innocent delights that make youth beautiful and its memory sweet.

I was a master, content to give little, while receiving all she could bestow.

Forgetting her loneliness, I fell back into my old way of life. I shunned the world because its gaieties had lost their zest. I did not care to travel, for home now possessed a charm it never had before. I knew there was an eager face that always brightened when I came, light feet that flew to welcome me, and hands that loved to minister to every want of mine. Even when I sat engrossed among my books, there was a pleasant consciousness that I was the possessor of a household sprite whom a look could summon and a gesture banish. I loved her as I loved a picture or a flower—a little better than my horse and hound—but far less than I loved my most unworthy self.

And she—always so blithe when I was by, so diligent in studying my desires, so full of simple arts to win my love and prove her gratitude—she never asked for any boon, and seemed content to live alone with me in that still place, so utterly unlike the home she had left. I had not learned to read that true heart then. I saw those happy eyes grow wistful when I went, leaving her alone; I missed the roses from her cheek, faded for want of gentler care; and when the buoyant spirit which had been her chiefest charm departed, I fancied in my blindness that she pined for the free air of the Highlands, and tried to win it back by transient tenderness and costly gifts. But I had robbed my lark of heaven's sunshine, and it could not sing.

I met Agnes again. She was a widow, and to my eye seemed fairer than when I saw her last and far more kind. Some soft regret seemed shining on me from those lustrous eyes, as if she hoped to win my pardon for that early wrong. I never could forget the deed that darkened my best years; but the old charm stole over me at times, and turning from the meek child at my feet, I owned the power of the stately woman whose smile seemed a command.

I meant no wrong to Effie, but looking on her as a child, I forgot the higher claim I had given her as a wife. Walking blindly on my selfish way, I crushed the little flower I should have cherished in my breast.

"Effie, my old friend Agnes Vaughan is coming here today, so make yourself fair, that you may do honor to my choice; for she desires to see you, and I wish my Scotch harebell to look lovely to this English rose," I said, half playfully, half earnestly, as we stood together looking out across the flowery lawn one summer day.

"Do you like me to be pretty, sir?" she answered, with a flush of pleasure on her upturned face. "I will try to make myself fair with the gifts you are always heaping on me, but even then I fear I shall not do you honor nor please your friend, I am so small and young."

A careless reply was on my lips, but seeing what a long way down the little figure was, I drew it nearer, saying with a smile, which I knew would make an answering one: "Dear, there must be the bud before the flower. So never grieve, for your youth keeps my spirit young. To me you may be a child forever, but you must learn to be a stately little Madam Ventnor to my friends."

She laughed a gayer laugh than I had heard for many a day, and soon departed, intent on keeping well the promise she had given. An hour later, as I sat busied among my books, a little figure glided in and stood before me, with its jeweled arms demurely folded on its breast. It was Effie, as I had never seen her before. Some new freak possessed her, for with her girlish dress she seemed to have laid her girlhood by. The brown locks were gathered up, wreathing the small head like a coronet; aerial lace and silken vesture shimmered in the light and became her well. She looked and moved like a fairy queen, stately and small.

I watched her in a silent maze, for the face with its shy blushes and downcast eyes did not seem the childish one turned frankly to my own an hour ago. With a sigh I looked up at Agnes's picture, the sole ornament of that room, and when I withdrew my gaze, the blooming vision had departed. I should have followed it to make my peace, but I fell into a fit of bitter musing and forgot it till Agnes's voice sounded at my door.

She came with a brother, and seemed eager to see my young wife. But Effie did not appear, and I excused her absence as a girlish freak, smiling at it with them while I chafed inwardly at her neglect, forgetting that I might have been the cause.

With Agnes at my side, we were pacing down the garden paths when our steps were arrested by a sudden sight of Effie fast asleep among the flowers. She looked a flower herself, lying with her flushed cheek pillowed on her arm, sunshine glittering on the ripples of her hair and the changeful luster of her dainty dress. Tears moistened her long lashes, but her lips smiled, as if in the blissful land of dreams she had found some solace for her grief.

"A 'Sleeping Beauty' worthy the awakening of any prince!" whispered Alfred Vaughan, pausing with admiring eyes.

A slight frown swept over Agnes's face, but vanished as she said with that low-toned laugh that never seemed unmusical before: "We must pardon Mrs. Ventnor's seeming rudeness if she welcomes us with graceful scenes like this. A child wife's whims are often prettier than the world's formal ways, so do not chide her, Basil, when she wakes."

I was a proud man then, touched easily by trivial things. Agnes's pitying manner stung me, and the tone in which I wakened Effie was far harsher than it should have been. She sprang up and, with a gentle dignity most new to me, received her guests and played the part of hostess with a grace that well atoned for her offense.

Agnes watched her silently as she went before us with young Vaughan, and even I, ruffled as my temper was, felt a certain pride in the loving creature who for my sake conquered her timidity and strove to do me honor. But neither by look nor word did I show my satisfaction; for Agnes demanded the constant service of lips and eyes, and I was only too ready to devote them to the woman who still felt her power and dared to show it.

All that day I was beside her, forgetful in many ways of the gentle courtesies I owed the child whom I had made my wife. I did not see the wrong then; but others did, and the deference I failed to show she could ask of them.

In the evening, as I stood near Agnes while she sang the songs we both remembered well, my eye fell on a mirror that confronted me, and in it I saw Effie bending forward with a look that startled me. Some strong emotion controlled her, for with lips apart and eager eyes she gazed keenly at the countenances she believed unconscious of her scrutiny.

Agnes caught the vision that had arrested the half-uttered compliment upon my lips, and, turning, looked at Effie with a smile just touched with scorn.

The color rose vividly to Effie's cheek, but her eyes did not fall—they sought my face and rested there. A half smile crossed my lips. With a sudden impulse I beckoned, and she came with such an altered countenance I fancied that I had not seen aright.

At my desire she sang the ballads she so loved, and in her girlish voice there was an undertone of deeper melody than when I heard them first among her native hills, for the child's heart was ripening fast into the woman's.

Agnes went at length, and I heard Effie's sigh of relief when we were left alone, but only bade her "go and rest" while I paced to and fro, still murmuring the refrain of Agnes's song.

The Vaughans came often, and we went often to them in the summer home they had chosen near us on the riverbank. I followed my own wayward will, and Effie's wistful eyes grew sadder as the weeks went by.

One sultry evening, as we strolled together on the balcony, I was seized with a sudden longing to hear Agnes sing and bade Effie come with me for a moonlight voyage down the river.

She had been very silent all the evening, with a pensive shadow on her face and rare smiles on her lips. But as I spoke, she paused abruptly and, clenching her small hands, turned upon me with defiant eyes—crying almost fiercely:

"No, I will not go to listen to that woman's songs. I hate her! Yes, more than I can tell! For till she came, I thought you loved me, but now you think of her alone and chide me when I look unhappy. You treat me like a child, but I am not one. Oh, sir, be more kind, for I have only you to love!" And as her voice died in that sad appeal, she clasped her hands before her face with such a burst of tears that I had no words to answer her.

Disturbed by the sudden passion of the hitherto meek girl, I sat down on the wide steps of the balcony and essayed to draw her to my knee, hoping she would weep this grief away, as she had often done a lesser sorrow. But she resisted my caress and, standing erect before me, checked her tears, saying in a voice still trembling with resentment and reproach:

"You promised Jean to be kind to me, and you are cruel. For when I ask for love, you give me jewels, books, or flowers, as you would give a pettish child a toy, and go away, as if you were weary of me. Oh, it is not right, sir! And I cannot, no, I will not bear it!"

If she had spared reproaches, deserved though they were, and humbly pleaded to be loved, I should have been more just and gentle. But her indignant words, the sharper for their truth, roused the despotic spirit of the man and made me sternest when I should have been most kind.

"Effie," I said, looking coldly up into her troubled face, "I have given you the right to be thus frank with me. But before you exercise that right, let me tell you what may silence your reproaches and teach you to know me better. I desired to adopt you as my child. Jean would not consent to that, but bid me marry you and so give you a home and win for myself a companion who should make that home less solitary. I could protect you in no other way, and I married you. I meant it kindly, Effie, for I pitied you—aye, and loved you, too, as I hoped I had fully proved."

"You have, sir—oh, you have! But I hoped I might in time be more to you than a dear child," sighed Effie, while softer tears flowed as she spoke.

"Effie, I told Jean I was a hard, cold man"—and I was one as those words passed my lips. "I told her I was unfitted to make a wife happy. But she said you would be content with what I could offer, and so I gave you all I had to bestow. It was not enough; yet I cannot make it more. Forgive me, child, and try to bear your disappointments as I have learned to bear mine."

Effie bent suddenly, saying with a look of anguish: "Do you regret that I am your wife, sir?"

"Heaven knows I do, for I cannot make you happy," I answered mournfully.

"Let me go away where I can never grieve or trouble you again! I will—indeed, I will—for anything is easier to bear than this. Oh, Jean, why did you leave me when you went?" And with that despairing cry Effie stretched her arms into the empty air, as if seeking that lost friend.

My anger melted, and I tried to soothe her, saying gently as I laid her tear-wet cheek to mine: "My child, death alone must part us two. We will be patient with each other and so may learn to be happy yet."

A long silence fell upon us both. My thoughts were busy with the thought of what a different home mine might have been if Agnes had been true; and Effie—God only knows how sharp a conflict passed in that young heart! I could not guess it till the bitter sequel of that hour came.

A timid hand upon my own roused me, and looking down, I met such an altered face, it touched me like a mute reproach. All the passion had died out, and a great patience seemed to have arisen there. It looked so meek and wan, I bent and kissed it; but no smile answered me as Effie humbly said:

"Forgive me, sir, and tell me how I can make you happier. For I am truly grateful for all you have done for me, and will try to be a docile child to you."

"Be happy yourself, Effie, and I shall be content. I am too grave and old to be a fit companion for you, dear. You shall have gay faces and young friends to make this quiet place more cheerful. I should have thought of that before. Dance, sing, be merry, Effie, and never let your life be darkened by Basil Ventnor's changeful moods."

"And you?" she whispered, looking up.

"I will sit among my books, or seek alone the few friends I care to see, and never mar your gaiety with my gloomy presence, dear. We must begin at once to go our separate ways, for with so many years between us we can never find the same paths pleasant very long. Let me be a father to you, and a friend—I cannot be a lover, child."

Effie rose and went silently away, but soon came again, wrapped in her mantle, saying, as she looked down at me, with something of her former cheerfulness: "I am good now. Come and row me down the river. It is too beautiful a night to be spent in tears and naughtiness."

"No, Effie, you shall never go to Mrs. Vaughan's again if you dislike her so. No friendship of mine need be shared by you if it gives you pain."

"Nothing shall pain me anymore," she answered with a patient sigh. "I will be your merry girl again and try to love Agnes for your sake. Ah, do come, *Father,* or I shall not feel forgiven."

Smiling at her April moods, I obeyed the small hands clasped about my own and, through the fragrant linden walk, went musing to the riverside.

Silently we floated down, and at the lower landing place found Alfred Vaughan just mooring his own boat. By him I sent a message to his sister while we waited for her at the shore.

Effie stood above me on the sloping bank, and as Agnes entered the green vista of the flowery path, she turned and clung to me with sudden fervor, kissed me passionately, and then stole silently into the boat.

The moonlight turned the waves to silver, and in its magic rays the face of my first love grew young again. She sat before me, with water lilies in her shining hair, singing as she sang of old, while the dash of falling oars kept time to her low song. As we neared the ruined bridge, whose single arch still cast its heavy shadow far across the stream, Agnes bent toward me, softly saying:

"Basil, you remember this?"

How could I forget that happy night, long years ago, when she and I went floating down the same bright stream, two happy lovers just betrothed? As she spoke, it all came back more beautiful than ever, and I forgot the silent figure sitting there behind me. I hoped Agnes had forgotten, too; for, cruel as she was to me, I never wished to think her hard enough to hate that gentle child.

"I remember, Agnes," I said with a regretful sigh. "My voyage has been a lonely one since then."

"Are you not happy, Basil?" she asked, with a tender pity thrilling her low voice.

"Happy?" I echoed bitterly. "How can I be happy, remembering what might have been?"

Agnes bowed her head upon her hands, and silently the boat shot into the black shadow of the arch. A sudden eddy seemed to sway us slightly from our course, and the waves dashed sullenly against the gloomy walls; a moment more and we glided into calmer waters and unbroken light. I looked up from my task to speak, but the words were frozen on my lips by a cry from Agnes, who, wild-eyed and pale, seemed pointing to some phantom which I could not see. I turned—the phantom was Effie's empty seat. The shining stream grew dark before me, and a great pang of remorse wrung my heart as that sight met my eyes.

"Effie!" I cried with a cry that rent the stillness of the night and sent the name ringing down the river. But nothing answered me, and the waves rippled softly as they hurried by. Far over the wide stream went my despairing glance, and saw nothing but the lilies swaying as they slept and the black arch where my child went down.

Agnes lay trembling at my feet, but I never heeded her—for Jean's dead voice sounded in my ear, demanding the life confided to my care. I listened, benumbed with guilty fear; and, as if summoned by that weird cry, there came a white flash through the waves, and Effie's face rose up before me.

Pallid and wild with the agony of that swift plunge, it confronted me. No cry for help parted the pale lips, but those wide eyes were luminous with a love whose fire that deathful river could not quench.

Like one in an awful dream, I gazed till the ripples closed above it. One instant the terror held me—the next I was far down in those waves so silver and fair above, so black and terrible below. A brief blind struggle passed before I grasped a tress of that long hair, then an arm, and then the white shape, with a clutch like death. As the dividing waters gave us to the light again, Agnes flung herself far over the boatside and drew my lifeless burden in. I followed, and we laid it down, a piteous sight for human eyes to look upon. Of that swift voyage home I can remember nothing but the still face on Agnes's breast, the sight of which nerved my dizzy brain and made my muscles iron.

For many weeks there was a darkened chamber in my house and anxious figures gliding to and fro, wan with long vigils and the fear of death. I often crept in to look upon the little figure lying there; to watch the feverish roses blooming on the wasted cheek, the fitful fire burning in the unconscious eyes; to hear the broken words so full of pathos to my ear; and then to steal away and struggle to forget.

My bird fluttered on the threshold of its cage, but Love lured it back, for its gentle mission was not yet fulfilled.

The *child* Effie lay dead beneath the ripples of the river, but the *woman* rose up from that bed of suffering like one consecrated to life's high duties by the bitter baptism of that dark hour.

Slender and pale, with serious eyes and quiet steps, she moved through the home which once echoed to the glad voice and dancing feet of that vanished shape. A sweet sobriety shaded her young face and a meek smile sat upon her lips, but the old blithesomeness was gone.

She never claimed her childish place upon my knee, never tried the winsome wiles that used to chase away my gloom, never came to pour her innocent delights and griefs into my ear or bless me with the frank affection which grew very precious when I found it lost.

Docile as ever and eager to gratify my lightest wish, she left no wifely duty unfulfilled. Always near me if I breathed her name, but vanishing when I grew silent, as if her task were done. Always smiling a cheerful farewell when I went, a quiet welcome when I came. I missed the April face that once watched me go, the warm embrace that greeted me again; and at my heart the sense of loss grew daily deeper as I felt the growing change.

Effie remembered the words I had spoken on that mournful night, remembered that our paths must lie apart—that her husband was a friend and nothing more. She treasured every careless hint I had given, and followed it most faithfully. She gathered gay young friends about her, went out into the brilliant world; and I believed she was content.

If I had ever felt she was a burden to the selfish freedom I desired, I was punished now, for I had lost a blessing which no common pleasure could replace. I sat alone, and no blithe voice made music in the silence of my room, no bright locks swept my shoulder, and no soft caress assured me that I was beloved.

I looked for my household sprite in girlish garb, with its free hair and sunny eyes, but found only a fair woman, graceful in rich attire, crowned with my gifts, and standing afar off among her blooming peers. I could not guess the solitude of that true heart, nor see the captive spirit gazing at me from those steadfast eyes.

No word of the cause of that despairing deed passed Effie's lips, and I had no need to ask it. Agnes was silent, and soon left us, but her brother was a frequent guest. Effie liked his gay companionship, and I denied her nothing—nothing but the one desire of her life.

So that first year passed. Though the ease and liberty I coveted were undisturbed, I was not satisfied. Solitude grew irksome and study ceased to charm. I tried old pleasures, but they had lost their zest—renewed old friendships, but they wearied me. I forgot Agnes and ceased to think her fair. I looked at Effie and sighed for my lost youth.

My little wife grew very beautiful to me, for she was blooming fast into a gracious womanhood. I felt a secret pride in knowing she was mine, and watched her as I fancied a fond brother might, glad that she was so good, so fair, so much beloved. I ceased to mourn the plaything I had lost, and something akin to reverence mingled with the deepening admiration of the man.

Gay guests had filled the house with festal light and sound one winter's night, and when the last bright figure had vanished from the threshold of the door, I still stood there looking over the snow-shrouded lawn, hoping to cool the fever of my blood and ease the restless pain that haunted me.

I shut out the keen air and wintry sky at length, and silently ascended to the deserted rooms above. But in the soft gloom of a vestibule my steps were stayed. Two figures in a flowery alcove fixed my eye. The light streamed full upon them, and the fragrant stillness of the air was hardly stirred by their low tones.

Effie was there, sunk on a low couch, her face bowed upon her hands; and at her side, speaking with impassioned voice and ardent eyes, leaned Alfred Vaughan.

The sight struck me like a blow, and the sharp anguish of that moment proved how deeply I had learned to love.

"Effie, it is a sinful tie that binds you to that man. He does not love you, and it should be broken—for this slavery will wear away the life now grown so dear to me."

The words, hot with indignant passion, smote me like a

wintry blast, but not so coldly as the broken voice that answered them: "He said death alone must part us two, and remembering that, I cannot listen to another love."

Like a guilty ghost I stole away and, in the darkness of my solitary room, struggled with my bitter grief, my newborn love. I never blamed my wife—that wife who had heard the tender name so seldom, she could scarce feel it hers. I had fettered her free heart, forgetting it would one day cease to be a child's. I bade her look upon me as a father; she had learned the lesson well; and now what right had I to reproach her for listening to a lover's voice when her husband's was so cold? What mattered it that slowly, almost unconsciously, I had learned to love her with the passion of a youth, the power of a man? I had alienated that fond nature from my own, and now it was too late.

Heaven only knows the bitterness of that hour—I cannot tell it. But through the darkness of my anguish and remorse, that newly kindled love burned like a blessed fire, and while it tortured, purified. By its light I saw the error of my life: Self-love was written on the actions of the past, and I knew that my punishment was very just. With a child's repentant tears I confessed it to my Father, and He solaced me, showed me the path to tread, and made me nobler for the blessedness and pain of that still hour.

Dawn found me an altered man; for in natures like mine the rain of a great sorrow melts the ice of years, and their hidden strength blooms in a late harvest of patience, self-denial, and humility. I resolved to break the tie which bound poor Effie to a joyless fate, and gratitude for a selfish deed which wore the guise of charity should no longer mar her peace. I would atone for the wrong I had done her, the suffering she had endured; and she should never know that I had guessed her tender secret, nor learn the love which made my sacrifice so bitter, yet so just.

Alfred came no more. As I watched the growing pallor of her cheek, her patient efforts to be cheerful and serene, I honored that meek creature for her constancy to what she deemed the duty of her life.

I did not tell her my resolve at once, for I could not give her up so soon. It was a weak delay, but I had not learned the beauty of a perfect self-forgetfulness. Though I clung to my purpose steadfastly, my heart still cherished a desperate hope that I might be spared this loss.

In the midst of this secret conflict, there came a letter from old Adam Lyndsay, asking to see his daughter's child; for life was waning slowly and he desired to forgive, as he hoped to be forgiven when the last hour came. The letter was to me, and as I read it, I saw a way whereby I might be spared the hard task of telling Effie she was to be free. I feared my new-found strength would desert me and my courage fail when, looking on the woman who was dearer to me than my life, I tried to give her back the liberty whose worth she had learned to know.

Effie should go, and I would write the words I dared not speak. She would be in her mother's home, free to show her joy at her release and smile upon the lover she had banished.

I went to tell her, for it was I who sought her now, who watched for her coming and sighed at her departing steps—I who waited for her smile and followed her with wistful eyes. The child's slighted affection was atoned for now by my un-seen devotion to the woman.

I gave the letter and she read it silently.

"Will you go, love?" I asked as she folded it.

"Yes—the old man has no one to care for him but me, and it is so beautiful to be loved."

A sudden smile touched her lips, and a soft dew shone in the shadowy eyes, which seemed looking into other and ten-derer ones than mine. She could not know how sadly I echoed those words, nor how I longed to tell her of another man who sighed to be forgiven.

"You must gather roses for these pale cheeks among the breezy moorlands, dear. They are not so blooming as they were a year ago. Jean would reproach me for my want of care," I said, trying to speak cheerfully, though each word seemed a farewell.

"Poor Jean! How long it seems since she kissed them

last!" sighed Effie, musing sadly as she turned her wedding ring.

My heart ached to see how thin the hand had grown and how easily that little fetter would fall off when I set my captive lark at liberty.

I looked till I dared look no longer, and then rose, saying, "You will write often, Effie, for I shall miss you very much."

She cast a quick look into my face, asking hurriedly, "Am I to go alone?"

"Dear, I have much to do and cannot go. But you need fear nothing. I shall send Ralph and Mrs. Prior with you, and the journey is soon over. When will you go?"

It was the first time she had left me since I took her from Jean's arms, and I longed to keep her always near me. But remembering the task I had to do, I felt that I must seem cold till she knew all.

"Soon—very soon—tomorrow. Let me go tomorrow, sir. I long to be away!" she cried, some swift emotion banishing the calmness of her usual manner as she rose with eager eyes and a gesture full of longing.

"You shall go, Effie" was all I could say, and with no word of thanks, she hastened away, leaving me so calm without, so desolate within.

The same eagerness possessed her all that day; and the next she went away, clinging to me at the last as she had clung that night upon the riverbank, as if her grateful heart reproached her for the joy she felt at leaving my unhappy home.

A few days passed, bringing me the comfort of a few sweet lines from Effie, signed "Your child." That sight reminded me that if I would do an honest deed, it should be generously done. I read again the little missive she had sent, and then I wrote the letter which might be my last—with no hint of my love beyond the expression of sincerest regard and never-ceasing interest in her happiness; no hint of Alfred Vaughan, for I would not wound her pride, nor let her dream that any eye had seen the passion she so silently surrendered, with no reproach to me and no shadow on the name I had given into her keeping. Heaven knows what it cost me, and heaven, through the suffering of that hour, granted me a humbler spirit and a better life.

It went, and I waited for my fate as one might wait for pardon or for doom. It came at length—a short, sad letter, full of meek obedience to my will, of penitence for faults I never knew, and grateful prayers for my peace.

My last hope died then, and for many days I dwelt alone, living over all that happy year with painful vividness. I dreamed again of those fair days and woke to curse the selfish blindness which had hidden my best blessing from me till it was forever lost.

How long I should have mourned thus unavailingly I cannot tell. A more sudden but far less grievous loss befell me. My fortune was nearly swept away in the general ruin of a most disastrous year.

This event roused me from my despair and made me strong again—for I must hoard what could be saved, for Effie's sake. She had known a cruel want with me, and she must never know another while she bore my name. I looked my misfortune in the face and ceased to feel it one, for the diminished fortune was still ample for my darling's dower. And now what need had I of any but the simplest home?

Before another month was gone, I was in the quiet place henceforth to be mine alone, and nothing now remained for me to do but to dissolve the bond that made my Effie mine. Sitting over the dim embers of my solitary hearth, I thought of this; and I looked around the silent room whose only ornaments were the things made sacred by her use, and the utter desolation struck so heavily upon my heart that I bowed my head upon my folded arms and yielded to the tender longing that could not be repressed.

The bitter paroxysm passed, and raising my eyes, the clearer for that stormy rain, I beheld Effie standing like an answer to my spirit's cry.

With a great start I regarded her, saying at length in a voice that sounded cold, for my heart leaped up to meet her and yet must not speak: "Effie, why are you here?"

Wraithlike and pale, she stood before me with no sign of

emotion but the slight tremor of her frame and answered my greeting with a sad humility: "I came because I promised to cleave to you through health and sickness, poverty and wealth, and I must keep that vow till you absolve me from it. Forgive me, but I knew misfortune had befallen you and, remembering all you had done for me, came, hoping I might comfort when other friends deserted you."

"Grateful to the last!" I sighed low to myself and, though deeply touched, replied with the hard-won calmness that made my speech so brief: "You owe me nothing, Effie, and I most earnestly desired to spare you this." Some sudden hope seemed born of my regretful words, for with an eager glance she cried:

"Was it that desire which prompted you to part from me? Did you think I should shrink from sharing poverty with you, who gave me all I own?"

"No, dear—ah, no!" I said. "I knew your grateful spirit far too well for that. It was because I could not make your happiness and yet had robbed you of the right to seek it with some younger and some better man."

"Basil, what man? Tell me, for no doubt shall stand between us now!" She grasped my arm, and her rapid words were a command.

I only answered, "Alfred Vaughan."

Effie covered up her face, crying as she sank down at my feet: "Oh, my fear! My fear! Why was I blind so long?"

I felt her grief to my heart's core; for my own anguish made me pitiful and my love made me strong. I lifted up that drooping head and laid it down where it might never rest again, saying gently, cheerily, and with a most sincere forgetfulness of self:

"My wife, I never cherished a harsh thought of you, never uttered a reproach, when your affections turned from a cold, neglectful guardian to find a tenderer resting place. I saw your struggles, dear, your patient grief, your silent sacrifice, and honored you more truly than I can tell. Effie, I robbed you of your liberty, but I will restore it, making such poor reparation as I can for this long year of pain. When I see you blessed in a happier home, my keen remorse will be appeased."

As I ceased, Effie rose erect and stood before me, transformed from a timid girl into an earnest woman. Some dormant power and passion woke; she turned on me a countenance aglow with feeling, soul in the eye, heart on the lips, and in her voice an energy that held me mute.

"I feared to speak before," she said, "but now I dare anything, for I have heard you call me 'wife' and seen that in your face which gives me hope. Basil, the grief you saw was not for the loss of any love but yours; the conflict you beheld was the daily struggle to subdue my longing spirit to your will; and the sacrifice you honor but the renunciation of all hope. I stood between you and the woman whom you loved, and asked of death to free me from that cruel lot. You gave me back my life, but you withheld the gift that made it worth possessing. You desired to be freed from the affection which only wearied you, and I tried to conquer it; but it would not die. Let me speak now, and then I will be still forever! Must our ways lie apart? Can I never be more to you than now? Oh, Basil! Oh, my husband! I have loved you very truly from the first! Shall I never know the blessedness of a return?"

Words could not answer that appeal. I gathered my life's happiness close to my breast and, in the silence of a full heart, felt that God was very good to me.

Soon all my pain and passion were confessed. Fast and fervently the tale was told, and as the truth dawned on that patient wife, a tender peace transfigured her uplifted countenance until to me it seemed an angel's face.

"I am a poor man now," I said, still holding that frail creature fast, fearing to see her vanish, as her semblance had so often done in the long vigils I had kept, "a poor man, Effie, and yet very rich, for I have my treasure back again. But I am wiser than when we parted, for I have learned that love is better than a world of wealth and victory over self a nobler conquest than a continent. Dear, I have no home but this. Can you be happy here, with no fortune but the little store set apart for you and the knowledge that no want shall touch you while I live?"

And as I spoke, I sighed, remembering all I might have done and dreading poverty for her alone.

But with a gesture soft yet solemn, Effie laid her hands upon my head, as if endowing me with blessing and with gift, and answered, with her steadfast eyes on mine: "You gave me your home when I was homeless. Let me give it back, and with it a proud wife. I, too, am rich, for that old man is gone and left me all. Take it, Basil, and give me a little love."

I gave not little, but a long life of devotion for the good gift God had bestowed on me—finding in it a household spirit the daily benediction of whose presence banished sorrow, selfishness, and gloom and, through the influence of happy human love, led me to a truer faith in the Divine.

BIBLIOGRAPHY

Flower Fables (1855) – stories
Hospital Sketches (1863) – sketches
The Rose Family (1864) – story
On Picket Duty, and Other Tales (1864) – stories
Moods (1865, 1882)[1] – novel
The Mysterious Key, and What It Opened (1867) – story
Morning-Glories, and Other Stories (1868) – stories
Three Proverb Stories (1868) – stories
Little Women (1868, 1869)[2] – novel
An Old-Fashioned Girl (1870) – novel
Will's Wonder Book (1870)[3] – stories
Little Men (1871) – novel
Aunt Jo's Scrap-Bag I (1872) – stories
Aunt Jo's Scrap-Bag II (1872) – stories
Work (1873) – novel
Aunt Jo's Scrap-Bag III (1874) – stories
Eight Cousins (1875) – novel
Silver Pitchers (1876) – stories
Rose in Bloom (1876) – novel
A Modern Mephistopheles (1877) – novel

1. Originally published by Loring in 1865. The revised version was published by Roberts Brothers in 1882.
2. *Little Women* originally appeared as two separate volumes. Part First was published in 1868 and Part Second in 1869.
3. Originally published anonymously; edited by Madeleine Stern and republished in 1975 as *Louisa's Wonder Book*.

Aunt Jo's Scrap-Bag IV (1878) – stories
Under the Lilacs (1878) – novel
Aunt Jo's Scrap-Bag V (1879) – stories
Jack and Jill (1880) – novel
Proverb Stories (1882) – stories
Aunt Jo's Scrap-Bag VI (1882) – stories
Spinning-Wheel Stories (1884) – stories
Lulu's Library Vol. I (1886) – stories
Jo's Boys (1886) – novel
Lulu's Library Vol. II (1887) – stories
A Garland for Girls (1888) – stories
Louisa May Alcott: Her Life, Letters, and Journals (1889) – letters and journals
Lulu's Library Vol. III (1889) – stories
Comic Tragedies (1893) – plays
Behind a Mask (1975) – stories
Plots and Counterplots (1976)[4] – stories
Diana and Persis (1978) – story
The Selected Letters of Louisa May Alcott (1987) – letters
A Double Life (1988) – stories
The Journals of Louisa May Alcott (1989) – journals
Freaks of Genius (1991) – stories
From Jo March's Attic (1993)[5] – stories
A Long Fatal Love Chase (1995) – novel
The Inheritance (1997) – novel
The Poems of Louisa May Alcott (2000) – poems (Ironweed, ISBN 0-9655309-5-7)

4. Republished in 1995 as *A Marble Woman*.
5. Republished in 1995 as *The Lost Stories of Louisa May Alcott*.

ORIGINAL PUBLICATION SOURCES

"The Rival Painters: A Tale of Rome": *Olive Branch,* May 8, 1852.

"The Masked Marriage": *Dodge's Literary Museum,* December 18, 1852.

"The Rival Prima Donnas": *Saturday Evening Gazette,* November 11, 1854.

"The Little Seed": In *Margaret Lyon, or, A Work for All* (Boston: Crosby, Nichols, 1854).

"A New Year's Blessing": *Saturday Evening Gazette,* January 5, 1856.

"The Sisters' Trial": *Saturday Evening Gazette,* January 26, 1856.

"Little Genevieve": *Saturday Evening Gazette,* March 29, 1856.

"Bertha": *Saturday Evening Gazette,* April 19 and 26, 1856.

"Mabel's May Day": *Saturday Evening Gazette,* May 24, 1856.

"The Lady and the Woman": *Saturday Evening Gazette,* October 4, 1856.

"Ruth's Secret": *Saturday Evening Gazette,* December 6, 1856.

"The Cross on the Church Tower": *Saturday Evening Gazette,* January 24, 1857. Reprinted as "The Cross on the Old Church Tower," *On Picket Duty, and Other Tales* (Boston: James Redpath, 1864).

"Agatha's Confession": *Saturday Evening Gazette,* March 14, 1857. Revised as "Thrice Tempted," *Frank Leslie's Chimney Corner,* July 20, 1867.

"Little Sunbeam": *Saturday Evening Gazette,* April 4, 1857.

"Marion Earle; or, Only an Actress!": *New York Atlas,* September 12, 1858. Originally appeared in *American Union,* ca. July–September, 1858.

"Mark Field's Mistake": *Saturday Evening Gazette,* March 12, 1859.

"Mark Field's Success": *Saturday Evening Gazette,* April 16, 1859.

"The Monk's Island: A Legend of the Rhine": *Saturday Evening Gazette,* September 3, 1859.

"Love and Self-Love": *The Atlantic Monthly,* March 1860.

A NOTE ON THE TEXT

The stories are drawn directly from their original publication sources. Obvious errors have been emended. In some instances words have been inserted or changed for clarity. Where appropriate, modern standards in spelling and punctuation have been imposed to enhance readability.